Financing the
2000 *Election*

Financing the 2000 Election

DAVID B. MAGLEBY
Editor

BROOKINGS INSTITUTION PRESS
Washington, D.C.

ABOUT BROOKINGS

The Brookings Institution is a private nonprofit organization devoted to research, education, and publication on important issues of domestic and foreign policy. Its principal purpose is to bring knowledge to bear on current and emerging policy problems. The Institution maintains a position of neutrality on issues of public policy. Interpretations or conclusions in Brookings publications should be understood to be solely those of the authors.

Copyright © 2002
THE BROOKINGS INSTITUTION
1775 Massachusetts Avenue, N.W., Washington, D.C. 20036
www.brookings.edu

Library of Congress Cataloging-in-Publication data

Financing the 2000 Election / David B. Magleby, editor.
   p.   cm.
Includes bibliographical references and index.
   ISBN 0-8157-0622-7 (cloth : alk. paper)
   ISBN 0-8157-0621-9 (paper : alk. paper)
   1. Campaign funds—United States. 2. Presidents—United States—Election—2000—
Finance. 3. United States. Congress—Elections, 2000—Finance. 4. United States—
Politics and government—1993–2001. I. Magleby, David B. II. Brookings Institution.
   JK 1991.F568 2002
   324.7'8'0973090511—dc21   2002000403

9 8 7 6 5 4 3 2 1
The paper used in this publication meets minimum requirements of the
American National Standard for Information Sciences—Permanence of Paper for
Printed Library Materials: ANSI Z39.48-1992.

Typeset in Sabon

Composition by Stephen D. McDougal
Mechanicsville, Maryland

Printed by R. R. Donnelly and Sons
Harrisonburg, Virginia

For
Linda Waters Magleby,
Joseph, Kathryn, Daniel, and Benjamin Magleby

Contents

Foreword

LONG BEFORE CONGRESS put teeth into laws requiring federal candidates to disclose their campaign finances, the Citizens Research Foundation (CRF) was in the business of providing reliable data on the costs of American democracy. CRF is the nation's oldest nonpartisan, nonprofit research center committed to public understanding of political finance. Now, thanks to federal and state disclosure laws and the Internet, dozens of public and private organizations flood the web with campaign finance data and reform proposals. CRF has consequently adapted its agenda and now seeks to focus less on the provision of raw data and more on the encouragement of solid analysis. Because CRF's chief concern is to promote quality research, it seeks to attract the participation of scholars with wide-ranging perspectives.

The role of an honest broker is important in a policy environment swirling with reform proposals, especially when calls for action precede the most basic appraisal of underlying problems. CRF is an organization without a vested interest in pursuing a particular path of reform. Instead, it provides a hospitable forum for scholars to review and debate the latest academic research and policy analysis on campaign finance. With a view toward the long term, CRF attempts to sustain a community of scholars dedicated to understanding the complexities of paying for democratic politics. This requires attention to the intellectual foundations of the field of study and a willingness to employ rigorous methods of social science research. Ultimately, CRF hopes to contribute to debates about reform by placing its research and resources in the hands of the public and its policymakers.

Financing the 2000 Election reflects these efforts. The CRF has been issuing the *Financing* series every four years since Herbert Alexander's inaugural edition in 1960. This continuity has created an invaluable historical record of American campaign finance trends. We know, for instance, that the costs of media have been the fastest growing expense for political campaigns during this period. In the 1960 presidential elections, the networks provided half as much free television time to candidates as candidates paid for, a proportion that could hardly be said to apply today. In the 1960 elections, the national parties relied on state party funding to maintain basic operations. Today, national parties send state parties millions of dollars to pay for issue ads and party-building activities.

This book continues the tradition by pulling together a comprehensive analysis of financing in the most recent U.S. elections. Numerous stories about the role of money in politics were told during the campaign, mostly by the nation's major news media organizations, but *Financing the 2000 Election* provides a definitive account of how money was raised and spent. In its breadth and depth, this book offers a perspective on political money that cannot be acquired from focusing only on a few races. To get this perspective, the foremost scholars in the field have been asked to help make sense of the numbers and to provide insights into how particular aspects of the campaign finance system affect American campaigns and elections.

The analyses in these chapters provide the empirical foundations for assessing the prospects of reform proposals. There has been much debate in Congress and in state capitals about campaign finance reform, but many of these discussions lack substantive grounding in the realities of American campaigns. An accounting of the costs of running effective campaigns such as is provided in this book can help bring sober judgment to the reform debate and support policies that achieve desired effects. In his pioneering study of American campaign finance in the middle of the twentieth century, Alexander Heard wrote:

> Public cynicism toward the legal regulation of money in elections has in fact become a cardinal feature of the whole subject. In the attempts made to remedy the abuses and overcome the dissatisfac-

tions associated with campaign finance, the functional necessity and ethical propriety of financing campaigns by some means have frequently become obscured. The ineffectiveness of the statutes has resulted basically from legislative intent out of harmony with the needs of the electoral system.[1]

In short, the *Financing* series provides a unique resource for students of elections, reformers, journalists, and interested citizens. In setting forth the contours of American political finance, this book contributes to public discourse about the role of money in politics. In his closing chapter ("Lessons for Reformers"), Thomas Mann draws on earlier analyses in the book and connects them to important issues in the reform debate. He notes the successes and failures of the Federal Election Campaign Act and raises questions that serious reformers need to address when embarking on the next experiment in regulating political money.

Past readers of this series may rest assured that this book contains the same sort of information as earlier editions but goes further. As usual, one chapter provides a macrolevel perspective on campaign spending in the 2000 elections, demonstrating patterns of change across different election categories and political organizations. Three subsequent chapters go into greater detail about financing the presidential nominations, the general election for president, and congressional elections, followed by chapters on parties and interest groups. David B. Magleby, a careful and enterprising editor, enriches this edition by adding a chapter about financing gubernatorial and state legislative contests and another on judicial elections.

Even the most casual observer of politics would not be surprised to learn that campaign spending increased in the 2000 elections, as it has done in every election cycle since our series began. We can point to the increasing costs of running modern campaigns, the difficulty of reaching voters, and the fact that a strong economy made it easier to raise money. But in the 2000 elections other factors must be considered. Certainly, the collection of electoral prizes at stake was rarely so rich. There was an open seat in the presidency, and the partisan balance in both houses of Congress was so narrow that a slight compositional change could have altered the majority. The outcome of the 2000 elections in state legislative and executive branches would also affect the bargaining process for the decennial reapportionment and legislative redistricting.

Besides documenting the usual trend of escalating campaign costs, the analyses in this book point to something far more interesting: the electoral terrain in highly contested races is now firmly occupied by groups other than candidates. Candidates no longer stand squarely against their rivals; they must also turn every which way to parry with the parties and assorted interest groups. While the content of American campaigns remains firmly candidate centered, control over campaigns and financing has moved away from candidates and toward organized interests. The reason for this shift has much to do with the campaign finance rules established by the Federal Election Campaign Act—rules that have been periodically refashioned by the courts.

An obvious if overlooked lesson of this development is that rules matter. Any set of reforms is bound to strengthen some political actors at the expense of others. The Federal Election Campaign Act (FECA) was written at a time when candidates shaped their own destinies and reformers were concerned with cleaning up problems associated with candidate-controlled campaigns, most notoriously the 1972 Committee to Reelect the President. To control the flow of funds into candidate committees, the FECA encouraged the formation of political action committees (PACs) as a way of limiting the worst abuses of a system that allowed unlimited contributions from wealthy individuals, corporations, and labor unions. To the dismay of many reformers, however, PACs proliferated in the 1980s, providing an increasing share of candidate funds, channeled primarily to incumbents.

The targets of reform in the most recent elections appear to be the political parties, which exploited vague language in the law and a series of FEC rulings to support their candidates with so-called soft money. The thrust of the McCain-Feingold reforms reflects this view. Banning soft money seeks to weaken the political parties relative to other actors, just as earlier reforms that constrained candidates gave additional leverage to parties and interest groups. It is to be expected that parties and other political actors will adapt in ways unforeseen. The next edition of *Financing* may document the unintended consequences of the most recently passed campaign finance laws, should new rules be enacted.

For this edition, we would like to acknowledge those who have made this book possible. We are grateful to our contributors, especially the Center for the Study of Elections and Democracy at Brigham Young University, where Magleby edited and coordinated the production of this volume.

We are thankful for generous grants from the Joyce Foundation, the Carnegie Corporation of New York, and the Open Society Institute, which made the production of this book possible. Finally, we are indebted to the Brookings Institution Press for publishing this latest addition to a long and valuable series.

Raymond J. La Raja
University of Massachusetts, Amherst

Nelson W. Polsby
University of California, Berkeley

Note

1. Alexander Heard, *The Costs of Democracy* (University of North Carolina Press, 1960), p. 9.

Acknowledgments

THIS PROJECT IS AN EXTENSION of a long series of books on campaign finance in presidential election years. Herbert E. Alexander was the author of the series from 1960 through 1992. All of us who study in this field are indebted to Herb for his pioneering work. The book on the 1996 election was edited by John C. Green, an author of a chapter in this volume. My involvement in this project stemmed from a request made by Nelson W. Polsby to advise him as the new director of the Citizens Research Foundation (CRF) on future research opportunities for CRF. I urged Nelson to take the long-standing *Financing* series and focus it on the likely historic 2000 election at all levels, including state and local and judicial elections. He liked the idea and pressed me to edit the book. Even with more than twenty years distance, it is hard to turn down one of your graduate school professors. I am grateful for the trust and confidence Nelson Polsby and CRF invested in my leading the project.

Funding for this project came from the Carnegie Corporation of New York, the Joyce Foundation, and the Open Society Institute. I am grateful for the trust and confidence of these foundations. Geraldine P. Mannion at Carnegie, Larry Hansen at Joyce, and Mark Schmitt at Open Society Institute were all wonderfully supportive. The project draws upon research that another team of scholars and I conducted on party soft money and issue advocacy in the 2000 presidential primaries and congressional general elections. I am grateful to the Pew Charitable Trusts for supporting that research.

xvi ACKNOWLEDGMENTS

Our aim was to produce this book in a timely manner in hopes it will be relevant to the ongoing campaign finance reform debate. I was greatly helped by a team of research assistants. Scott Cameron, a recent BYU graduate, edited and re-edited the entire manuscript. Scott helped coordinate the coverage and worked to minimize duplication across chapters. Emily Walsh and C.W. Ross, also recent BYU graduates, assisted me and all authors with data concerns and verified all data statements in the book. Elizabeth Esty, Analisa Underdown, Brian Smith, and Chris Rees, all of BYU, provided research assistance. Editorial assistance was provided by Anna Nibley Baker. Work on completing the project was assisted by Stephanie Perry Curtis and Jennifer Jensen. The authors of the chapters in this book worked in a concerted and coordinated effort to produce a book with as much data from the 2000 election as possible. I appreciate their willingness to work together, read each other's chapters, and meet deadlines. While more and more of campaign finance in federal elections is "off the books," we were greatly aided in our work by Bob Biersack, senior statistician at the Federal Election Commission, who helped us integrate the FEC data in several chapters. We also express appreciation to three reviewers who provided detailed and helpful comments on the book.

A common feature across chapters of the book is the involvement of talented and hardworking research assistants. Candice J. Nelson was assisted at American University by Valerie Martin as well as by C.W. Ross and Emily Walsh at the Center for the Study of Elections and Democracy at BYU. John C. Green wishes to thank his coauthor, Nathan S. Bigelow, for his help. He would also like to acknowledge the assistance of the Ray C. Bliss Institute of Applied Politics at the University of Akron for collecting and preparing the data for his chapter. Sarah Barclay and Heitor Gouvea of Colby College assisted Anthony Corrado in his work on the presidential general election. Paul S. Herrnson, coauthor of the congressional elections chapter, acknowledges the assistance of Peter Francia and Atiya Stokes of the Center for American Politics and Citizenship at the University of Maryland. Diana Dwyre, coauthor of the party financing chapter, expresses appreciation to Joe Picard and Quinn Picard. Anthony Gierzynski, author of the chapter on state elections, wishes to thank Leslie-Anne Hinton for her help with data on gubernatorial elections and Stefanie Lynch for her assistance with data on legislative races. In the research on judicial elections, as with the book generally, we were fortunate to have access to experts and practitioners. Roy A. Schotland also benefited from the assistance of Brian Henninger and Janice Hoggs. Thomas E. Mann was assisted by Larissa Davis in his concluding chapter.

At the Brookings Institution Press, Christopher Kelaher acquired the book, Theresa Walker edited it, and Carlotta Ribar proofread it. Enid Zafran prepared the index.

Finally, I wish to thank my wife and children for their patience and understanding as this project was added to an already full summer. I dedicate the book to them.

Financing the
2000 *Election*

ONE   *A High-Stakes Election*

DAVID B. MAGLEBY

A LOT WAS AT STAKE for a wide range of partici-
pants in the 2000 elections. Candidates, parties, interest groups, and individual donors saw 2000 as an unusually important year to invest in
campaigns. The White House had no incumbent running, Republican control of the House and Senate was shaky, and many of the constraints on
money in American politics had been lifted owing to a series of court and
administrative rulings.

Quite naturally, presidential elections, especially when no incumbent
is running, foster intense competition between the parties and allied interest groups. That tendency was amplified in 2000 for the Republicans because of their visceral dislike for Bill Clinton and a strong desire to win
back the White House after eight years of Democratic control. As George
W. Bush said at a campaign event, "We're going to win the state of West
Virginia and we're going to do so because this nation is sick and tired of
the politics of personal destruction. This nation is looking for an administration that will appeal to our better angels, not our darker impulses."[1]
Republican elites felt that their party should not have lost the 1992 election to Clinton and that he stole GOP issues like welfare reform to win re-
election in 1996.[2]

The Republican disregard for Clinton had an added edge, an anger
over the dishonor they felt Clinton had brought to the office of president through his affair with a White House intern, Monica Lewinsky,
and his efforts to conceal it. The protracted investigation, House impeachment, and Senate trial failed to remove Clinton from office and

reinforced Republican outrage. For many, especially those who contribute money to the Republican Party, Clinton had besmirched the presidential office, and replacing him with a Republican was important. Among voters, the direct assault on Clinton stressing the impeachment and his character flaws flopped for House Republicans in their 1998 Operation Breakout.[3] As a result, Republicans used more veiled references to Clinton in their campaign against Al Gore in 2000; among GOP elites, however, returning "dignity and honor" to the White House was a common phrase that helped unify the party and motivate financial support.[4]

The possibility of winning back the White House motivated Republicans and allied interest groups to find and rally around a winning candidate. George W. Bush exploited this unifying motive and asserted his leadership through strong, early fund-raising. And, like Clinton, he moved to co-opt issues usually identified with the other party: Social Security, health care, and education.

As a lame duck president, Clinton still had a large impact on the 2000 election, especially by assisting his party with fund-raising. He was also actively involved in Hillary Clinton's successful U.S. Senate bid in New York.[5] In his 1996 race against Bob Dole, Clinton's expanded use of party soft money for candidate definition purposes transformed how parties spend soft money, making it a powerful tool in candidate-specific promotions and attacks. Clinton's soft-money fund-raising involved giving favors to large donors, such as granting access to policy briefings in the White House, and for some, a night in the Lincoln Bedroom. Vice President Gore also was involved in questionable and possibly illegal fund-raising, including a visit to a Buddhist temple where the Democratic National Committee raised $140,000.[6] Footage of Vice President Gore's visit to the temple was used against him in a Republican National Committee ad attacking his veracity and was the "first political attack ad of the general presidential campaign."[7]

The stakes of the 2000 election were high in terms of controlling both houses of Congress. If Bush won the presidential election and the GOP held their majorities in both houses of Congress, the Republicans would achieve unified party control over Congress and the presidency for the first time in forty-six years. The possibility of a sweep excited Republicans and their interest group allies; it also motivated Democrats and allied groups like labor unions to contribute to Democrats.[8]

At the start of the 1999–2000 election cycle, the Republican House majority was razor thin, only a thirteen-seat majority, the narrowest majority in forty-five years. The Democrats came out of the 1998 election with high spirits because they had picked up a net gain of five seats in a midterm election, something neither party had done while controlling the White House since 1934. Recognizing how important money would be in 2000, they appointed Patrick Kennedy to head the Democratic Congressional Campaign Committee (DCCC). Minority Leader Dick Gephardt kept Democratic House retirements and departures by incumbents so they could run for other office to a minimum, creating few open-seat opportunities for Republicans. In contrast, Speaker J. Dennis Hastert had to defend twenty-four open seats. Hastert reportedly was not aware of the retirement of John Edward Porter (R-Ill.) until it was announced.[9] Political pundits agreed that the House was up for grabs.

Early on, the Republicans seemed more likely to hold their majority in the U.S. Senate. But that changed on July 18, 2000, with the death of Georgia Republican Senator Paul Coverdell, who was replaced by the popular former governor Zell Miller, a Democrat. A combination of vulnerable Republican incumbents like Spence Abraham (Mich.), John Ashcroft (Mo.), Rod Grams (Minn.), and Rick Santorum (Pa.), plus opportunities to gain open seats formerly held by Republicans in states like Florida and Nebraska, gave the Democrats real hope for a majority following the election. The Democrats enhanced their chances of multiple victories by recruiting strong candidates, including three who could finance their own races: John Corzine in New Jersey, Mark Dayton in Minnesota, and Maria Cantwell in Washington.[10]

To individuals and interest groups, the 2000 congressional elections provided a rare election in which either party could credibly argue that with resources, they could take or retain control of Congress. On many policy fronts this meant groups and individuals invested heavily in their preferred party, and even safe incumbents were called into fund-raising duty to help their party in this effort. The real possibility of either party controlling Congress, or even one chamber, was a frequent refrain in fund-raising appeals from all four party congressional campaign committees.

Because the 2000 elections fell on the eve of the decennial reapportionment and redistricting, parties and allied interest groups also looked ahead to 2002 and beyond by positioning themselves to secure a party advantage through redistricting. Both parties identified state legislature or gubernatorial races in which an investment would improve their political leverage for redistricting in 2001 and 2002. Examples of battleground states for this effort were Iowa, Illinois, Washington, Tennessee, and Missouri.[11]

This heightened competition even carried over into state judicial elections. States often have more than three times as many judges as legislators. With rare exceptions, judicial elections in the past were different than executive or legislative elections because of their largely invisible nature. This was true despite the large number of judicial elections on the typical general election ballot. This invisibility results in part because many judicial elections are nonpartisan affairs that often involve a vote to retain or not retain a sitting judge, rather than offer a choice between competing judicial candidates. But money is becoming increasingly important in state judicial elections. For example, Alabama spent the most on the state judicial elections, with $12.5 million spent on twelve candidates in 2000.[12] As Roy Schotland discusses in chapter 9, interest groups, recognizing the importance of the judiciary in policymaking, are also investing in judicial elections, and campaign professionals, sensing a new market for their wares, are eager to put that money into campaign communications. Indeed, the tone and nature of many judicial election television commercials is strikingly similar to ads voters see in competitive candidate and ballot initiative contests.

Thus, on all fronts, 2000 was a high-stakes election in terms of partisan and ideological control of government not only for the short run but potentially for the next decade. Individuals and groups who invest in politics understood this dynamic and gave money in extraordinary amounts.

The Regulatory Environment for Money and Politics in 2000

The regulatory environment for campaign finance has gradually changed since the major reforms of the early 1970s. In 1971 Congress enacted the Federal Election Campaign Act (FECA), which was significantly modified following the Watergate scandal with amendments in 1974, 1976, and 1979. The act was also greatly altered by the 1976 landmark *Buckley* v. *Valeo* decision, which held parts of the FECA unco titutional.[13] In response to requests from both parties, the FECA was amended in 1979 to permit parties to spend money raised under FECA rules on party building activities like pins, bumper stickers, voter registration, and get-out-the-vote drives. Under the amended law, such party expenditures do not count against the party contribution or coordinated expenditure limits for any candidate. The Federal Election Commission in subsequent advisory opinions permitted parties at the state and federal levels to set up separate accounts for fund-raising (called nonfederal or "soft money") for party activities not expressly connected to candidates. The regulatory regime in place at the end of this decade of reform included three basic elements: disclosure, contribution limits, and expenditure limits (when linked to public financing).

Disclosure

The premise of disclosure is that the public has a right to know who is funding the candidates, parties, and interest groups involved in elections. Furthermore, if opposing candidates, parties, and the media can gain access to information about who is funding campaigns, voters can hold candidates accountable for how they fund their campaigns. The Supreme Court also noted the need to deter corruption and undue influence. Prior efforts at reform, like the Federal Corrupt Practices Act and the Publicity Act of 1910, had included some form of disclosure in their provisions. But these acts provided incomplete disclosure at best. Recommendations for reform of campaign finance from a presidential commission appointed by President John F. Kennedy were made more salient by the 1968 elections and by President Richard M. Nixon's veto of the Political Broadcasting Act of 1971. Finally, the Watergate scandal called attention to money-filled suitcases transferred to candidate campaigns and added momentum to campaign finance reform efforts.[14]

A fundamental element of the FECA is that money for election activities going to candidates, parties, and interest groups must be disclosed. Money flowing from any of these entities to another must also be disclosed. Candidates are obligated to fully disclose how they fund their campaigns, including full disclosure of how much of their own money they are giving or loaning their campaigns. The disclosure provisions in the FECA withstood constitutional challenge. As the authors in this book demonstrate, disclosure of who is advocating the election or defeat of candidates through noncandidate electioneering is far from complete. Individuals and groups can mask their identity through issue advocacy. Groups and individuals can also communicate with voters through the political parties by way of party soft money. A common element of recent reform legislation is enhanced disclosure, but not all legislation includes issue advocacy, and without greater disclosure of the true sources of issue advocacy, disclosure will remain limited.

Contribution Limitations

A centerpiece of the FECA is that money given to parties or candidates can be limited. This provision was deemed constitutional by the courts. The 1974 amendments to the FECA set aggregate contribution limits for individuals at $25,000 per year or $50,000 per two-year cycle; the amendments also specified that individuals can only give a candidate $1,000 for the primary election and $1,000 for the general election, or $2,000 per election cycle.[15] The contribution limits for political action committees (PACs) were set at $5,000 for the primary and $5,000 for the general election, or $10,000 per routine election cycle. The amendment also limited direct-party contributions to candidates and any money spent in coordination with them. One purpose of contribution limitations is to limit the influence large donors exert on candidates and political parties. Contribution limitations, like disclosure, have been breached by issue advocacy and party soft money. Large donors have many means to influence elections and communicate with voters. Under the *Buckley* v. *Valeo* decision they could spend unlimited money independent of the candidate or parties. But that electioneering was fully disclosed and the source of the communication known. In the aftermath of issue advocacy by the candidates through party soft money in 1996 and issue advocacy by interest groups in that same year we have effectively removed contribution limits.

Expenditure Limitations

The Supreme Court held expenditure limitations on candidates to be constitutional as long as these limits were voluntary and tied to some form of public financing.[16] Presidential elections are the only part of the FECA that include public funds. Every major party nominee since the FECA took effect has accepted federal funding in the general election, including outspoken critics of public financing like Ronald Reagan. Public funding in presidential primaries is partial and comes in the form of matching funds. When candidates accept matching funds, they must abide by aggregate and state-by-state spending limits, although the state-by-state limits have come to be loosely interpreted.[17]

These forms of regulation were meant to reduce the importance of large and undisclosed donors to candidates and political parties and elevate other forms of electoral competition.[18] However, the FECA did not clearly differentiate campaign communications from other forms of speech. It fell to the Supreme Court to attempt to craft a "bright line" definition of electioneering or what it called express advocacy. In *Buckley* v. *Valeo* the Court defined "express advocacy" in terms of word choice. Ads that use words like " 'vote for,' 'elect,' 'support,' 'cast your ballot for,' 'Smith for Congress,' 'vote against,' 'defeat,' or 'reject'" constitute express advocacy.[19] The Court held that nonelection communications, or issue advocacy, are not subject to contribution limits or disclosure, while independent expenditures, which use express advocacy language, are subject to disclosure requirements.

By the 1996 election cycle, interest groups had found ways to effectively communicate election messages without using the "magic words" of express advocacy. Groups like the American Federation of Labor and Congress of Industrial Organizations (AFL-CIO) spent $35 million on issue ads without disclosure constraints or spending limitations. Other groups followed suit in 1996, including business groups, some with innocuous names like "Triad" and "The Coalition: Americans Working for Real Change."[20]

Not only did the Court uphold individual and group rights to speak out on an issue, but it also upheld the right of groups and individuals to comment expressly on political elections. In *Buckley* v. *Valeo* the Court permits unlimited express advocacy electioneering by individuals and groups, requiring only full disclosure, as long as there was no coordination or collusion with the candidate or parties. These so-called independent expenditures have been a relatively small, but sometimes consequential, part of the campaign finance mosaic ever since 1976 and were a precursor to issue advocacy in 1996. For example, in the 1980 election the National Conservative Political Action Committee (NCPAC) made independent expenditures against five Senate Democrats and may have been a factor in their defeat.[21] Groups like the National Rifle Association and the National Education Association use independent expenditures as a primary means of electioneering.

In *FEC* v. *Colorado Republican Federal Campaign Committee*, the Republican Party successfully argued that if individuals and PACs can spend unlimited amounts in independent expenditures, parties should be able to do the same. In the 1999-2000 election cycle the parties largely bypassed independent expenditures. The Democratic Congressional Campaign Committee (House Democrats) spent under $2 million in independent expenditures. The other party committees lagged far behind—the

National Republican Senatorial Committee spent $267,000 independently, mostly in Nebraska. The Democratic Senatorial Campaign Committee spent $133,000 independently, with more than half that amount spent in the New York Senate race. One state party, the Utah Republicans, spent $375,503 in independent expenditures in the Utah second congressional district.

Party Soft Money and Interest Group Issue Advocacy

Parties experience greater latitude in spending money on elections through soft money. In 1979 Congress recognized the parties' right to support their candidates and strengthen party infrastructure. As noted, the FECA was amended to permit party committees to fund some generic party activities with hard dollars (subject to the contribution limits of FECA). These expenditures are not counted toward any candidate's party contribution or coordinated expenditure limits. The advisory opinions of the Federal Election Commission (FEC) went much further, permitting state and national parties to raise money for party building to be spent as nonfederal or "soft money." Donations to the parties for nonfederal or soft money accounts are disclosed but unlimited.

The use of soft money grew in new ways during the 1996 election cycle when the Clinton-Gore campaign used soft money to promote their candidacy; the Republicans mimicked this move and widely applied it to competitive federal contests in 1998 and again in 2000.[22] The ability to use soft money to promote or attack candidates has given the parties a powerful new tool and makes soft money fund-raising more important.

Record-setting spending by candidates, as well as noncandidates, brings into question the efficacy of campaign finance regulation. The FEC is widely perceived as slow and prone to deadlock.[23] These problems with the FEC can often be traced back to those being regulated—Congress and the president. Congress structured the FEC to have an even number of partisan commissioners and has consistently left the agency underfunded for enforcement and other activities.

Lax enforcement by the FEC is clearly part of the reason individuals, candidates, parties, and interest groups circumvented the intent of the FECA, as clearly demonstrated by Anthony Corrado in chapter 4 and Thomas Mann in chapter 10. But the commission is not alone to blame for the demise of the FECA. The seeds of the demise of the FECA were sown by Congress in failing to clearly define election speech and differentiate it from nonregulated speech. Others would contend that the problem with the FEC is that it has pursued the wrong enforcement issues in cases involving the Christian Action Network, among others.[24] During the past few election cycles the ability of campaign participants to circumvent the FECA has grown. In the broad spectrum of change, two developments in the 2000 elections stand out as most important in the growing campaign finance free-for-all: party soft money and issue advocacy by interest groups.

The soft money exemption to contribution limits and the parties' ability to spend that money in ways clearly linked to the election or defeat of certain candidates has effectively removed contribution limits. Moreover, with the widespread use of joint fund-raising committees or "victory funds" in 2000, candidates could go to a donor and seek the maximum individual contribution to the candidate account, a hard money contribution to the party, and a soft money contribution with the understanding that the soft money raised through the candidate's victory fund would be spent in that candidate's contest. A visible example of a candidate using the victory fund device in 2000 was Hillary Clinton's New York Senate race.[25] The use of victory funds by candidates removes the fig leaf that soft money contributions are not candidate contributions.

Individuals are not constrained by contribution limits or disclosure provisions when they seek to influence an election's outcome through issue advocacy. For example, in 2000 one or more donors gave the National Association for the Advancement of Colored People (NAACP) Voter Fund more than $10 million to fund election activities, including an ad that graphically reminded viewers of the dragging death of James Byrd Jr. and attacked George W. Bush for not supporting hate crimes legislation in Texas.[26] Also in 2000, Jane Fonda gave $12.5 million to pro-choice ($12 million) and environmental groups ($500,000) to run ads aimed at electing candidates friendly to her perspective on these issues.[27] An early harbinger of issue advocacy came in the presidential primaries when a group calling itself Republicans for Clean Air ran ads attacking John McCain. The ad was actually funded by Texas businessman Sam Wyly.[28] No doubt other large donors contribute to issue advocacy groups, but because of the lack of disclosure, we do not know who they are.

Limits on interest group and PAC contributions have been seriously eroded. For direct contributions to candidates, PACs are still limited. But PACs may also give to congressional leadership PACs, who in turn may give to other candidates (143 leadership PACs made contributions in 2000), and, even more important, their sponsoring corporations or unions can give unlimited money to the political parties for soft money purposes.[29] For example, unions composed six of the ten largest soft money donors to the Democratic Party committees in 2000.[30] Unions, interest groups, or individuals who fund PACs can avoid limits and disclosure by spending money on issue advocacy. Hence, the pharmaceutical industry gave an estimated $10.7 million directly to candidates and parties through their PACs and individual contributions, contributing an estimated $15.8 million in soft money to the parties and then spent an estimated $40 million through a group calling itself "Citizens for Better Medicare," which ran some pure issue ads but also aggressively supported and opposed some candidates.[31] With the advent of electioneering through issue advocacy, increasing campaign activity is going undisclosed. Some groups like the Sierra Club and Americans for Limited Terms announce the amounts they spend, seeking added publicity for their issue, while other groups spend millions communicating their message but insisting that they are communicating about issues, not electioneering.

Issue advocacy is often conducted by groups such as Foundation for Responsible Government, American Family Voices, Coalition to Make Our Voices Heard, Hands across New Jersey, and Committee for Good Common Sense. These groups use innocuous names to avoid disclosing any recognizable group affiliation. Until Congress required some disclosure through legislation enacted in July 2000, some groups campaigned anonymously by exploiting the issue advocacy distinction in *Buckley* to avoid disclosure to the FEC and section 527 of the Internal Revenue Code that exempted groups with assets in noninterest-bearing accounts from reporting anything about their organizations to the Internal Revenue Service. The most visible "section 527 organization" in the 2000 election was Republicans for Clean Air, which attacked Arizona senator John McCain's environmental record. Republicans for Clean Air ran its ads only in California, Ohio, and New York in the days before the March 7, 2000, presidential primary. Most of the $2.5 million they were estimated to have spent was used in New York City.[32] The McCain campaign angrily attacked the claims in the ad and insisted it must be connected to the Bush campaign. After two days of intense media investigation, Texas billionaire Sam Wyly acknowledged that he had funded Republicans for Clean Air.[33] The controversy surrounding section 527 organizations pressured Congress to enact legislation that requires an initial notice, periodic reports on contributors and expenditures, and modified annual returns, legislation that was signed into law in July 2000 by President Clinton.[34]

Section 527 organizations continued to affect the 2000 general elections, however, because the funds raised before the legislation took effect fell outside of any disclosure provision of the congressional action. For example, Citizens for Better Medicare used their section 527 status to buy $65 million in television, radio, and newspaper ads.[35]

At the state level, participants often have even more latitude to spend money on campaigns. For example, candidates in some jurisdictions can still convert campaign funds to personal uses.[36] Even in judicial elections—a domain long thought to be removed from the taint of money and influence, the 2000 campaigns were increasingly expensive elections with active campaigning by interest groups and parties in ways that force debate on the role of electoral democracy in the judiciary.

The Supply Side

The high volume of overall spending is evidence that for individuals and groups inclined to spend money on campaigns, the 2000 elections were worth investing in. The sources of this incredible spending remain diverse but not broadly representative. Some have argued that the robust economy and the success of dot-com entrepreneurs are reasons for the high spending in the 2000 elections.[37] Added to this "new money" were the staples of campaign finance—organized labor, teachers, environmental groups, pro-choice groups, and trial lawyers supporting Democrats and business groups, trade associations, pro-life, and socially conservative groups supporting Republicans.

The Bush campaign not only exploited the depth of Republican resentment over Clinton but used a hierarchal structure with titles and levels as a fund-raising tool. Although this was not a new idea, Bush used this method on an unprecedented scale. He set up a group of two hundred individuals, whom he called the "Pioneers." Each pioneer committed to raising $100,000 in $1,000 increments. This group provided Bush "with about one-fifth of his total funds."[38] Gore had a similar structure to his fund-raising, the "Board of Directors," but he was not nearly as successful.

As a party, the Republicans continued to utilize their successful small donor program. This program worked especially well in raising hard money for the Republican National Committee (RNC) and National Republican Congressional Committtee (NRCC). The RNC more than doubled the amount of hard money it raised in 1998, from $104,048,689 to an impressive $212,798,761 in 2000. The NRCC also did well by raising $97,314,513 in 2000 compared with $72,708,311 in 1998.

Another important source of money in politics is candidates' personal wealth, which they can spend in unlimited amounts on their own campaigns. In the presidential primaries, candidate self-financing was most evident in the Republican candidacy of Steve Forbes, who spent $48 million on his own campaign.[39] Forbes's substantial personal investment in seeking office was surpassed by the more than $60 million spent by Democrat John Corzine in his successful bid for the U.S. Senate from New Jersey.[40] Both parties have long courted self-financed candidates, but the Senate Democrats clearly did better at this game in 2000 than the Republicans.[41] Mark Dayton in Minnesota and Maria Cantwell in Washington were also largely self-financed candidates. Dayton spent $11.7 million of his own funds, and Cantwell spent $10.3 million of hers.[42] Three largely self-financed candidates in key races helped the DSCC target its massive soft money war chest elsewhere.

But the most dramatic demonstration of an expanded supply of political money in the 2000 elections was the House and Senate Democratic campaign committees' success in fund-raising, especially soft money fund-raising. For the first time, the Democratic Senatorial Campaign Committee (DSCC) surpassed the National Republican Senatorial Committee (NRSC) in soft money receipts and was much better at deploying the party money into competitive races.[43]

Interest groups also found 2000 to be a year in which money seemed more abundant. The context of the election—open seat for the presidency, close margins of party control in both houses, a pending redistricting, a closely divided U.S. Supreme Court with the new president likely to make one or more appointments—gave groups many themes to raise with donors when they were asking for money. Moreover, interest groups now invest money in campaigns in many ways. They can hedge their bets when they contribute hard money, which clearly business and trade associations are inclined to do; they can invest more ideologically in party soft money contributions; and they can spend anonymously through issue advocacy.

This is not to say that all potential donors were happy with the increased pressure to give more political money to more entities. Some corporate leaders have spoken out against the "influence of large donors and special interest groups." Calling itself the Committee for Economic Development (CED), this group of corporate leaders comes from corporations like Xerox, Citigroup, General Electric, Exxon Mobil, and Liberty Mutual Insurance. The committee would ban soft-money donations, increase individual contribution limits, provide public financing for congressional races, and limit campaign spending.[44]

Implications for Reform and Future Elections

Assessing how campaigns were financed in 2000 is a principal focus of this book. This book also explores the implications of current campaign finance as viewed by voters, candidates, parties, organized groups, and institutions, and addresses the question: how can the debate over campaign finance reform be informed by the way the 2000 elections were financed? The Federal Election Campaign Act, as noted, has been greatly altered from its underlying premises by campaign practices. Despite the few changes made in federal campaign laws, the state and local level has seen serious campaign finance reform activity, which offers important lessons. Finally, in recent years judicial elections, a domain in which money was not seen as very important, have seen increasingly contested elections, issue advocacy, and a new political culture. Will courts see issue advocacy differently when it involves electing state supreme court justices and other judges than when it involves legislative or executive candidates?

At the presidential level, the implications for reform that flow from the 2000 elections include whether candidates will continue to build their strategies around partial public funding. Or will they pursue the Bush strategy and avoid the constraints of matching funds in the nomination phase, yet reap the bonus without the meaningful strings of the public grant in the general election?

One major reason why candidates might forgo matching funds and limits in the primary while accepting full public funding and expenditure limits in the general election is that expenditures in the latter are effectively unlimited with party soft money electioneering. Both parties demonstrated in 1996 and 2000 that the national parties can effectively carry the candidates' message through ads funded largely by soft money, thereby permitting the candidates to accept the federal grant without real constraints. Hence, expenditure limitations are no longer meaningful at the federal level. At the state level, expenditure limits exist in several states with some form of public financing, but these are often circumvented through party spending or issue advocacy. A few candidates before 2000 turned down the matching funds, most notably John Connally in 1980 and Steve Forbes in 1996. However, George W. Bush was the first frontrunner to turn down matching funds, a move he justified in part by having to run against Steve Forbes who also turned down matching funds in his 2000 campaign.

While correcting a part of the issue advocacy problem, the legislation relating to section 527 organizations has not stopped interest groups from exploiting the Supreme Court's "magic words" dictum and investing un-limited amounts of money in presidential elections. This loophole was exploited early in the 2000 primary season when the Sierra Club and the National Abortion and Reproductive Rights Action League (NARAL) ran ads against George W. Bush in an effort to raise doubts about his candi-dacy and perhaps start a fight within the Republican Party on environ-mental and abortion issues. In some respects, the Republicans for Clean Air attacks on McCain in March 2000 were a response to the early Sierra Club environmental attacks on Bush. One lesson future candidates will likely take from 2000 is that they will need even more money in their campaign treasuries to counter not only their opponents but the opposing party and issue advocacy groups as well.

Congressional elections now fall into two different categories. The more common type of congressional election is a safe seat, in which the incum-bent or candidate from the dominant party in the district or state will win. Only in a small set of contests is there real competition. Competitive campaigns have a very different dynamic. In these, noncandidate cam-paign activity roughly equals the spending and volume of communication by the candidate campaigns. Campaigns funded by outside money are often more strident and sometimes create problems for the intended ben-eficiaries.[45] Because the battle for party control of Congress centers on only a few House and Senate races, all players—parties, interest groups, safe-seat incumbents elsewhere, and leadership PACs—focus on winning these races. With so much at stake and so much being spent, the costs of advertising rise, and air time becomes scarce.

In these highly contested elections, candidate and noncandidate cam-paigns diversify their approach and use more mail, telephone, Internet, and personal contact. In some House races in 2000, more than eighty unique mailings and an estimated 2 million pieces of mail were sent for the two candidates.[46] Candidates in contested races should assume that at least as much will be spent against them by their opponent's allies (party soft money and issue advocacy) as by their opponent. It is also safe for them to assume that money spent by their party and allied groups will not always be to their advantage. The net effect is that candidates need to raise and spend as much money as possible because they control that money, and they will need it to compete against those allied against them.

This growth in noncandidate campaigning questions assumptions made by political scientists and voters about our candidate-centered politics. Political scientist Martin Wattenberg has argued that American elections are candidate centered, an argument reinforced by the historic pattern of weak political parties.[47] But in competitive races, campaigning is now a team sport with candidates no longer in control. The growth in joint fund-raising or victory committees is a good example. But the analogy of politics as a team sport could be taken too far because competitive federal elections are contests without a coach, a clearly defined set of rules, or referees that consistently call penalties.

To the voter, however, the presumption remains that the candidates are in control.[48] When relatively few races are seriously contested, as in 2000, recruiting high-quality candidates for these races remains important. With so much of the money spent in contested races coming from party soft money, the power of congressional campaign committees has grown because they allocate that money in whatever amounts they choose. How are these decisions made? By whom? And what are the implications for legislative behavior given this enlarged role played by large soft money donors? Will the party caucuses as a whole be more friendly to large party donors?

Issue advocacy too carries important implications for voters. These campaigns are much noisier, and issue advocacy from groups with masked identities is difficult to unravel during the heat of the campaign. In races with substantial issue advocacy and party spending of soft money, there is anecdotal evidence that voters "tune out" politics and ignore much of the mail and telephone contact directed their way.[49] Unfortunately, the media have often not given voters much help. If substantial electioneering is conducted by way of issue advocacy, shouldn't there be greater disclosure from the groups about who they are? Should groups be able to campaign anonymously?

Political scientists have long been strong advocates of strengthened political parties. On the surface it seems that the infusion of so much soft money into the parties has the salutary effect of strengthening parties, but soft money's effect on party strength depends a great deal on how the soft money is spent. In competitive environments almost all soft money is spent on candidate-centered strategies, and to an extent, the parties are merely bank accounts used by political professionals to mount campaigns for and against candidates.[50] In these cases, even large amounts of soft money do not strengthen parties appreciably. Whether the small fraction of soft money spent on voter lists, party organizing, and so forth, is great enough to have made a difference is open to debate. Clearly parties are less important than they once were in funding candidates outside the highly competitive environments. The emphasis on soft money communications may therefore have reduced the parties' willingness to invest in promising but not clearly competitive candidates. Hence, any assessment of soft money implications needs to include how it is spent, who benefits, and what it does for the parties.

The array of noncandidate campaigning from interest groups through independent expenditures, internal communications within group membership, and issue advocacy has been important in competitive races, and in the view of some, when combined with the party spending, it is determinative.[51] Because of its nature, this type of campaigning is difficult to monitor, and as groups have shifted from independent expenditures to issue advocacy, interest group campaigning has avoided disclosure. One way to track part of the activity is through a broadcast monitoring service like the Campaign Media Analysis Group (CMAG), which has the technological means to identify every television commercial in the seventy-five largest media markets. Assuming sound coding of the commercials by professional coders, we have a means to estimate the frequency of issue advocacy in the more populated markets. Using this technology in 1998, Jon Krasno and Ken Goldstein conducted studies for the Brennan Center and found nearly half of all political ads were not run by candidates (46 percent), and ads run by parties and interest groups were more negative in tone.[52] As helpful as the CMAG data are, they clearly underestimate the costs of issue advocacy, because as election day approaches stations raise their fees for noncandidate entities. The CMAG data are also limited because they only examine television activity in large markets, and as my colleagues and I have demonstrated in research on the 1997–98 and 1999–2000 election cycles, a great deal of issue advocacy takes place in the mail, on the phone, and in person.[53]

Much remains to be learned about issue advocacy. We have evidence that in the 2000 presidential race, voters perceived issue ads as indistinguishable from party and candidate ads.[54] This fact sparks several questions: is this equally true in congressional races? Assuming that the "magic words" test is inadequate to distinguish electioneering from nonelectioneering in the real world of campaigns, what are meaningful standards or definitions of electioneering? Given the importance of issue advocacy to elections, how might a disclosure requirement work? If Congress enacts a ban on soft money and does nothing about disclosure of issue advocacy, will voters end up knowing less about who is trying to influence the outcome of elections?

The constitutional question of whether issue advocacy is protected speech and therefore not subject to limitation or regulation also arises. Analysis of 2000 data shows that most issue advocacy centered on electing or defeating candidates.[55] This has profound consequences for reform and eventual judicial review of those reforms.

Far more elections occur at the state and local levels than at the federal level, yet much less attention is paid to these contests regarding implications for reform. States have enacted a wide range of campaign finance reform and provide a wealth of data. Reform is also affected because the campaign finance problem now clearly confronts the judiciary. The judicial branch, a bystander in the past, may alter its thinking. Evidence of the issue's importance to state supreme court justices is the fact that chief justices of fourteen of the seventeen largest states with judicial elections attended a recent conference to discuss reform of judicial campaign finance.[56]

Overview of the Book

Participation in this volume was not based on a common perspective on campaign finance reform. Indeed, the authors' views vary widely.

In chapter 2 Candice J. Nelson examines spending in the 2000 elections overall, giving aggregate spending estimates and comparing them to previous election cycles. This estimating process is much more difficult than at any time since 1972 because so much activity is now undisclosed. The chapter also explores the implications of dramatically rising spending for matters like static contribution limits, the time candidates spend raising money, the length of the campaign, and the growing importance of personal wealth and outside money.

This book divides the financing of the 2000 presidential elections into nomination and general election phases. John C. Green and Nathan S. Bigelow explore the nomination phase in chapter 3, and Anthony Corrado focuses on the general election phase in chapter 4. Green and Bigelow discuss how fund-raising innovations sharply increased the costs of the nomination campaigns in 2000. They also discuss the relationship among campaign finance laws, candidate resources, and structure of competition and the financing of the 2000 nomination campaigns. Unlike the presidential primaries, which saw no soft money influence, Corrado finds soft money a major component of the general election. Corrado also discusses an unprecedented use of money in politics—the financing of the Florida recount battle, including the protracted litigation. The provisions of the FECA in relation to presidential general elections are according to Corrado "ineffective and meaningless."

Paul S. Herrnson and Kelly D. Patterson examine the close party balance in the House and Senate as factors in financing the 2000 congressional elections. Other important developments in congressional campaign finance in 2000 include soft money, issue advocacy, victory committees, the continued tendency of PACs to give to incumbents, and the strategic advantages of self-financed candidates.

Much of the story of 2000 is one of party soft money and the role of the parties in our electoral process. In chapter 6, Diana Dwyre and Robin Kolodny put the role of the political parties in the 2000 election in perspective. As important as soft money is, without hard money it is not nearly as potent for electioneering. Dwyre and Kolodny explain this important interaction as well as the changing dynamics of party finance.

Interest groups influence federal elections in many ways. In chapter 7, Allan J. Cigler explores these interest group investment options and how groups may choose to behave differently in candidate contributions than in issue advocacy or soft money allocations. Cigler describes the actions of groups and organizations, in disclosed and undisclosed electioneering, that were most active in financing the 2000 elections.

With redistricting looming in 2001 and 2002, the financing of gubernatorial and state legislative elections had significance at the state and federal levels. As Anthony Gierzynski demonstrates in chapter 8, the political parties and interest groups understood this importance and invested more heavily as a result. Gierzynski summarizes an impressive collection of data on gubernatorial and legislative campaign finance and compares it with the empirical regularities at the federal level.

This is the first in this series of books on financing elections to include a chapter on financing judicial elections. Roy A. Schotland thoroughly examines recent history and the growing trend toward expensive campaigns marked by issue advocacy by outside groups. Now, unlike in the past, judicial elections are starting to resemble the other elections examined in this book. Interestingly, the courts, which will ultimately decide the fate of any legislatively enacted reform, must now confront many of the same issues in an area much closer to home, their own branch of government.

Finally, Thomas E. Mann, in chapter 10, assesses the realities of financing and the implications for reform that emerge from the remarkable election in 2000. Mann explains why the most pragmatic strategy is more effective regulation on the model of McCain-Feingold rather than deregulation or full public financing.

Notes

1. Alison Mitchell, "The Republicans: The Texas Governor; Bush Concentrates on Clinton, but Keeps an Eye on Gore," *New York Times*, August 2, 2000, p. A17.

2. James A. Barnes, "Pressure on Clinton to Turn Leftward," *National Journal,* vol. 29, April 26, 1997, p. 836.

3. David B. Magleby, ed., *Outside Money: Soft Money and Issue Advocacy in the 1998 Congressional Elections* (Rowman and Littlefield, 2000).

4. George W. Bush used the "restore honor and dignity" language frequently when discussing the 2000 race, and his website issue page uses this phrase. See ⟨www.georgewbush.com/ [July 2, 2001]⟩.

5. Center for Responsive Politics, "White House Guests Database" ⟨www.opensecrets.org/whitehouse/index.htm [June 21, 2001]⟩.

6. Ruth Marcus and Ira Chinoy, "A Fund-Raising 'Mistake'; DNC Held Event in Buddhist Temple," *Washington Post,* October 17, 1996, p. A1.

7. David B. Magleby, ed., *Election Advocacy: Soft Money and Issue Advocacy in the 2000 Congressional Elections* (Brigham Young University, Center for the Study of Elections and Democracy, February 2001). See note 22.

8. Thomas B. Edsall, "Unions in High-Tech Fight for the Future," *Washington Post*, October 31, 2000, p. A8.

9. Lynn Sweet, a reporter from the *Chicago Sun Times,* interview by Barry Rundquist, January 18, 2001. Barry Rundquist and others, "The 2000 Illinois Tenth Congressional District Race," in Magleby, *Election Advocacy*, pp.161–73; and David B. Magleby, ed., "The e-Symposium: Outside Money in the 2000 Presidential Primaries and Congressional General Elections" ⟨www.apsanet.org/ps/ [June 2001]⟩.

10. Corzine set a new record in self-financing by spending more than $35 million in the primary and another $25 million in the general election. See Andrew Jacobs, "Primary in New Jersey: The Democrats; Low-Key End on Both Sides as Corzine Gets Nomination," *New York Times*, June 7, 2000, p. B9.

11. See chapter 8 for a detailed analysis of gubernatorial and state legislative elections.

12. See Roy Schotland, chapter 9, in this volume.

13. *Buckley* v. *Valeo*, 424 US 1(1976).

14. Nancy Lammers and John L. Moore, eds., *Dollar Politics*, 3d ed. (Washington: Congressional Quarterly, 1982) p.10; and Robert L. Peabody and others, *To Enact a Law: Congress and Campaign Financing* (Praeger, 1972).

15. When there is a runoff election, individuals can contribute an additional $1,000, and PAC limits rise to $15,000.

16. *Buckley* v. *Valeo*, 424 U.S. 1(1976).

17. Evidence of the FEC concern for state-by-state limits is found in the states' repeated requests to Congress to abolish them. Federal Election Commission, *Legislative Recommendations* (Government Printing Office, 2001), p. 47.

18. Patricia A. O'Connor, ed., *Congress and the Nation*, vol. 4 (Washington.: Congressional Quarterly, 1977) p. 985.

19. *Buckley* v. *Valeo*, 424 U.S.1 (1976), note 52.

20. David B. Magleby, "Interest-Group Election Ads," in Magleby, *Outside Money* (Rowman and Littlefield, 2000), p. 54.

21. Thomas B. Edsall, "Financial Woes, Legal Fights Weaken Conservative PACs; For Some, Fund-Raising Drops as Debts Rise," *New York Times*, October 29, 1986, p. A1.

22. Magleby, *Outside Money;* Magleby, *Election Advocacy;* and David B. Magleby, ed., *The Other Campaign: Soft Money and Issue Advocacy in the 2000 Congressional Elections* (Rowman and Littlefield, 2002).

23. Brooks Jackson, *Broken Promise: Why the Federal Election Commission Failed* (Priority Press Publications, 1990), pp. 59–62.

24. Eliza Newlin Carney. "Besieged FEC Gets Dissed on All Sides," *National Journal,* May 24,1997, p.1038.

25. "Money Games in the Senate Race," *New York Times*, January 5, 2000, p. A20.

26. John Mintz, "The Interest Groups; Liberals Mobilize against Bush, GOP," *Washington Post*, November 3, 2000, p. A22.

27. Ruth Marcus, "Costliest Race Nears End; Bush, Gore Running Close; U.S. Campaigns Fuel $3 Billion in Spending," *Washington Post*, November 6, 2000 p. A1; and John Mintz and Susan Schmidt, "Stealth PACs' Report Campaign Financing; First Data Available under New Reform Law," *Washington Post*, November 1, 2000, p. A17.

28. Richard W. Stevenson and Richard Perez-Pena, "The 2000 Campaign: The Tactics; Wealthy Texan Says He Bought Anti-McCain Ads," *New York Times,* March 4, 2000, p. A1.

29. Center for Responsive Politics, Washington, D.C.

30. Brody Mullins and Charlie Mitchell, "Soft Money Unleashed," *National Journal*, February 17, 2001, p. 501.

31. The $10.7 and $15.8 million figures come from the Center for Responsive Politics, Washington, D.C. The $40 million dollar figure comes from Mintz and Schmidt, "Stealth PACs' Report Campaign Financing," p. A17.

32. Mike Allen, "McCain Foe Gives $100,000 to GOP Committee," *Washington Post*, April 21, 2000, p. A5.

33. John Mintz, "Texan Aired 'Clean Air' Ads: Bush's Campaign Not Involved, Billionaire Says," *Washington Post,* March 4, 2000, p. A6.

34. "Filing Requirements—Political Organizations," *IRS 2001* (www.irs.ustreas.gov/prod/bus_info/eo/pol-file.html [20 Jun 2001]).

35. "Clinton Signs Law to End Anonymous Political Ads," *Florida Times Union*, July 2, 2000, p. A13.

36. Council of State Governments, *The Book of the States*, pp. 211–28.

37. Chapter 2 explores spending in the 2000 elections in depth; and see Marcus, "Costliest Race Nears End," p. A1.

38. Susan B. Glasser, "George W. Bush's Dash for Cash," *Washington Post's Weekly Edition*, April 19, 1999, p. 10.

39. Data compiled from the Federal Election Commission, Washington (www.fec.gov [July 10, 2001]).

40. Jacobs, "Primary in New Jersey: The Democrats," p. B5.

41. David B. Magleby and Candice J. Nelson, *The Money Chase* (Brookings, 1990), p. 45.

42. Federal Election Commission, "FEC Reports on Congressional Finance Activity for 2000," Washington, May 15, 2001(www.fec.gov/press/051501congfinact/051501congfinact.html [July 10, 2001]).

43. Magleby, *Election Advocacy*; and Magleby, *The Other Campaign*.

44. Committee for Economic Development, "Business Leaders Launch Campaign Finance Reform Effort," press release, Washington, March 19, 1999.

45. Magleby, *Outside Money*; and Magleby, *The Other Campaign*.

46. Todd Donovan and Charles Morrow, "The 2000 Washington Second Congressional District Race," in *Election Advocacy*, pp. 259–74.

47. Martin Wattenberg, *The Rise of Candidate-Centered Politics: Presidential Elections of the 1980's* (Harvard University Press, 1991).

48. David B. Magleby, *Dictum without Data: The Myth of Issue Advocacy and Party Building* (Brigham Young University, Center for Study of Elections and Democracy, 2000).

49. Dana Milbank, "Mercilessly Multiplying Election Ads," *Washington Post*, October 31, 2000, p. C01.

50. Jonathan S. Krasno and Daniel E. Seltz, *Buying Time: Television Advertising in the 1998 Congressional Elections* (New York University School of Law, Brennan Center for Justice, 2000).

51. Michael W. Traugott, "The 2000 Michigan Senate Race," in Magleby, *Election Advocacy*, p. 62.

52. The Brennan Center for Justice at New York University Law School with Kenneth Goldstein, "Press Release March 13, 2001."

53. Magleby, *Election Advocacy* ; Magleby, *Outside Money*; and Magleby, *The Other Campaign*.

54. Magleby, *Dictum without Data*.

55. Ibid.; and Brennan Center for Justice with Kenneth Goldstein of the University of Wisconsin—Madison conducted an ongoing study consisting of six press releases from September 19 to October 30, 2000, titled *Brennan Center Releases Real Time Data on Ads in 2000 Campaign*.

56. The conference, Summit on Improving Judicial Selection, was held in Chicago, Illinois, December 2000.

TWO   *Spending in the*
          2000 Elections

CANDICE J. NELSON

THE 2000 ELECTIONS shattered spending and
contribution records. Not only did the candidates and parties spend money
in record numbers, but so did interest groups and unaffiliated organizations. Fueled by the unprecedented amounts of soft money in this election
cycle, issue advocacy spending by political parties and interest groups com-
peted with spending by candidates, and in some contested House and Senate
races, effectively doubled overall spending.[1] From the Bush presidential
campaign dwarfing the receipts of all other presidential candidates in the
prenomination phase, to Jon Corzine spending $60 million of his per-
sonal fortune on his successful New Jersey Senate race, spending figures
in the 2000 election redefined the costs of elections in the United States.

In looking at spending in the 2000 elections, two themes stand out.
One is that almost across the board, more money found its way into the
political system than in past elections. The second, but just as important,
is that it is becoming harder and harder to document the amount of money
in the political system.

The Federal Election Campaign Act of 1971 (FECA) and amendments
to the act passed in 1974 established campaign finance disclosure and
contribution limits for federal elections, as well as voluntary spending limits

I am grateful to my research assistant at American University, Valerie Martin,
for her help in compiling the tables in this chapter and to C.W. Ross and Emily
Walsh at the Center for Study of Elections and Democracy at Brigham Young
University for help in adjusting the tables for inflation.

for presidential elections. During the past decade all three elements of the FECA—disclosure, contribution limits, and spending limits—have eroded.

Although disclosure of contributions by individuals to federal candidates and to the national political parties and contributions for express advocacy independent expenditures continues, disclosure of spending by interest groups and unaffiliated organizations for issue advocacy is not required. The Supreme Court, in its 1976 *Buckley* v. *Valeo* decision, ruled that only funds spent on broadcast or print advertisements that expressly advocate the election or defeat of a candidate by using words such as "vote for," "support," "vote against," and "defeat" are considered spending subject to the disclosure requirements of the FECA. Although the Court made this distinction in a footnote, which received little attention at the time, that decision has led to the creation of issue advocacy campaigns, one of the largest areas of nondisclosure in elections today.

Groups have found they can communicate election messages while avoiding the "magic words" standard enumerated in *Buckley* v. *Valeo*.[2] The Annenberg Public Policy Center of the University of Pennsylvania and the Center for the Study of Elections and Democracy at Brigham Young University, among others, have attempted to estimate how much money interest groups and political parties spend on issue advocacy.[3] However, because the FECA places disclosure requirements only on express advocacy, we simply do not know how much interest groups spend on issue advocacy.

Although the 1974 contribution limits remain in place, Congress amended the FECA in 1979 to allow spending beyond the candidate contributions and coordinated expenditures by political parties for "party-building" activities like bumper stickers, voter registration drives, and get-out-the-vote efforts. The Federal Election Commission (FEC) in a series of advisory opinions went further to allow state and national party committees to establish "nonfederal" or soft money accounts to be used for joint state and federal party activity not coordinated with the candidates. Individuals and business interests, such as corporations and labor unions, can give hundreds of thousands of dollars to political parties for these soft money accounts, unfettered by contribution limits. Much of this soft money is spent for the promotion or attack of particular candidates, a clear departure from the 1979 amendments, and activity the FEC has chosen not to limit.[4]

Although partial public funding of the presidential prenomination and public funding of the party conventions and the presidential general elec-

Table 2-1.   *Campaign Spending in 2000*
Millions of dollars

Category	Spending
Presidential	607[a]
Congressional	1,006[b]
Party (federal)	693[c]
Soft money	498[d]
Issue ads	509[e]
State (nonfederal)	329[f]
Judicial elections	62[g]
Ballot initiatives	225[h]
Total	3,929,000

a. Spending by primary and general election candidates. Calculated from Center for Responsive Politics, Washington, and the Federal Election Commission, Washington.

b. FEC, press release, Washington, May 15, 2001.

c. Expenditures by the Democratic and Republican national, state, and local party committees.

d. Includes money transferred from the Republican and Democratic national party committees to state party committees, money contributed to state and local candidates, and joint federal/nonfederal expenses. FEC press release, May 15, 2001.

e. See: "Issue Advocacy in the 1999–2000 Elections," report issued by the Annenberg Public Policy Center of the University of Pennsylvania.

f. Includes spending on 2000 gubernatorial elections and spending on legislative races in twenty-five states. See chapter 8 of this volume for data sources and list of states.

g. See chapter 9 of this volume.

h. Estimate provided to the author by Dane Waters, president, Initiative and Referendum Institute, Washington, June 25, 2001.

tion were put in place to remove much of the private money that tainted President Richard M. Nixon's re-election campaign, private money is now back in the presidential election, just as it was in elections before 1976. The disclosure requirements of the FECA initially documented campaign contributions and expenditures, but now the explosion of soft money and issue advocacy has undercut the capacity to fully document election spending.

Categories of Spending

Spending in the 2000 elections can be divided into the eight categories listed in table 2-1: spending by the presidential election candidates, spending by congressional candidates, party spending in hard dollars (contributions and spending limited by the FECA), soft money spending (unlimited contributions and expenditures), issue advocacy spending, spending in state elections, spending in judicial elections, and spending on ballot initiatives.

Presidential candidates spent $607 million during the 2000 election.[5] This sum includes primary and general election spending by major party candidates, as well as primary and general election spending by Pat Buchanan, the Reform Party candidate, Ralph Nader, the Green Party candidate, and Harry Browne, the Libertarian Party candidate. This figure includes federal matching funds in the primary elections and public funding in the general election. Spending for the Democratic, Republican, and Reform party conventions is included in the figure. This figure does not include spending on behalf of candidates by parties and interest groups.

Congressional candidates collectively spent more than a billion dollars during the 1999–2000 election cycle.[6] This figure does not include issue advocacy expenditures, nor does it include independent expenditures on behalf of candidates or in opposition to candidates.

The national, state, and local Democratic and Republican party committees spent $692 million during the 2000 elections; this is hard money falling under the restrictions of the Federal Election Campaign Act.[7] Contributions directly to candidates and coordinated expenditures for such items as polls and media production made on behalf of candidates are included.

In soft money, the six Democratic and Republican national party committees disbursed $498 million during the 1999–2000 election cycle. This money was spent at the federal, state, and local levels, and includes transfers to state party committees and contributions to state and local candidates.

The Annenberg Public Policy Center at the University of Pennsylvania estimated that $509 million was spent on issue advocacy advertising campaigns during the 1999–2000 election cycle.[8] However, because spending on issue advocacy does not have to be disclosed, this estimate is probably much lower than the actual amount spent on issue advocacy. This estimate is higher than that of the Brennan Center, which relied exclusively on data from the Campaign Media Analysis Group. The Annenberg estimate includes any self-reporting to the media of issue advertising expenditures by interest groups.

At least $329 million was spent in state gubernatorial and legislative elections in 2000.[9] However, because there is no central location where state level election data are kept, the actual figure for spending in state elections is likely much higher. For example, this estimate does not include spending in California legislative elections in 2000, and the costs of legislative elections in California have, in the past, often rivaled spending in congressional elections in some districts.

Spending in judicial elections is just as hard to trace as spending in state legislative elections. Roy A. Schotland estimates in chapter 9 of this volume that at least $62 million was spent on judicial elections. Again, the total figure spent on judicial elections is likely higher.

Finally, the Initiative and Referendum Institute estimates that approximately $225 million was spent on ballot initiatives across the country during the 2000 election cycle.[10]

In these eight categories, listed in table 2-1, $3.9 billion was spent on the 2000 elections. Aggregating estimates of spending by categories (state legislative, judicial, issue advocacy, and so on) is imprecise and provides at best a gross estimate of total spending. The estimate of the authors in this volume is close to the $4 billion estimate frequently mentioned in the media but well below some other estimates. More important than providing some gross estimate is that the state of campaign finance disclosure in the 2000 elections does not permit an accurate estimate.

The data provided by the FEC in some categories are more comparable over time. Table 2-2 examines the increases in money in elections during the past eight years in four categories: spending in congressional elections, PAC contributions to congressional candidates, federal or hard money spending by political parties, and nonfederal or soft money spending by both parties. Even after adjusting for inflation, spending in all six categories exceeds spending in all previous elections.

Table 2-2 shows that the amount raised and spent in congressional elections has skyrocketed during the past five election cycles. Both receipts and expenditures rose approximately one-third over the previous election cycle.

As congressional spending has increased, so have the contributions of political action committees (PACs) to congressional candidates. These committees contributed $259.8 million to candidates running for office during the 1999–2000 election cycle, a 12 percent increase compared with the 1997–98 election cycle.[11] The Democratic and Republican parties each raised more in both hard and soft money in 1999–2000 congressional contests than in the previous election cycle, and more than they did in the previous presidential election cycle.

Patterns of Political Spending

Before the 2000 elections campaign professionals, journalists, and political scientists expected that spending in the elections would set record levels, and those expectations were met. Spending by presidential candidates, congressional candidates, political parties, PACs, and issue advocacy

Table 2-2. *Money in Elections, 1992–2000*
Millions of dollars adjusted for inflation in 2000 dollars

Item	2000	1998	1996	1994	1992
Congressional elections[a]	1,047.3	825.4	867.6	860.4	809.2
PAC contributions[b]	259.8	232.3	239.0	220.3	231.9
Democratic federal[c]	275.2	169.0	243.2	154.3	200.4
Republican federal[c]	465.8	301.1	457.1	283.6	325.1
Democratic nonfederal[d]	245.2	98.0	136.0	57.1	44.6
Republican nonfederal[d]	249.9	139.0	151.7	61.0	61.1

a. Total amount raised by all congressional candidates. FEC, press release, May 15, 2001.
b. PAC contributions to all federal candidates. FEC, press release, May 31, 2001.
c. Hard dollars raised by the Democratic and Republican parties. FEC, press release, May 15, 2001.
d. Soft money raised by the Democratic and Republican parties. FEC, press release, May 15, 2001.

groups exceeded past spending records. The pattern was established early in 1999, when George W. Bush began raising millions of dollars from individual contributors. As early as April 1999, before Bush even announced his candidacy, his exploratory committee had raised more than $7 million in contributions of $1,000 or less.[12] The pattern was confirmed when Jon Corzine spent $60 million of his personal fortune on his successful Senate race, including spending $3 million a week during the last six weeks of the election.[13]

The Presidential Election

The Federal Election Campaign Act provides for partial public funding of presidential nominations, funding for the Democratic and Republican conventions, and full public funding for major party general election candidates who forgo private contributions. Table 2-3 shows payouts from the Presidential Election Campaign Fund from 1976 through the 2000 election.

To qualify for partial public funding in the prenomination phase of the campaign, candidates must raise $5,000 in amounts of $250 or less in twenty different states. In the 2000 election, candidates who qualified for federal matching funds had a prenomination spending limit of $40.536 million.[14] Only John McCain came close to reaching this limit; McCain spent $39.81 million on his primary campaign.[15]

Before the June 30, 1999, FEC quarterly filing, it was rumored that George W. Bush would report receipts of $20 to $23 million.[16] In fact,

Table 2-3. *Payouts from the Presidential Election Campaign Fund,*
1976–2000
Millions of dollars, adjusted for inflation in 2000 dollars

Year	Payout
1976	216.1
1980	212.3
1984	219.8
1988	257.5
1992	215.3
1996	256.8
2000	208.3

Source: Data for 1976–96 from John C. Green, ed., *Financing the 1996 Election* (M. E. Sharpe, 1999), p. 18; 2000 data from FEC, press releases, August 4, 2001, August 18, 2001, September 14, 2001, and September 29, 2001.

Bush's campaign receipts for that filing totaled $37 million, a sum equal to the combined receipts of the other ten Republican candidates, and more than the combined receipts of Democratic candidates Bill Bradley and Al Gore.[17] Bush's remarkable fund-raising ability effectively narrowed the field of Republican candidates vying for the presidential nomination. Just four months after the June 30 filing, five Republican contenders had withdrawn from the race—former vice president Dan Quayle, former Tennessee governor Lamar Alexander, Representative John Kasich, Senator Bob Smith, and former secretary of labor Elizabeth Dole. In announcing her withdrawal, Dole said, "The bottom line is money."[18]

Both the Democratic and Republican parties were given $13.512 million in federal funds for their nominating conventions.[19] In practice, however, millions more were spent on each convention. With the nominations decided in advance, the nominating conventions became opportunities for corporate interests to woo convention delegates, including members of Congress. The Center for Responsive Politics estimated at least $15 million in corporate contributions to the Republican convention and at least $12 million in corporate contributions to the Democratic convention.[20] Moreover, a number of corporations contributed to both conventions. AT & T, General Motors, and Microsoft each contributed a million dollars to both major party conventions.[21]

Both major party candidates accepted public funding in the general election campaign, and each received a check for $67.56 million from the federal treasury. In addition, the Reform Party candidate, Pat Buchanan, and his running mate, Ezola Foster, received $12,613,452 in federal funds for their general election campaign.[22] In total, the Democratic and Re-

Table 2-4. *Congressional Campaign Expenditures, 1972–2000*
Millions of dollars, adjusted for inflation in 2000 dollars

Year	Total	Senate	House
1972	318.5	126.5	191.6
1974	308.1	121.2	186.9
1976	349.5	133.2	216.4
1978	514.5	225.0	289.5
1980	499.5	215.0	284.4
1982	611.0	247.0	364.0
1984	620.0	282.6	337.4
1986	708.4	332.5	375.9
1988	666.2	292.9	373.3
1990	588.0	237.7	350.3
1992	832.5	333.4	499.1
1994	841.5	370.7	472.0
1996	839.9	315.5	524.4
1998	782.2	304.0	478.1
2000	1,005.6	434.7	572.3

Source: 1972–96 data from Green, *Financing the 1996 Election*, p, 23; 1997–98 data from FEC, press release, April 28, 1999; and 1999–2000 data from FEC, press release, May 15, 2001.

publican presidential nominees spent more money in the 2000 election than in any previous presidential election. The Center for Responsive Politics estimated that George W. Bush spent almost $186 million on his primary and general election campaigns, and Al Gore spent $120 million on his entire campaign.[23] These figures do not include monies spent by the political parties and other groups on behalf of the two candidates.

As mentioned earlier, one of the assumptions behind federal funding of presidential elections was that the bulk of the election would be financed with public, rather than private, funds. However, in the 2000 election cycle, as a result of George W. Bush's departure from the norm in the primaries by forgoing partial public funding, with its obligatory spending limits, only 35 percent of Bush's presidential campaign came from public funds. Gore accepted partial public funding in the prenomination phase of the campaign, and 62.5 percent of his presidential campaign was funded by U.S. Treasury funds.[24]

Congressional Elections

The 2000 congressional elections were the most expensive in the history of the United States. Table 2-4 shows congressional campaign expenditures during the past three decades.

Even after adjusting for inflation, the 2000 congressional elections were the most expensive in history. Both receipts and expenditures by congressional candidates increased approximately one-third over receipts and expenditures in the 1997–98 cycle.[25] House candidates spent $572.3 million, 26 percent more than was spent by House candidates in the previous election cycle. Senate candidates spent $434.7 million, 51 percent more than was spent in 1997–98, though it is difficult to compare Senate spending across election cycles because the mix of states in each cycle varies. For example, election cycles that include races in California and New York, as the 2000 cycle did, usually have higher expenditures than election cycles that do not include such large and costly states. Rick Lazio and Hillary Rodham Clinton together spent $70 million dollars in the New York Senate race,[26] and that, coupled with the previously mentioned $63 million spent by Jon Corzine in New Jersey, undoubtedly helps to explain the 50 percent increase in Senate expenditures in the 2000 election cycle over the previous cycle.[27] If spending in the 2000 Senate race is compared with spending in the 1994 Senate elections, when New York, New Jersey, and California also had Senate elections, spending in the 2000 races is still much higher, even after adjusting for inflation. Spending by the Corzine, Clinton, and Lazio campaigns contributed to the increases in 2000 but does not entirely explain the increases over spending in 1994.

Not only was congressional election spending the highest on record, but successful congressional candidates were, in the vast majority of cases, those who outspent their opponents. The Center for Responsive Politics found that 85 percent of Senate candidates and 94 percent of House candidates who spent the most money were elected.[28] Competitive House candidates routinely spent $1 million or more, and while Jon Corzine's $63 million Senate campaign dramatically exceeded all records, $5 million or more is now the expected price of a competitive Senate race in many states.[29] The cost of a competitive House race has doubled during the past decade, while the increase in the cost of a competitive Senate race has increased somewhat more slowly. In 1990 a competitive House race was half a million dollars, while competitive Senate races were $3.5 to $4 million.[30]

Political Parties

The Republican Party continued to outraise the Democratic Party in hard money in 2000. The Republican Party committees raised $465.8 million in hard dollars, compared with the Democratic Party committees' $275.2

million. Although the Democratic Party committees raised fewer total federal dollars than did the Republican Party committees, Democratic Party fund-raising increased 13 percent over the 1996 presidential cycle, while Republican Party fund-raising increased only 1 percent over 1996.[31]

However, the bigger story of the 2000 election cycle about party fund-raising was soft money. Both parties raised record amounts of soft money. The Republican Party raised $249.9 million in soft money, a 65 percent increase over the 1995–96 presidential election cycle, and the Democratic Party raised $245.2 million in soft money, an 80 percent increase over the last presidential election cycle.[32] Moreover, in soft money receipts, the Democratic Party was, for the first time since 1994, essentially on par with the Republican Party. In the 2000 election cycle almost one-half, 47 percent, of the money raised by the Democratic Party was soft money, compared with one-third of the money raised by the Republican Party.[33] In light of these figures a ban on soft money, as proposed by the McCain-Feingold bill, coupled with an increase in the amount of hard money the parties could raise, has very different implications for the two parties. Because the Republican Party is less dependent on soft money than the Democratic Party, the Republican Party would lose less revenue than the Democratic Party, and, with higher contribution limits, would have opportunities to increase its hard money contributions.

Political Action Committees

Just as congressional, presidential, and party spending increased in 2000, so did PAC contributions to candidates. The PACs contributed $259.8 million to federal candidates, a 12 percent increase over PAC contributions in the 1997–98 election cycle.[34] As in past elections, the majority of PAC money went to incumbents; 75 percent of PAC contributions were given to incumbents, 11 percent to challengers, and 14 percent to candidates for open seats.[35] Corporate, trade association, and health PACs were the most likely to contribute the bulk of their money to incumbents. Eighty eight percent of corporate PAC contributions went to incumbents, while trade, membership, and health PACs gave 83 percent of their PAC money to incumbents. Labor PACs gave 70 percent of their contributions to incumbents, 18 percent to challengers, and 12 percent to open-seat candidates. Nonconnected PACs were the most likely to support nonincumbent candidates. Nonconnected PACs gave 21 percent of their money to challengers and 23 percent of their contributions to open-seat candidates; 56 percent of their contributions went to incumbents.[36]

The PACs were more supportive of Senate Republicans than Senate Democrats; Republicans received 61 percent of PAC contributions, compared with 39 percent for Senate Democrats. This is similar to the pattern of PAC contributions to Senate candidates in the previous two election cycles. In 1997–98 PACs gave 57 percent of their contributions to Republicans and in 1995–96 PACs gave 63 percent of their contributions to Republican candidates. In 1993–94 PAC contributions were almost evenly divided between Democrats and Republicans; Democrats received 51 percent of PAC contributions and Republicans 49 percent.[37] PAC contributions to House candidates were almost evenly divided between Democrats and Republicans, repeating a pattern of the last two election cycles. Democrats received 51 percent of PAC money and Republicans 49 percent, a mirror image of the 1997–98 election cycle, in which Republicans received 51 percent of PAC money and Democrats received 49 percent. In 1995–96, PAC money was evenly divided between House Democrats and Republicans.[38]

Besides direct contributions to candidates, PACs also made $21 million in independent expenditures as reported to the FEC.[39] Of those expenditures, approximately three-fourths were on behalf of candidates, and one-fourth was in opposition to candidates.[40]

Issue Advocacy

Issue advocacy burst onto the political scene in 1993, when the insurance industry ran ads in ten states to raise questions in citizens' minds about President Bill Clinton's health reform proposals. The Health Insurance Association of America spent millions of dollars on these ads, which featured an ordinary couple, Harry and Louise, asking questions and raising doubts about health insurance under the Clinton plan.[41] While the "Harry and Louise" ads were pure issue advocacy, candidates and interest groups soon adopted the issue advocacy technique to more directly advocate candidates. Under the stewardship of Dick Morris, a political adviser to President Clinton's 1996 re-election campaign, the Democratic National Committee ran issue ads during the spring and summer of 1996 to set the stage and introduce Clinton's message for the fall campaign.[42] Issue advocacy campaigns by interest groups also leaped into the political environment in 1996, when the AFL-CIO announced it planned to spend $35 million to defeat seventy-five Republican candidates.[43] In 1998 the Democratic and Republican parties' congressional committees joined the issue advocacy arena.[44] By the 2000 election cycle issue advocacy campaigns were a strong component of the political arsenal of parties and interest groups.

There were three major studies of issue advocacy in the 2000 elections. The Center for the Study of Elections and Democracy at Brigham Young University examined issue advocacy in seventeen very competitive House and Senate races in the 2000 elections.[45] The Annenberg Public Policy Center at the University of Pennsylvania examined issue advocacy spending by 125 groups in the 2000 election and tracked television spending on issue ads in the top seventy-five media markets in the country between Super Tuesday and Election Day.[46] The Brennan Center for Law and Justice at the New York University Law School coded all political ads in the seventy-five largest media markets using data provided by the Campaign Media Analysis Group (CMAG) to assess the extent and costs of candidate, party, and interest group issue advocacy communications.[47] Although some overlap undoubtedly occurs in the three studies, all of them indicate a surge in spending on issue ads in the 2000 elections.

The Brennan Center found that as of October 30, 2000, all ads funded by the Republican and Democratic parties mentioned a candidate, but none referenced a party, "even though the soft money paying for the ads is restricted by law to party-building activities."[48] They also found that interest groups and parties together spent more than candidates in key U.S. House races. In these races, the Republican and Democratic parties and independent groups spent $32.6 million on ads. Candidate-combined spending in these races totaled $23.9 million.

The Center for the Study of Elections and Democracy (CSED) found that, contrary to past cycles, the Democrats experienced the most dramatic growth in soft money spending, at $243 million for the 1999–2000 election cycle. The RNC and the NRCC spent $244 million in soft money in the same cycle. The center also found that interest groups often doubled their soft money spending in 2000 over any previous cycle and that in the top races, parties and interest groups outspent their candidates two-to-one in television and radio advertising. Most of these monies were spent on issue advocacy. On the ground, an unprecedented average of seventy-two different (unique) pieces of direct mail (mostly issue advocacy) and at least seven different telephone communications went to targeted voters in each of these same campaigns.

The Annenberg study found that $509 million was spent on broadcast issue advocacy in the 2000 elections.[49] However, the study estimates that this figure is only "a fraction of the total expenditures,"[50] because issue ads need not be disclosed. This study found that almost $248 million was spent on broadcast issues ads in the top seventy-five media markets between March 8 and November 7.[51] These ads mentioned a candidate by name and generally included some form of attack against the candidate. However, because the ads did not specifically advocate the election or defeat of a candidate, the ads were not considered election spending.

Clearly, as these studies found, issue advocacy was an important, yet unregulated and undisclosed, part of spending in the 2000 elections. Issue advocacy has clearly become an important influence in the outcome of elections in the United States and is seen as an important tool by interest groups and political parties. Election issue advocacy[52] has become a way for political parties and interest groups to interject their own messages into campaigns, without the constraints of the contribution limits of the FECA.

Patterns of Political Giving

There seems to be some evidence that political giving by individuals also increased during the 2000 elections. Table 2-5 shows that according to respected national polls 12 percent of the American public report making a contribution to a political candidate or a political party, twice the number of people who reported making a political contribution in 1996. However, undoubtedly, considerable overlap occurs among those who report making contributions to candidates and parties, so the actual percentage of political contributors in the 2000 elections was likely somewhat lower than 12 percent.

Table 2-5 presents survey data on Americans who report making political contributions. Given the consistency in the data over time, it seems fair to assume that somewhere between 5 and 10 percent of Americans participate financially in elections in any given election cycle. Table 2-6 looks at the distribution of types of political contributions during the past twenty years. In most years, including 2000, individual contributions to candidates and parties are generally evenly divided between the two types. In 2000, 5.7 percent of the population reported making contributions to candidates, and 5.5 percent reported making contributions to party organizations.

Both the Republican Party and Republican candidates fare better than their Democratic counterparts in the percentage of people who report making contributions. Of the 5.7 percent making contributions to candi-

Table 2-5.   *Percentage of National Adult Population Making Political Contributions, 1952–2000*

Year	Polling organization	Contributed to Republican	Contributed to Democratic	Total[a]
1952	SRC	3	1	4
1956	Gallup	3	6	9
1956	SRC	5	5	10
1960	Gallup	4	4	9
1960	Gallup			12
1960	SRC	7	4	12
1964	Gallup	6	4	12
1964	SRC	5	4	10
1968	SRC	3	3	8[b]
1972	SRC	4	5	10[c]
1974	SRC	3	3	8[d]
1976	Gallup	3	3	8[e]
1976	SRC	4	4	9[f]
1980	CPS	2	2	4
1984	CPS	2	2	4
1988	CPS	4	2	6
1992	CPS	2	2	4
1996	CPS	3	2	6
2000	CPS	6	4	12

Source: Survey Research Center (SRC), and later the Center for Political Studies (CPS), both at the University of Michigan; data direct from the center or from Angus Campbell, Philip E. Converse, and Donald E. Stokes, *The American Voter* (John Wiley and Sons, 1960), p. 91; 1980 data from Ruth S. Jones and Warren E. Miller, "Financing Campaigns: Macro Level Innovation and Micro Level Response," *Western Political Quarterly*, vol. 38, no. 2 (1987, pp. 187–210); 1984 data from Ruth S. Jones, "Campaign Contributions and Campaign Solicitations: 1984" (paper presented at the meeting of the Southern Political Science Association, November, 1985); and Gallup data direct or from Roper Opinion Research Center, Williams College, and from the American Institute of Political Opinion (Gallup poll).

a. The total percentage may add to a total different from the total of Democratic and Republican contributors because of individuals contributing to both major parties, or to candidates of both major parties, nonparty groups, or combinations of these.

b. Includes 0.7 percent who contributed to the American Independent Party (AIP).

c. Includes contributors to the American Independent Party.

d. Includes 0.7 percent who contributed to both parties and 0.8 percent who contributed to minor parties.

e. Includes 1 percent to another party and 1 percent to "do not know" or "no answer."

f. Republican and Democratic figures are rounded. The total includes 0.6 percent who gave to both parties, 0.4 percent to other, and 0.3 percent to "do not know."

dates, 3 percent reported making contributions to Republicans, while only 1.8 percent reported making contributions to Democrats. Similarly, of the 5.5 percent who reported making contributions to party organizations, almost 3 percent (2.8) reported making contributions to the Republican Party, compared with 1.9 percent to the Democratic Party.

The more important point from these data, however, is that very few Americans contribute to political parties and candidates in the United

Table 2-6. *Mode of Political Contributions, 1990–2000*
Percent

Item	1980 (N = 1,395)	1982 (N = 1,418)	1984 (N = 1,944)	1986 (N = 2,176)	1988 (N = 1,775)	1990 (N = 2,000)	1992 (N = 2,252)	1994 (N = 1,795)	1996 (N = 1,714)	2000 (N = 1,807)
Federal tax checkoff[a]	26	30	31	32	26	25	26	n.a.*	n.a.*	n.a.
State tax checkoff[b]	6	7	n.a.	n.a.	n.a.	n.a.	n.a.	n.a.	n.a.	n.a.
Candidate organization[c]	6	7	5	5	6	5	6	4.6	4.9	5.7
Republican	3.8	2.8	2.1	2.1	2.7	2.2	2.2	2.1	2.6	3
Democrat	2	4	2.4	2.4	2.6	2.5	3	1.7	1.8	1.8
Both	n.a.	n.a.	0.3	0.2	0.4	0.2	0.4	0.5	0.2	0.3
Other[d]	0.5	0.4	0.2	0.2	0.2	0.2	0.4	0.1	0.2	0.5
Party organization[e]	4	4	5	5	6	4	4	4.4	5.6	5.5
Republican	3	2.7	2.6	2.7	4	1.9	1.9	2.5	2.8	2.8
Democrat	1	1.3	2	1.9	1.9	1.8	1.8	1.3	2.2	1.9
Both	n.a.	n.a.	0.2	0.3	0.1	0.1	0.1	0.3	0.2	0.3
Other[f]	0	0	0.2	0.1	0	0.1	0.1	0.3	0.4	0.4

PAC[g]	7	8	n.a.	n.a.	n.a.	n.a.	n.a.	n.a.	n.a.	n.a.
Ballot issue[h]	n.a.	n.a.	2	3	4	5	5	5	n.a.	n.a.
Other group[i]	n.a.	n.a.	2	3	4	5	5	5	5	n.a.
Summary										
Noncontributor[j]	68	63	65	64	68	69	69	89.0**	88.0**	n.a.
Checkoff only[k]	20	21	26	27	20	20	20	n.a.*	n.a.*	n.a.
Organizational giver[l]	11	15	10	9	12	10	11	11	12	80

Source: National Election Studies, University of Michigan.

Note: Entries do not always total 100 percent because of rounding.

n.a. Not available.

*This question no longer asked by National Election Studies.

**These entries are an index of those who made no organizational contributions.

a. "Did you use the $1 checkoff option on your federal income tax return to make a political contribution?" The entries are those who said yes.

b. "Did you make a political contribution by checking off that item on your state income tax return?" The entries are those who said yes.

c. "Did you give money to an individual candidate?" The entries are those who said yes.

d. "Which party did that candidate belong to?" Missing values are not included.

e. "Did you give money to a political party?" The entries are those who said yes.

f. "To which party did you give money?" Missing values are not included.

g. "Did you give money to political action groups?" The entries are those who said yes.

h. "Did you give money to help support or oppose any ballot proposition this election year?" The entries are those who said yes.

i. "Did you give any money to any other group that supported/opposed candidates?" The entries are those who said yes.

j. The entries are an index that counts those who did not make political contributions at all.

k. The entries count those who make only checkoff contributions.

l. The entries count those who make other kinds of contributions and may have used the checkoff.

States, and the percentage who do contribute has remained relatively stable during the past twenty years, even as the costs of elections have increased. Consequently, candidates need to spend more and more time trying to raise money from a very narrow donor base.

Besides self-reported survey data, there is one other measure of financial participation in elections. When the Federal Election Campaign Act of 1971 established voluntary public funding of presidential elections, it created the Presidential Election Fund to provide a mechanism to fund presidential elections. Americans filing tax returns were allowed to designate one dollar (changed to three dollars in 1993) to be put into the Presidential Election Fund. Table 2-7 presents data on the percentage of returns that designate funds to the Election Fund, the dollar amount designated over time, and the fund balances for every year between 1973 and 1999.

The percentage of returns that check off a designation to the fund has declined steadily since 1973. In 1999 the percentage of returns designating a contribution to the fund was slightly higher than in 1998, but the amount designated was somewhat lower.

These data together suggest that very few Americans contribute money to politics, and the percentages of those who do participate have remained steady, in the case of self-reported activity, or declined, in the case of the Presidential Election Fund. With no expanding participation base, candidates and parties have had to rely on those individuals who do participate to contribute more generously. The wealthy individuals whom the FECA amendments of 1974 were designed to limit in the political system have been invited back into the system and welcomed with open arms by candidates and parties, through such devices as soft money, victory funds, leadership PACs, and issue advocacy.

Public Perceptions about Campaign Finance

Campaign finance reform was a more visible element of the 2000 election than any election in more than two decades in part because of John McCain's presidential candidacy. In the New Hampshire primary especially, McCain not only stressed his leadership on the issue but linked it to his opposition to wasteful federal spending, concern about the power of special interests, and independence from special interests and the party establishment. McCain described Bush "as the unwitting pawn." McCain said, "If he won't support fundamental reform of the system then he becomes part of the problem."[53]

Table 2-7. *The Federal Income Tax Checkoff*

Calendar year	Returns[a] (percent)	Dollar amount	Fund balances
1999	10.4	61,000,000	165,514,976
1998	8.2	63,300,000	133,194,012
1997	12.4[b]	66,347,632	69,907,162
1996	12.5[b]	66,903,797	3,657,886
1995	12.9	67,860,127	146,862,732
1994[c]	13	71,316,995	101,664,547
1993	14.5	27,636,982	30,779,386
1992	17.7	29,592,735	4,061,061
1991	19.5	32,322,336	127,144,469
1990	19.8	32,462,979	115,426,713
1989	20.1	32,285,646	82,927,013
1988	21	33,013,987	52,462,359
1987	21.7	33,651,947	177,905,677
1986	23	35,753,837	161,680,423
1985	23	34,712,761	125,870,541
1984	23.7	35,036,761	92,713,782
1983	24.2	35,631,068	177,320,982
1982	27	39,023,882	153,454,501
1981	28.7	41,049,052	114,373,289
1980	27.4	38,838,417	73,752,205
1979	25.4	35,941,347	135,246,807
1978	28.6	39,246,689	100,331,986
1977	27.5	36,606,008	60,927,571
1976	25.5	33,731,945	23,805,659
1975	24.2	31,656,525	59,551,245
1974[d]	0	27,591,546	27,591,546
1973[d]	0	2,427,000	2,427,000

Source: Compiled from FEC data.

a. The percentages refer to the tax returns of the previous year. For example, the 17.7 percent of 1991 tax returns that indicated a checkoff of $1 or $2 directed $29,592,735 into the Presidential Election Fund in calendar year 1992.

b. The participation rates for 1996–99 were taken from the Taxpayer Usage Study (TPUS), a sample-based analysis generated by the Internal Revenue Service.

c. 1994 (1993 tax year returns) was the first one in which the checkoff value was $3.

d. The 1973 tax forms were the first to have the checkoff on the first page; in 1972 taxpayers had to file a separate form to exercise the checkoff option. To compensate for the presumed difficulty caused by the separate form, taxpayers were allowed to designate $1 for 1972 as well as 1973 on the 1973 forms. Given these circumstances, total and percentage figures for these returns would be misleading.

When interest groups like National Right to Life and Americans for Tax Reform (ATR) attacked McCain for his position on campaign finance reform in New Hampshire, McCain exploited the attack to reinforce his themes. He then took the offensive by making an issue of Grover Norquist's (of ATR) visit to New Hampshire, identifying him as a lobbyist for foreign interests and a "Washington insider." By characterizing his attackers in this way, McCain was able to claim "outsider" status.[54] Interestingly, after McCain won New Hampshire by 18 percent, Norquist dropped off the scene and National Right to Life shifted its attack on McCain to his support of fetal tissue research. In the Democratic presidential nomination battle, candidates Gore and Bradley supported reform and had very few differences on the issue, though Bradley may have been more identified with campaign finance reform than Gore, in part because of Gore's association with the 1996 Clinton-Gore campaign's questionable fund-raising techniques. This left McCain as the most identifiable reform candidate.

Clearly the issue was perceived to have some traction with voters as George W. Bush countered McCain in the primaries after New Hampshire by emphasizing his "reformer with results" message. Bush's position on campaign finance reform was to ban unions and corporations from giving soft money to the parties, require union members to authorize annually the use of their contributions for political purposes (paycheck protection), raise the limits on individual contributions, require rapid disclosure of contributions on the Internet, prohibit federally registered lobbyists from contributing to members of Congress while Congress is in session, and preserve the right of individuals and groups to engage in issue advocacy.[55]

Not surprisingly, the topic of the Clinton-Gore campaign finance scandals became a part of the general election when the Republican National Committee (RNC) in a television soft money funded ad attacked Gore for his inconsistency on the issue, juxtaposing footage of Gore attending a fundraiser at a Buddhist Temple with a clip of him stating his support for campaign finance reform. Interest groups also used this issue against Gore, including one group that ran an ad made to look like the television game show *Jeopardy,* but calling the show *Hypocrisy.*

However, in polling during and after the election, campaign finance was not a driving issue in the election. A national poll conducted by ABC News in late March and early April, 2000, asked voters, "How important will reforming election campaign finance laws be to you in deciding how to vote in the 2000 presidential election in November?" Seventy percent said important (34 percent very important and 36 percent somewhat important).[56] But when the salience of campaign finance reform is compared with that of other issues, it is not as important. For example, campaign finance reform was the second from the last in relative importance of nineteen issues included in a January 2001 Gallup poll.[57] Issues more important than campaign finance reform included education, health care, and the economy.

In most congressional races, campaign finance was not a pressing issue. However, McCain traveled extensively, endorsing Republican candidates and seeking to raise the issue while helping some candidates assert credibility as reformers. In the highly contested congressional races where spending often hit new highs, the issue was more prominent. Editorial pages, for example, often railed against the influence of outside money, negative campaigning, and the high levels of spending by outside groups. In the Montana Senate race, for example, several spats over who was responsible for Democratic- and Republican-funded ads led the *Helena Independent Record* to write in an editorial: "What is getting most boring is the practice of candidates; when asked about negative ads, to shrug their shoulders and explain that their campaign had no control over those ads."[58]

Although candidates and political elites can discern whether communications are from candidates, parties, or interest groups, voters cannot. David Magleby found in a national survey conducted by Knowledge Networks that voters cannot tell candidate ads from party or issue advocacy ads. Moreover, voters presume that candidates are in control of ads in their races.[59]

A direct measure of how voters see campaign finance reform is when they vote on ballot propositions on the topic. In 2000, as in previous years, voters approved ballot propositions on campaign finance reform. Since 1972, voters have approved roughly 90 percent of CRF initiatives on statewide ballots, a much higher percentage than the roughly one-third of all initiatives that pass.[60]

Implications

The 2000 election cycle saw increases in spending across the political landscape. George W. Bush spent more than any previous presidential candidate to contest the nomination and general election. Congressional candidates spent more than a billion dollars in hard-fought battles to control the House and Senate. Contributions from PACs to congressional candidates continued their upward spiral. Hard money spending by the Democratic and Republican parties increased over previous election cycles. The growth in soft money spending, particularly by the Democratic Party, was essential to the party's success in some key congressional races.

Finally, issue advocacy, unheard of just six years ago, accounted for at least one-half billion dollars in election spending.

There were some unique characteristics of the 2000 elections, which contributed to the rise in election costs. First, George W. Bush made the decision not to accept federal matching funds in the prenomination phase of the election. In 1996 Bob Dole, the eventual Republican presidential nominee, accepted federal matching funds, but because Republican presidential candidate Steve Forbes chose to fund his campaign with his personal wealth, Dole had to spend his entire prenomination limit to match Forbes's spending, leaving Dole with essentially no money to spend between April of 1996 and the Republican convention in August.[61] Determined not to be financially squeezed by Forbes in the 2000 race, Bush decided to forgo federal funds and consequently was not bound by the prenomination spending limit. By the time of the Republican convention, Bush had outraised Forbes by almost two to one.[62]

The 2000 elections were a fight over the control of the House, and, eventually, the Senate. With every contested seat potentially the difference between Republican or Democratic control of the House and Senate, millions were spent in closely contested House and Senate races. For example, Congressman Rush Holt, who was a surprise winner in the 1998 elections, and who was seen as one of the most vulnerable incumbents in 2000, spent almost $2.6 million to reclaim his seat, and his opponent, former congressman Dick Zimmer, spent almost $2.2 million.[63] On the Senate side, incumbent Senator Spencer Abraham spent $13 million in his unsuccessful effort to retain his seat, and his opponent, Congresswoman Debbie Stabenow, spent $8 million to defeat him.[64]

Lingering feelings over the impeachment of President Clinton contributed to the increase in spending in the 2000 elections. Representatives James Rogan and Bob Barr were House managers during the impeachment trial, and their races were targeted by both political parties. Rogan spent almost $6.9 million in his losing effort, and Barr spent almost $3.5 million to retain his seat.[65] Adam Schiff spent $4.3 million to defeat Rogan, and Roger Kahn spent $3.8 million in his unsuccessful effort to defeat Barr.[66]

The willingness of candidates to contribute their personal fortunes to their congressional races affected spending in several Senate races. Former Goldman Sachs executive Jon Corzine's spending in New Jersey has been discussed earlier in this chapter, but department store heir Mark Dayton and former Microsoft executive Maria Cantwell each spent more than $10 million of their own money in their successful Senate races.[67]

The growth in soft money in the 2000 election cycle by both political parties contributed to the increased cost of this election. Both the Democratic and Republican national party committees, and their House and Senate counterparts, aggressively sought soft money donors. Moreover, the amount of soft money solicited from individuals continued to climb. Although both parties used to reward their $100,000 contributors with special memberships and access to top party and administration officials, in 2000 it was the $250,000 contributors who were the most coveted. After 1996 the GOP announced a million dollar club and that became a new target. In 2000 at least fifty donors gave a million dollars or more in soft money.[68]

Finally, issue advocacy plays a major role in understanding the costs of the 2000 election. The three studies cited earlier in this chapter do an excellent job of describing issue advocacy campaigns in selected states and congressional districts and done by selected interest groups in media markets. However, these studies recognize that they have measured only the tip of the iceberg. Without required disclosure of issue advocacy, it is impossible to know how much was really spent on issue advocacy in the 2000 elections.

With ever-increasing election costs and fixed limits on the amounts individuals can contribute to federal candidates, candidates need to spend more and more time raising money to fund their election campaigns. For incumbents, this means more time spent on fund-raising calls and attending fund-raising events and less time spent on legislative business. For challengers and open-seat candidates, it means only candidates with the personal resources or financial connections to raise a million dollars or more have a realistic chance to successfully participate in campaigns.

With limits on the amounts of hard dollars individuals can contribute to political parties and with the importance of issue advocacy campaigns to the parties' success in elections, soft money has become increasingly important to the Democratic and Republican parties. Ironically, the Democrats, the erstwhile proponents of campaign finance reform, were the most dependent on soft money in the 2000 elections. As discussed above, almost half of the money raised by the Democratic Party was raised in soft money. A ban on soft money, as proposed in the McCain-Feingold bill, coupled with an increase in the amount of hard money that could be contributed to the political parties, as included in the bill that passed the Senate in April 2001, would, at least in the short term, benefit the Republican Party much more than the Democratic Party. The Republican Party is less dependent on soft money than the Democratic Party, so a ban on such money would remove only approximately one-third of their party's support, compared with almost one-half the resources of the Democratic Party. In addition, of those individuals who report contributing to candidates and parties, a slightly larger percentage contribute to the Republican Party and Republican Party candidates than to the Democratic Party and its candidates. It is ironic that there is considerably more support for McCain-Feingold among Democrats in Congress than among Republicans, because if McCain-Feingold were to be enacted, Democratic fund-raising efforts would probably be hurt much more severely than Republican fund-raising. Soft money, which Democrats are now just as successful as Republicans in raising, would disappear, leaving Democrats to have to raise hard money dollars to compete with Republicans. Democrats have never been able to raise as much money in hard dollars as Republicans.

Without soft money to fund issue ads, the parties would essentially cede spending on issue advocacy to interest groups and unaffiliated groups. These groups often have their own agendas in a particular race and are often not welcome by the candidates they are trying to help, either by supporting a candidacy or targeting an opponent. Issue ads can introduce new messages into a campaign, forcing candidates to discuss messages they did not want to focus on or risk having their own messages drowned out in the debate.

With no disclosure of issue ads and no limits on the amounts that can be spent on them, voters find it more difficult to sort through who is saying what in an election. While issue ads purport to be about issues, in fact, the vast majority of issue ads in the 2000 elections were what Magleby has called "election issue advocacy."[69] These ads avoid the Supreme Court's magic words test, but are clearly aimed at influencing the outcomes of elections, and voters see them as such. Until issue advocacy is recognized for what it is, spending to influence the outcome of elections, voters will not have a full accounting of the costs of spending in elections in the United States.

In many ways spending has come full circle in the past thirty years. Donors willing and able to give hundreds of thousands of dollars are active participants in the electoral process. Corporate contributions are welcomed by the political parties. There is no required disclosure of interest group spending on issue advocacy. We can estimate spending in the 2000 election as more than $4 billion but suspect that actual spending was even greater.

Notes

1. David B. Magleby, ed., *Election Advocacy: Soft Money and Issue Advocacy in the 2000 Congressional Elections* (Brigham Young University, Center for the Study of Elections and Democracy, 2001).

2. 424 U.S. 1 (1976).

3. Magleby, *Election Advocacy;* "Annenberg Public Policy Center Tracks over $509 Million in Reported Expenditures on Issue Advocacy," Annenberg Public Policy Center of the University of Pennsylvania, press release, February 1, 2001.

4. David B. Magleby, ed., *Outside Money: Soft Money and Issue Advocacy in 1998 Congressional Elections* (Rowman and Littlefield, 2000); David B. Magleby, "Outside Money in the 2000 Presidential Primary and Congressional General Elections," *PS: Political Science and Politics,* vol. 34 (June 2001) pp. 203–04; and Jonathan S. Krasno and Daniel E. Seltz, *Buying Time: Television Advertising in the 1998 Congressional Elections* (Brennan Center for Justice at New York University School of Law, 2000).

5. Calculated from Center for Responsive Politics, Washington; and data from the Federal Election Commission, Washington.

6. FEC, press release, Washington, May 15, 2001.

7. FEC, "FEC Reports Increase in Party Fundraising for 2000," press release, Washington, May 15, 2001.

8. Kathleen Hall Jamieson, *Issue Advocacy in the 1999–2000 Election Cycle* (Annenberg Public Policy Center of the University of Pennsylvania, 2001).

9. See chapter 8 of this volume for data sources.

10. Estimate provided to the author by M. Dane Waters, president, Initiative and Referendum Institute, Washington, June 25, 2001.

11. FEC, "PAC Activity Increases in 2000 Election Cycle," press release, Washington, May 31, 2001.

12. Dan Balz, "Bush Is Already 'Misspoken' For," *Washington Post,* April 29, 1999, p. A3.

13. Ben White, "Raising the Standards for Personal Spending on a Political Race," *Washington Post,* December 10, 2000, p. A10.

14. FEC, "FEC Announces 2000 Presidential Spending Limits," press release, Washington, March 1, 2000.

15. "Disbursements of 1999–2000 Presidential Campaigns through July 31, 2000" (*www.fec.gov/finance/pdism8.htm* [June 5, 2001]).

16. Howard Kurtz, "Media Misled by Silence on Fund-Raising," *Washington Post,* July 2, 1999, p. C2.

17. "Financial Activity of 1999–2000 Presidential Campaigns through June 30, 1999" (*www.fec.gov/finance/prsq299.htm* [September 27, 1999]).

18. Ruth Marcus, "Dollars Dictate Field's Early Exits," *Washington Post*, October 21, 1999, p. A1.

19. FEC, "Republican and Democratic Parties to Receive Additional Funds for Party Nominating Conventions," press release, Washington, March 28, 2000.

20. Compiled from Center for Responsive Politics Data; and Holly Bailey, "Donor Double Take at the Conventions," *Capital Eye*, vol. 7 (Summer 2000).

21. Bailey, "Donor Double Take at the Conventions."

22. FEC, "FEC Certifies General Election Public Funds for Buchanan-Foster Ticket," press release, Washington, September 14, 2000.

23. "2000 Presidential Race: Total Raised and Spent" (*www.opensecrets.org/2000elect/index/AllCands.htm* [June 28, 2001]).

24. "President George W. Bush" (*www.opensecrets.org/2000elect/index/P00003335.htm* [April 11, 2001]); "2000 Presidential Candidate Al Gore" (*www.opensecrets.org/2000elect/index/P80000912.htm* [April 11, 2001]).

25. FEC, "FEC Reports on Congressional Financial Activity for 2000," press release, Washington, May 15, 2001.

26. "1999–2000 Top 50 Senate Disbursements" (*www.fec.gov/press/051501congfinact/top50/sendisb.htm* [June 11, 2001]).

27. "1999–2000 Top 50 Senate Disbursements" (*www.fec.gov/press/051501congfinact/top50/sendisb.htm* [June 28, 2001]).

28. Center for Responsive Politics, "Money Wins Big in 2000 Elections," press release, Washington, November 8, 2000.

29. Compiled from FEC data. "1999–2000 Top 50 House Disbursements" (*www.fec.gov/press/051501congfinact/top50/hsedisb.htm* [June 28, 2001]); "1999–2000 Top 50 Senate Disbursements" (*www.fec.gov/press/051501congfinact/top50/sendisb.htm* [June 28, 2001]).

30. Frank J. Sorauf, *Inside Campaign Finance: Myths and Realities* (Yale University Press, 1992), pp. 187–88; and see David B. Magleby and Candice J. Nelson, *The Money Chase: Congressional Campaign Finance Reform* (Brookings, 1990), pp. 27–47.

31. FEC, "FEC Reports Increase in Party Fundraising for 2000."

32. Ibid.

33. Ibid.

34. FEC, "PAC Activity Increases in 2000 Election Cycle," press release, Washington, May 31, 2001.

35. Ibid.

36. Ibid.

37. Ibid.

38. Ibid.

39. Ibid.

40. Ibid.

41. Michael Weisskopf, "Health Reform Advocates Add Visibility to Insurance Industry Group's Message," *Washington Post*, November 4, 1993, p. A8.

42. Dick Morris, *Behind the Oval Office: Getting Reelected against All Odds* (Renaissance Books, 1999).

43. David B. Magleby, ed., *Outside Money: Soft Money and Issue Advocacy in the 1998 Congressional Elections* (Rowman and Littlefield, 2001).

44. Magleby, *Outside Money*.

45. Magleby, *Election Advocacy*.

46. Jamieson, *Issue Advocacy*.

47. Brennan Center for Justice in conjunction with Kenneth Goldstein of the University of Wisconsin–Madison conducted an ongoing study consisting of six press releases from September 19 to October 30, 2000, titled *Brennan Center Releases Real Time Data on Ads in 2000 Campaign*. For more information see (www.brennancenter.org/presscenter/presscenter_pressrelease.html).

48. Amanda Cooper, "Brennan Center Finds 'Soft Money' Spending on TV Ads Continues to Dominate Both Presidential and Congressional Contests," *Brennan Center for Justice*, press release, October 30, 2000 (www.brennancenter.org/presscenter/pressrelsease_2000_1030cmag.html [9 July 2001]).

49. Jamieson, *Issue Advertising in the 1999–2000 Election Cycle*.

50. "Issue Ad Spending (1999–2000)" (*www.appcpenn.org/issueads/estimate.htm* [April 11, 2001]).

51. "Issue Ad Spending (1999–2000)."

52. For a definition of election issue advocacy, see Magleby, *Election Advocacy*, p. 7.

53. Alison Mitchell, "Bush and McCain Exchange Sharp Words over Fund-Raising," *New York Times*, February 10, 2000, p.A26.

54. Linda L. Fowler, Constantine J. Spiliotes, and Lynn Vavreck, "The Role of Issue Advocacy Groups in the New Hampshire Primary," in David B. Magleby, *Getting Inside the Outside Campaign*, report presented at the National Press Club, Washington, July 7, 2000.

55. "Campaign Finance Reform" (www.georgewbush.com/issues/campaignfin.html [July 1, 2001]).

56. "Public Opinion on Campaign Finance" (www.igs.berkeley.edu:8880/research_programs/CRF/Basics/opinion.html [July 1, 2001]).

57. "Widespread Public Support for Campaign Finance Reform" (www.gallup.com/poll/releases/pr010320.asp [July 2, 2001]).

58. Craig Wilson, "Montana 2000 Senate and House Races," in David B. Magleby, ed., *Soft Money and Issue Advocacy in the 2000 Congressional Elections* (Rowman and Littlefield, forthcoming).

59. David B. Magleby, *Dictum without Data: The Myth of Issue Advocacy and Party Building* (Brigham Young University, Center for the Study of Elections and Democracy, 2000).

60. Anthony Corrado and Daniel Ortiz, *Campaign Finance Reform: A Sourcebook* (www.brook.edu/gs/cf/sourcebk/chap9.htm).

61. Candice J. Nelson, "Money in the 1996 Elections," in William Crotty, ed., *America's Choice: The Election of 1996* (Dushkin/McGraw-Hill, 1997).

62. "Receipts of 1999–2000 Presidential Campaigns through July 31, 2000" (*www.fec.gov/finance/precm8.htm*) [June 29, 2001]).

63. "1999–2000 Top 50 House Disbursements."

64. "1999–2000 Top 50 Senate Disbursements."

65. "1999–2000 Top House Disbursements."

66. Ibid.

67. "1999–2000 Top Senate Disbursements."

68. Sheila Krumholz, Center for Responsive Politics, Washington, telephone interview by David B. Magleby, July 16, 2001.

69. Magleby, *Election Advocacy*.

THREE   *The 2000 Presidential Nominations: The Costs of Innovation*

JOHN C. GREEN

NATHAN S. BIGELOW

PRESIDENTIAL NOMINATION contests are among
the most dynamic aspects of American politics, with innovations in campaign finance central to this dynamism.[1] Financial creativity in the 2000
presidential nomination campaign contributed to a dramatic increase in
spending over 1996. Although it did not set a record in real terms, the
campaign marked two milestones: the largest amount ever spent by a single
campaign and a sharp expansion of "outside" money—direct spending
by interest groups. When combined with other aspects of the 2000 campaign, these two feats further eroded the legitimacy of the federal campaign finance regime.

The record-setting performance was by George W. Bush, who spent an
unprecedented $89 million in his quest for the Republican presidential
nomination (and raised a record-breaking $94 million). Bush's decision
to forgo matching funds made this level of spending possible by freeing
his campaign from spending limits. Indeed, Bush is one of the few major
party candidates to ever bypass public financing and the only one to then
win the nomination. This innovation was rooted in the context of the
2000 campaign, including campaign finance rules, decisions of rival candidates, and access to resources. It also represented the increased influence of the GOP establishment and their allies. An increased role for party
insiders was also evident in Al Gore's successful campaign for the Democratic nomination, and the growth of "outside" spending by interest groups
characterized both parties' primary contests. Spirited challenges from John
McCain and Bill Bradley showed that it is possible to oppose this growing

49

influence of party and interest group organizations, but the success of such opposition remains in doubt.

Rules, Rivals, and Resources in 2000

Federal campaign finance laws, the structure of competition, and candidate resources help account for the financing of the 2000 nominations.

Federal Campaign Finance Laws

Federal campaign finance is governed by the Federal Election Campaign Act (FECA) of 1971 as amended in 1974 and 1976, interpreted by the federal courts, and implemented by the Federal Election Commission (FEC).[2] These laws create two important features in presidential nomination campaigns. First, they impose mandatory fund-raising regulations on all candidates and most other political organizations. Second, they create a voluntary public financing program, which includes additional regulations for participating candidates. Unlike previous years, the fact that these two features are not linked was critical in 2000, largely because of Bush's decision to forgo matching funds in the presidential primaries.

The campaign act mandates full disclosure of funds raised (donations of more than $200 from any one source must be itemized) and expended by all candidates and political organizations that are engaged in "express advocacy," that is, specifically advocating the election or defeat of a federal candidate. The timing and details of these reports have become part of presidential nomination politics.[3]

The act also mandates that in nomination campaigns, presidential candidates may accept a maximum contribution of $1,000 per election from any one individual and a maximum of $5,000 from any one party or political action committee (PAC). Although the FECA imposes a number of limits, none apply to candidates' contributions or loans to their own campaigns, nor to how much their campaigns spend overall—unless they agree to accept public funds.

Additional rules cover direct campaign expenditures by interest groups and parties. As discussed further in chapter 7, political action committees (PACs) may engage in: unlimited express advocacy for or against a candidate via "independent expenditures": unlimited express advocacy; "internal communications" with their own members; and unlimited and undisclosed issue advocacy that often supports or opposes a candidate.[4] Given modern communications technology, there is also a fine line between issue advocacy and more traditional grassroots campaigning, an activity that is also largely unregulated.

The second major FECA provision is that participating candidates can receive public funds for nomination campaigns if they follow appropriate procedures and abide by additional regulations. The first step is to qualify for public funds by raising $100,000 in amounts of $250 or less, with $5,000 coming from at least twenty states. Once qualified, the first $250 of every individual contribution raised in the election cycle (election year and year prior) is matched dollar per dollar with public funds, up to one-half of the federal spending limits for that year. Political action committee (PAC) and party donations cannot be matched. Like other contribution limits, the matching fund amounts are not adjusted for inflation, so that by 2000, the original $250 maximum match had declined to roughly $75 in real terms. Qualified candidates receive federal funds after January 1 of the election year. However, they can lose qualification if they receive less than 10 percent of the vote in two successive primaries or caucuses and requalify if they receive 20 percent in a subsequent contest.

In return for matching funds, candidates must abide by state-by-state and overall spending limits. The state limits are based on the voting-age population and are adjusted for inflation; the overall limit is the sum of the adjusted state limits. Candidates allocate expenditures to particular states by means of complex rules, and such allocations are regularly manipulated to maximize candidate spending in key states—a practice encouraged by the FEC's reluctance to strictly enforce the state limits (chapter 1).[5] Thus, within the context of the public financing regime, individual state limits usually do not pose a major problem for the campaigns, although self-financed candidates and outside spending by interest groups can make state limits problematic for candidates who abide by them. In any event, the overall spending limit carries considerable weight, effectively determining what candidates can legally raise and spend for the entire prenomination period.

Besides these campaign funds, candidates accepting matching funds are allowed to raise an additional 20 percent of the overall limit for fund-raising purposes. Another 15 percent of the overall limit is allowed for "compliance" expenses, such as accounting and legal costs. (Once a candidate withdraws from the campaign, other expenses are exempt from the limits.) Clever campaigns can use compliance funds to maximize operational spending, and it often makes sense to raise such funds simultaneously with other campaign contributions.[6] Finally, candidates who accept matching funds are limited to giving or lending $50,000 of their own money to their campaigns.

In 2000 the FEC set the overall spending limit for candidates accepting public funds at $33.8 million, with an additional $6.8 million for fund-raising and $5.0 million for compliance expenses, for a grand total of $45.6 million.

Structure of Competition

Candidate finances are also influenced by the structure of competition, which has three basic elements. The first element is the means by which the national convention delegates (who formally nominate major party presidential candidates) are chosen. With some minimum guidance from the national parties, each state sets the type of contest (such as a caucus or primary), determines who may participate (such as whether it is open to all voters or closed to all but party members), and decides the actual date of the contest. Thus the nomination calendar varies from election to election.

The 2000 calendar represented another step in a long-term trend to-ward "front loading," that is, the clustering of nomination contests early in the election year. Following custom, the 2000 election calendar began with events for both major parties, the Iowa caucuses on January 24 and the New Hampshire primary on February 1. For the Republicans, a series of contests followed, including South Carolina (February 19), Michigan and Arizona (February 22), while the Democrats had no contests. Both parties participated in "Titanic Tuesday" on March 7 with primaries in about a dozen states, including California, New York, and Ohio. One week later both parties also held contests on Super Tuesday, mostly in the South. Thus the nomination was likely to be settled by the Ides of March, leaving a five-month "postprimary" period until the national conventions in August. Since the presumptive nominees would need to campaign in the postprimary period, the early end to the primary season created additional pressures to raise funds.

The presence or absence of an incumbent is also important. Elections in which a sitting president seeks renomination and re-election differ from contests in which there is no incumbent. The 2000 election was an open-seat race, and this factor affected nomination politics of both major parties.

A third element in the structure of competition is the number of candidates. Multicandidate races (like that in 1988 with an open seat and six

Republicans and seven Democrats competing) call for different strategies than two-candidate races with a "front-runner" and a "challenger."[7] All other things being equal, most candidates would rather run in a two-candidate race because it is more predictable than a multicandidate race. This generalization holds for well-established "front-runners" who benefit from facing a single opponent but also applies to challengers who seek to unite the opposition. So, most candidates have incentives to "winnow" the field of rivals. For example, a crowded pool can reduce the funds raised by all of the less well-known candidates, to the benefit of the front-runner, and once the field is narrowed, supporters of the departed candidates can then swell the coffers of the remaining challenger.

Campaign Resources

The campaign finance laws and the structure of competition set the basic parameters for candidates' finances. And in the context of these parameters, each candidate has a different calculation of how much money he or she will need and how to acquire it, but there were some commonalities as the 2000 race began.

On the fund-raising side, the disjunction between the rising cost of campaigns (evidenced by the adjusted overall spending limits) and the unadjusted contribution limits (including the matching funds threshold) put pressure on all candidates to innovate in fund-raising.[8] One innovation was to raise more money in larger amounts, preferably the $1,000 maximum. This result could be accomplished by early and frequent solicitations by candidates of wealthy individuals, asking allied politicians to ask their donors to give, involving many "solicitors" who ask their networks of friends and associates to give, and having more fund-raising events. Another option was to raise more money in small amounts by impersonal means—direct mail, telephone, and the Internet. The availability of public funds was central to these calculations, since matching money doubles all individual donations up to $250.

However, some alternatives did not involve matching funds. For example, candidates could also forgo public funds, and under this circumstance, wealthy candidates could substantially fund their own campaigns, or well-connected candidates could raise and spend unlimited amounts of money. Candidates could raise extensive funds from PACs or encourage interest groups to campaign on their behalf. One strategy used in past election cycles was for candidates to form "leadership" PACs, allowing them to prepare for fund-raising before the cycle began.[9] Although many of the prospective candidates in 2000 had leadership PACs, this technique was not especially important in 2000, perhaps because Bush, McCain, Gore, and Bradley were already well prepared for the race.

On the expenditure side, front loading and the prospect of multicandidate races in both parties pressured candidates to raise large sums of money early in the process. Campaign professionals concluded that successful candidates would need to raise at least $20 million in 1999 to be competitive in 2000.[10] This conclusion involved assumptions about campaigning costs in the early contests, as well as the lack of time to raise additional funds once the contests began. It also reflected the symbolic power of money: an ample war chest would signal to the media, rival politicians, voters—and most importantly, prospective donors—that the candidate was viable. Indeed, fund-raising was a critical aspect of the "invisible primary," the name given to the process of narrowing the field of candidates before the contests begin.[11] A final consideration was the need for funds with which to compete in the long "post-primary" season. Thus the conventional wisdom strongly advised against a much celebrated (but rarely successful) "momentum" strategy: winning an early contest and then raising the needed funds to obtain the nomination. Of course, defying the conventional wisdom could give a clever candidate the element of surprise.

The Costs of the 2000 Nomination Campaigns

Before we consider the Republican and Democratic campaigns in detail, it is useful to describe the overall dimensions of 2000 nomination finances. As table 3-1 reports, major and minor party candidates raised $343 million and expended $326 million. In nominal dollars, these figures represent a spending increase of $92 million over 1996, a dramatic growth of 39 percent.[12] In constant or real dollars (figures adjusted for inflation), the 2000 spending represented a still-large 26 percent gain over 1996. However, this amount was about 12 percent lower in real terms than spending in 1988, the last open-seat presidential election.

Much of the spending increase came on the Republican side, where expenditures by all candidates totaled $224 million, a modest 12 percent constant dollar increase over 1996, and a similarly modest 8 percent growth from 1988. Most of the increase came from George W. Bush, whose $89 million was an all-time spending record by any measure—and an impressive one, since it included neither public funds nor the candidate's per-

Table 3-1. *Presidential Prenomination Receipts and Spending, 2000*
Dollars

Party	Receipts	Spending
Republican		
Bush	94,466,341	89,135,337
Forbes	48,144,976	47,846,044
McCain	45,047,937	44,614,846
Bauer	12,136,548	11,761,561
Keyes	10,999,752	10,575,767
Quayle	6,317,695	5,922,577
Dole	5,127,832	5,122,723
Alexander	3,085,631	3,085,632
Hatch	2,552,723	2,509,154
Kasich	3,191,083	2,335,793
Smith	1,614,198	1,795,231
Democratic		
Gore	49,202,745	42,478,461
Bradley	42,142,565	41,088,547
LaRouche[a]	4,505,658	4,481,792
Reform		
Buchanan	10,536,435	10,629,640
Green		
Nader	1,463,567	993,506
Libertarian		
Browne	1,248,198	1,254,213
Natural Law		
Hagelin	1,179,980	770,257

Source: Compiled from Federal Election Commission data, Washington.
a. LaRouche is a right-wing fringe candidate who ran in Democratic presidential primaries, 1980–2000.

sonal wealth. Several comparisons help put the Bush spending in perspective. It was about twice the size of the total expenditures of each of his two principal nomination rivals, publisher Steve Forbes ($47.8 million) and Senator John McCain ($44.6 million), and about twice the size of all the remaining Republican candidates combined. In constant dollars, it was roughly twice the spending of the 1996 GOP presidential nominee, Senator Bob Dole, about one-third higher than former president George Bush spent in his successful 1988 nomination campaign, and almost twice as high as Bush's spending in 1992.

There was, however, some stability and relative decline in Republican spending compared with that in 1996, reducing the overall impact of Bush's record expenditures. On the first count, Steve Forbes's expenditures, in constant dollars, were only marginally greater than his 1996 spending. On the second count, the combined spending of conservative Christian candidates, former Family Research Council head, Gary Bauer ($11.7 million) and Ambassador Alan Keyes ($10.5 million), was less than what former commentator Pat Buchanan spent in 1996. Spending in 2000 by Keyes was more than double what he spent in 1996, perhaps because of the absence of Buchanan. Many of the "also ran" candidates spent markedly less money than their counterparts in 1996. The best example is former Tennessee governor Lamar Alexander, who ran in both elections, spending just $3 million in 2000 compared with $16 million in 1996. Most of these candidates fell victim to the invisible primary and withdrew from the race in 1999. Bush's war chest absorbed much of the money that funded such candidacies in previous elections.

The Democrats experienced an even larger, 97 percent, increase over 1996, with Vice President Al Gore's ($42.4 million) and former senator Bill Bradley's ($41 million) spending together nearly doubling President Bill Clinton's 1996 total in constant dollars. Of course, Clinton faced no opposition in 1996, and in fact, Gore's 2000 spending was equivalent to Clinton's 1996 funds in real terms. A more apt comparison is with 1992, when Clinton won the nomination over a field of eight candidates. Overall, the 2000 Democratic nomination cost just about the same amount as the 1992 contest in real terms. The last open-seat contest for president was in 1988. Overall, the 2000 Democratic nomination cost a little more than one-half of the 1988 contest in constant dollars. In 1980 the Democrats also had a competitive two-candidate race. But the 2000 Democratic spending was about 29 percent higher than 1980. Thus the Democrats may have experienced an upward creep in campaign spending largely because candidates have become more adept at meeting the legal maximum in fund-raising.

However, table 3-1 does not report "outside" money spent by interest groups to influence the nominations. Reports filed with the FEC document just the tip of this electioneering iceberg. The PACs reported spending $1.2 million on independent expenditures (11 percent) for and (89 percent) against presidential candidates. Another $3.3 million was reported as internal communication costs (99 percent) for and (1 percent) against candidates in the primaries, a figure that understates such expenditures owing to the vagaries of disclosure. Nevertheless, these reported funds are about twice the size of similar 1996 spending in constant dollars.

But the bulk of outside money was submerged from easy view in the form of issue advocacy and traditional grassroots campaigning. For example, a study of five presidential primaries in 2000 found that 102 different groups had participated in one way or another, ranging from the AFL-CIO to the Christian Coalition.[13] Some three-fifths of this spending was directly associated with a presidential candidate, and only about two-fifths was pure issue advocacy. The nature of such spending varied enormously, with some groups attacking or supporting a candidate in a particular contest, others mobilizing their followers overall, and still others preparing for the fall campaign. Of course, the full impact of such funds depended on when, where, and how they were spent. Indeed, considerable disagreement exists over the impact of such spending. Some observers note that outside money is often spent in relatively small amounts, dubbed "vanity buys," designed mostly to generate media coverage; other observers believe that substantial outside spending by rival groups tends to produce little impact, as each side cancels out the other's message. Still others argue that outside spending often harms the candidate on whose behalf it is deployed, undermining the candidate's message. However, some observers believe that heavy outside spending in a short time span by a number of allied groups can have an enormous impact on particular races.[14]

Because of the lack of official reports, one can guess at the magnitude of this outside spending by estimating low and high figures. A study of outside money in the New Hampshire primary estimated that nine major groups spent a combined total of at least $429,000.[15] One can develop a low estimate of outside money by assuming that this New Hampshire figure was typical of the twenty-one contests through Titanic Tuesday (some were fiercely contested and some were not). By this assumption, outside money would have totaled about $9 million in the primaries. Alternatively, one can develop a high estimate by assuming that the typical figures were twice as much, or $858,000 per contest (consistent with the increase in independent expenditures and internal communications over 1996). Under this assumption, the comparable estimate would be $18 million in outside money. Adding the FEC figures on independent expenditures and internal communications costs produces a low estimate of $13.5 million and a high estimate of $22.5 million—a little less than what McCain and Bradley each raised in 1999. These are not trivial figures and surely represent a sharp increase over 1996. Judging by the much larger level of outside spending in the 2000 general election, it could expand greatly in future nomination campaigns.

The final entries in table 3-1 report the nomination spending of minor parties, including the Reform, Green, Libertarian, and Natural Law parties. Pat Buchanan faced an uphill struggle to obtain the Reform Party nomination and ended up spending a little more than Ross Perot spent in 1996. Like Perot, Buchanan spent much of this money just gaining ballot access. The remaining candidates had a much less daunting task to secure their nominations. With the exception of the Libertarians, the minor party candidates accepted matching funds, and all made substantial personal contributions to their own campaigns.

The Republicans

The extraordinary fund-raising of George W. Bush reflects the interaction of the rules, rivals, and resources. The most critical decision—to forgo public funds—was debated extensively within the Bush campaign. Two factors weighed strongly in its favor. The first was the experience of Bob Dole in 1996, whose campaign had been seriously damaged by Steve Forbes's heavy expenditure of his personal fortune, which was exempt from spending limits. Bush feared Forbes's self-financed campaign would be able to dramatically outspend him in key early contests if he abided by the spending limits. Second, the Bush campaign wanted funds for a "postprimary" campaign leading up to the national convention. In 1996 Dole had exhausted his funds by the end of the primary season and could not compete with Bill Clinton, who had ample funds. The Bush campaign was aware of Al Gore's fund-raising prowess and expected the Democrats to be well funded in the postprimary period. Thus the Bush camp wanted as much flexibility as possible to prepare for the general election.[16]

There were also two critical factors against forgoing public funds. The first was largely logistical: could the Bush campaign actually raise enough money to make up for the loss of public money? Campaign officials worried that Bush would not raise enough extra money to justify forgoing public funds. Interestingly, Bush did not decide to bypass public money until mid-1999, when his fund-raising efforts had proved far more successful than anticipated. As one aide put it: "For every dollar we went out and raised, another $2 came in, unexpected, over the transom."[17] An initial goal of becoming competitive by raising a war chest of $20 million was transformed into a goal of running a classic frontrunner campaign.

The Bush campaign was able to plan on a full-scale primary campaign in thirty states, an adequate postprimary effort, and early investments for the general election campaign.

A second concern was strictly political: would criticism over forgoing public funds hurt Bush with the voters? Campaign officials worried about a negative reaction from the media, especially the accusation that Bush was violating the spirit of the campaign finance laws. They also noted the danger of reinforcing the stereotypes of the GOP as "the party of the rich" and Bush as the candidate of the GOP "establishment." Bypassing public funds did become an issue in the primaries, aiding McCain's spirited challenge, but it did not prove to be a serious liability with core Republican constituencies.

George W. Bush was the very definition of a well-connected party insider, and he based his fund-raising strategy on exploiting his unique connections with the Republican establishment. Having been active in his father's presidential campaigns, he could lay claim to the extensive network of supporters acquired over three decades in public life (an estimated 50,000 persons). Furthermore, Bush was a recently re-elected governor of Texas, a state rich in donors (he raised $41 million in his 1994 and 1998 gubernatorial campaigns). And Bush was well liked by Republican leaders and office-holders, especially GOP governors (in fact, the Republican Governors Association's endorsement helped launch his campaign). Bush sought to tap these numerous connections by means of the Pioneers, a group of solicitors who pledged to each raise $100,000 in $1,000 donations from pyramids of friends and associates. Similar groups of solicitors had been deployed in previous campaigns and by party committees, but nothing on this scale.[18] Of the 400 people who took the pledge in July 1999, 226 eventually met or exceeded the $100,000 goal, providing Bush with about one-fourth of his total funds.[19]

Who were the Pioneers? Overall, they represented a broad cross section of the GOP establishment. Many Pioneers were business leaders, representing the finance, energy, real estate, and manufacturing sectors in roughly equal numbers, followed by a wide array of other industries; they included chief executive officers of major corporations, entrepreneurs, and venture capitalists. However, the largest group of Pioneers was lawyers and lobbyists, professional "brokers" in the political process.

The Pioneers also included a number of prominent political leaders, social issue activists, and other Bush family members. As one might expect, the largest number of Pioneers (more than one-quarter) came from

Texas, but thirty-four other states and the District of Columbia were represented.[20] Bush benefited from an unusual unity among Republican notables; in most elections, these notables and insiders would have been divided among competing candidates.

How was this massive network organized? James Francis, a Dallas lawyer and Bush confidant, developed and managed the Pioneer operation. According to one observer, the secret to its success was a combination of "accountability and competition."[21] Each Pioneer had his or her own personal account code with the Bush campaign, so that each person could get credit for money he or she raised. The Bush campaign carefully monitored the incoming contributions, bestowing praise and status to Pioneers who met the $100,000 pledge. This system of monitoring and rewards created strong incentives among the Pioneers that tapped into the competitive drive of business executives, lawyers, and politicians.

The Pioneers wanted the things major donors typically want in politics: ideological, social, and material rewards.[22] Ideological motivations were reinforced by a deep resentment of the Clinton administration and a strong desire for a return to more conservative government. The Republicans had been out of the White House for eight years, and many of the Pioneers simply wanted their side to win. They viewed "Dubya" as one of their own. No doubt many had specific policy changes in mind, and others wanted appointments in a Bush administration. One Pioneer, Elaine Chao, wife of Kentucky Republican senator Mitch McConnell, was appointed secretary of labor, and fourteen Pioneers were nominated as ambassadors. Of course, realizing all of these goals depended on a Republican victory, and so the perception that Bush was going to win the nomination and the general election was critical.

The Pioneers were also part of the Bush campaign's broader effort to prepare for the general election. They were central to the hard dollar fundraising of the GOP, with many having served on Team 100, a Republican National Committee fund-raising network, or in similar state party programs. The Bush campaign used these connections to raise funds for general election activities. A good example was the establishment of a "joint fund-raising committee" between the Bush campaign and twenty state Republican parties in July 1999. This effort allowed the state parties to raise an estimated $5 million in hard dollars from Bush donors by encouraging donors to "max out" their total hard dollar contributions for 1999. These funds might otherwise have gone untapped, and they proved valuable as a match for soft money in the 2000 general election. The Pioneers were critical to soft-money fund-raising too. Overall, they provided some $28 million in soft money to Republican Party committees in 2000, up from $25 million in 1996.

While Bush pursued his front-runner campaign, McCain set out to run a classic "momentum" campaign, which in some key respects was the opposite of the Bush front-runner model. A genuine war hero with a maverick style, McCain hoped to energize moderate Republicans and independents on the basis of government reform, especially campaign finance reform, and use them against the party establishment. He originally planned to raise a total of $19 million, including public financing—about what the conventional wisdom advocated for the preprimary season. McCain believed that such funds would allow him to win the first four primaries (New Hampshire, South Carolina, Michigan, and Arizona), all of which were open contests, and that these victories would drive the front-runner from the field.

The McCain plan assumed that his initial successes would allow him to raise a large portion of the needed funds, but it never envisioned competing head-to-head with a frontrunner on Titanic Tuesday or thereafter. Indeed, the McCain campaign had no plans for funding a postprimary campaign. The early emergence of Bush as the clear frontrunner only helped the McCain "outsider" strategy. The campaign was also helped by the fall 1999 publication of McCain's autobiography, *Faith of My Fathers*. The initial public response to McCain was so encouraging that the campaign invested heavily in telephone, direct mail, and Internet fundraising, decisions that paid off handsomely once primary contests began. Before the campaign was over, McCain had raised more than twice his original goal and nearly reached the legal maximum.[23]

The scope of Bush's 'connections' campaign is shown in table 3-2. All told, he received maximum $1,000 donations from some 63,000 individuals, accounting for two-thirds of his total. This figure was roughly equal to the number of $1,000 donations raised by all other major party candidates combined and was nearly three times larger than all such donations to the other GOP candidates. Another $12.5 million (roughly one-eighth of the total) came from individual donations of $500 to $999, which was also far larger than all the other Republican candidates. His smallest category was $200 to $499, but even here, his $5.3 million was greater than all other candidates except Al Gore. And although donations under $200 were hardly Bush's strength (making up one-tenth of the total), his $10 million in this category was second only to McCain. Bush also raised almost $2 million in PAC money, the most of any candidate.

Table 3-2. *Republican Presidential Prenomination Receipts, 2000*

Candidate	$1,000 contributions	$500-$999 contributions	$200-$499 contributions	$199 and less contributions	Matching funds	Contributions and loans from the candidate	Political action committees
Bush	63,205,000	12,499,238	5,354,383	10,273,330	0	0	1,960,060
Forbes	1,742,000	496,258	570,410	2,943,482	0	42,330,000	0
McCain[a]	10,008,000	3,930,780	3,756,431	10,448,402	14,467,788	0	405,599
Bauer	1,192,000	753,234	1,318,529	4,289,554	4,632,803	0	6,000
Keyes	452,000	353,318	945,290	5,912,645	3,325,340	0	10,100
Quayle	1,724,000	357,697	317,768	1,683,736	2,087,748	1,000	43,200
Dole	3,114,000	706,542	410,232	770,861	0	735	118,292
Alexander	1,391,000	223,962	104,120	582,665	0	666,417	80,383
Hatch	1,162,000	244,157	95,375	623,175	0	0	173,016
Kasich	1,315,000	161,580	72,575	153,513	0	0	77,224
Smith	95,900	39,371	25,458	1,361,399	0	0	17,070

Source: Compiled from FEC data.
a. McCain transferred $2,000,000 from his Senate campaign.

These patterns present a sharp contrast to the other Republican candidates. As table 3-2 shows, the Forbes campaign was once again largely self-financed, with $42.3 million in gifts and loans accounting for nearly 90 percent of the total. One can see why Forbes inspired respect: his own money was nearly equal to all the funds McCain raised. As in 1996, Forbes hoped that his personal wealth would make up for his lack of public office, name recognition, and connections with the party establishment. Besides his own money, Forbes planned to raise between $5 and $10 million; this goal was met, allowing the campaign to reach its financial goals. Like McCain, Forbes's strategy was to defeat Bush early (in Iowa, New Hampshire, Delaware, and Arizona) and drive him from the race. The dynamics of the campaign, including McCain's decision to bypass Iowa and his surge in New Hampshire, undermined Forbes's strategy. While Forbes's defeat may deter some self-financed candidates in the future, particular combinations of rules, rivals, and resources are likely to encourage wealthy candidates to spend their own funds. All told, Forbes's decision to forgo public funds may have helped legitimize the Bush campaign.[24]

McCain had a more varied source of funds, reflecting his maverick style and momentum strategy. He began by transferring $2 million from his Senate campaign and raised $10 million in $1,000 donations, which together accounted for one-quarter of his funds. That McCain was the chairman of the Senate Commerce Committee was an asset in obtaining these larger donations. Another one-sixth of McCain's funds came from donations between $200 and $999, and he had a major success with donations under $200, which provided almost another one-quarter of his funds. Five million dollars of McCain's money was reported to have been raised over the Internet, the most successful Internet effort to date.[25] The largest portion of McCain's funds, almost one-third, came from matching funds, revealing the importance of public money to insurgent candidates.

Two patterns describe the rest of the GOP field. First, Gary Bauer, Alan Keyes, and New Hampshire senator Bob Smith relied heavily on raising donations under $200 from religious conservatives through direct mail—all matched with public funds. However, this approach was used to greater effect by Pat Robertson in 1988 and Pat Buchanan in 1992 and 1996. These monies accounted for three-quarters of Bauer's money and some 90 percent of Keyes's and Smith's funds. The other candidates, Elizabeth Dole, Dan Quayle, Orrin Hatch, Lamar Alexander, and John Kasich, were starved for cash. This point is well illustrated by the paucity of $1,000 donors for these well-connected insiders: none of them received as much

Figure 3-1.   *Republican Primary Fund-Raising, 1999–2000 (Bush and McCain)*

Millions of dollars

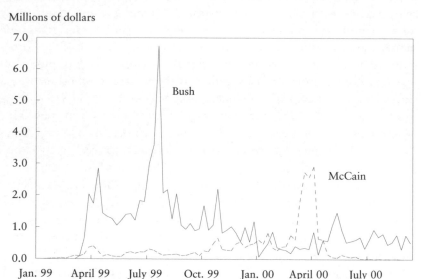

Source: Compiled from Federal Election Commission data, Washington.

as one-twentieth of the Bush total. Still other candidates, such as former California governor Pete Wilson, declined to enter the race owing to Bush's fund-raising. Most of these candidates had the same general approach to fund-raising as Bush but were simply unable to execute it in the face of the Bush juggernaut.[26]

The dynamics of Republican fund-raising are shown in figure 3-1, which plots the funds raised by week over the course of the campaign by Bush and McCain. Bush implemented his fund-raising efforts early in 1999, producing some startling results.[27] Early peaks came during the weeks of March 17 and April 1, and his best week was June 30, when he raised almost $7 million—more than many of his rivals raised in the entire election cycle. Subsequent peaks occurred in the weeks of September 30 and November 8. When combined with extensive endorsements and good poll numbers, this extraordinary fund-raising established Bush as the clear frontrunner for the nomination early in the campaign. Interestingly, the McCain fund-raising effort did not really begin until the preprimary season was nearly over.

A final hurdle for Bush came with the Iowa "straw poll" in August 1999. Designed as a fund-raiser for the Iowa GOP, the various candidates purchased $25 tickets so their supporters could express their presidential preferences. Bush had three advantages: a paid organization, ample cash for tickets, and no need to worry about the Iowa spending limits, against which such expenses could be charged. Bush spent at least $750,000 on the straw poll and finished first with 30 percent. Many of the other candidates also spent heavily, with the hope that a good showing would jumpstart their campaigns and their fund-raising efforts. Thus, it came as no surprise when most candidates left the race shortly after the Iowa straw poll.[28] Since McCain had not participated in the straw poll, he was unaffected by the results and probably benefited from the sudden narrowing of the field.

By year's end, Bush had clearly won the invisible primary. He had raised $69 million dollars, more than three times his initial goal of $20 million, and about the same as the public financing grant given to Bush and Gore for the 2000 general election. His remaining rivals, Forbes ($28 million) and McCain ($16 million) were far behind. Bush's fund-raising efforts then declined, so by January 2000 he was raising funds at about the same level as McCain, whose take had begun to rise. Besides helping to narrow the field, Bush was able to spend lavishly on a national organization, including thirty-four state offices across the country, 174 paid staff, and detailed plans to run in every state.[29] Much of this spending was directed beyond the primaries to the general election.

Bush assumed, correctly as it turned out, that he would defeat Forbes and the remaining conservative candidates in Iowa and New Hampshire. In the Iowa caucuses Bush was aided by TV and radio ads from the Republican Leadership Council (RLC) warning Forbes against becoming "too negative" in the campaign. Some analysts believe that these ads pre-empted a Forbes attack on Bush similar to his 1996 assault on Dole, although others believe it had little effect on the Forbes campaign.[30] In any event, Bush's margins over Forbes and Bauer in the early contests quickly drove them from the race. But the Bush campaign miscalculated with regard to McCain, who bypassed Iowa, and was well positioned to unite the lingering opposition.

A shrewd use of campaign resources allowed McCain to conduct his "momentum" campaign effectively. Using his time and personal charisma in place of money, McCain spent seventy-two days in the Granite State, riding his "Straight Talk Express" campaign bus to 114 open town meetings. Campaign finance reform was a central issue for McCain, and its appeal was reinforced by Bush's big war chest. However, it is also true that McCain had husbanded enough money to wage an effective media campaign in New Hampshire.[31]

Although Bush outspent McCain in New Hampshire, the Arizona senator won decisively, based largely on his support from independent voters.[32] Outside spending played a role in New Hampshire: conservative groups attacked McCain, and liberal groups criticized Bush. These efforts may have hurt the candidates with conservative and independent voters, respectively, but the spending by liberal interest groups against Bush may have helped solidify his credentials with conservatives.[33] Unlike many New Hampshire victors in past years, however, McCain experienced a dramatic fund-raising windfall. As figure 3-1 reveals, McCain's fund-raising picked up in the week following New Hampshire, producing $1.8 million and then improving to his best week at the end of February, when he collected $2.9 million. As a consequence, McCain's total receipts in February were $14.5 million, nearly as much as he obtained in 1999. These funds were acquired in many ways, but his Internet donations were especially noteworthy. These gains gave McCain the money to continue his campaign plan in the South Carolina and Michigan primaries.

McCain's surge coincided with the steady depletion in Bush's campaign coffers, so that he had fewer resources than anticipated with which to respond. This fact can be seen in figure 3-2, which shows the rapid descent of Bush's cash on hand. Although McCain never enjoyed appreciable surpluses in his campaign coffers, his post-New Hampshire gains appeared to match Bush's existing funds, a prime goal of the "momentum" campaign. Journalists, as well as Republican insiders, began to ask: what had Bush's money bought? The frontrunner status acquired by the spectacular fund-raising in 1999 had greatly diminished as an asset. However, Bush's investment in campaign infrastructure probably paid off on Titanic Tuesday.[34]

The next major confrontation was in South Carolina, where Bush and McCain faced off in a bitter campaign, widely recognized as one of the most negative on record. Once again Bush outspent McCain and received critical assistance from conservative interest groups, which strongly attacked McCain's conservative credentials.[35] These groups included prolife, Christian conservative, and tobacco groups; and their efforts built a wall between social conservatives and McCain, allowing a solid Bush win. In a sense, McCain faced two opponents in South Carolina and did not

Figure 3-2. *Republican Primary, Cash on Hand (Bush and McCain)*

Millions of dollars

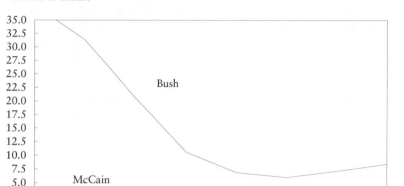

Source: Compiled from FEC data.

have the funds to fight both. After South Carolina, the campaign shifted almost immediately to Michigan, where McCain obtained an unexpected victory. As in South Carolina, Bush outspent McCain and conservative interest groups attacked McCain; but as in New Hampshire, McCain won with strong support from independents.[36] On the same day McCain also won in his home state of Arizona (where Bush had earlier led in the polls).

Worries about his emptying coffers led Bush to reconsider his spending plans and begin fund-raising again, an effort he maintained throughout the spring (figure 3-1).[37] The McCain camp faced funding problems of its own and decided on a major gamble to change the dynamics of the campaign; McCain attacked Pat Robertson and Jerry Falwell with the hope of rallying opponents of the Christian Right against Bush. This gamble turned out to be a major mistake because it alienated a key GOP constituency: Christian conservatives.[38] This error, plus high levels of spending by Bush and his conservative allies, produced solid Bush victories in Virginia, Washington, and North Dakota, abruptly ending McCain's momentum. McCain's fund-raising plummeted the following week, right before the most expensive day of the year, Titanic Tuesday (figure 3-1).

Although McCain won primaries in New England on Titanic Tuesday, Bush's organization and spending produced major wins in New York,

Ohio, and California. Once again, Bush received outside financial help. Texas millionaire Sam Wyly (brother of Pioneer Charles Wyly) funneled $2.5 million through a group entitled "Republicans for Clean Air" for television ads attacking McCain's environmental record.[39] McCain then faced daunting prospects: the next primaries, including Texas, were largely in the South, and McCain's campaign was running up against the spending limits. Thus he folded his "momentum" campaign.

In the end, Bush's superior funds allowed him to outlast McCain's post-New Hampshire fund-raising surge. This pattern can be seen in a comparison of total 2000 spending by month. In January, Bush outspent McCain two-to-one ($12.8 versus $6.7 million), but the two campaigns were essentially even in February ($13.1 for Bush and $13.5 for McCain). In March, Bush edged McCain ($10.1 to $8.5 million). These figures probably understate Bush's advantage because they do not include organization expenditures made earlier in the campaign or the expenditures from outside groups in principal states. In this sense, the conventional wisdom about early fund-raising was borne out, despite the initial success of McCain's momentum strategy.

When he clinched the GOP nomination on March 14, Bush had $10 million remaining in his campaign, about the same amount as Gore had when he secured the Democratic nomination following Titanic Tuesday. But without an overall spending limit, Bush was able to raise and spend an additional $13 million after March to use against his Democratic rival in the postprimary season. It is hard to tell what effect this advantage had on the ultimate outcome, but it did allow Bush to campaign effectively against Gore before the national conventions.

What were the lessons of the 2000 Republican nomination contest? For one thing, there was no serious backlash against Bush's and Forbes's decisions to forgo public financing, or against Bush's unprecedented war chest. Future Republican frontrunners will surely consider following Bush's example. Of course, relatively few candidates will be able to duplicate Bush's fund-raising feat. To oppose the establishment candidates, some challengers may want to follow the McCain model, which was the best "momentum" campaign to date, and other challengers may follow the Forbes's model of self-financing. No matter what model they choose, frontrunners and challengers alike will need to be aware of the impact of outside money. If 2000 is any guide, a united party establishment will be nearly impossible to beat.

The Democrats

Unlike Bush, Gore planned from the beginning to winnow the Democratic field by raising an insurmountable war chest. There is no evidence, however, that Gore ever considered forgoing public funds, a decision that would have provoked a strong, negative reaction among the party faithful. Instead, Gore fully exploited the matching funds system to raise the maximum funds quickly and efficiently. Early in 1999, campaign officials referred to the vice president as "the $55 million man," making a plausible case that they could raise this unheard-of amount.[40] The goal was to run a classic frontrunner campaign and discourage potential rivals from even entering the race.

Gore's plan was plausible because, like Bush, he was well connected to the powers within his party. The son of a prominent senator, Gore had grown up in politics, eventually serving in the House of Representatives and the Senate, collecting thousands of supporters along the way. He made a credible run for the presidency in 1988 and then spent eight years as vice president, where he fell heir to President Clinton's extensive network. Although a founding member of the "New Democrats," Gore had forged close connections with many liberal groups, including environmentalists, feminists, and the African American community. He had some early difficulties with organized labor but then received labor's enthusiastic backing. His association with Democratic office-holders and party leaders produced many early endorsements. These connections produced a fund-raising effort that resembled Bush's emphasis on $1,000 contributions. Gore even had a modest version of the Pioneers, a group of $100,000 solicitors known as the Board of Directors, but unlike Bush, Gore's approach put more stress on smaller donations and avoided PAC donations altogether, with an eye toward matching funds.

Gore was more successful than Bush in narrowing the field: most potential rivals never entered the race. These potential candidates included House Minority Leader Richard Gephardt, Senators Bob Kerrey, John Kerry, and Paul Wellstone, and Reverend Jesse Jackson. Although it was not the only factor, Gore's fund-raising prowess clearly influenced their decisions not to enter the race. However, Gore did draw one strong opponent, former senator Bill Bradley. Ironically, Gore's nearly clean sweep of the field gave Bradley the early opportunity to unite the opposition. Bradley proved an effective fund-raiser. Although out of office since 1996, he

Table 3-3. Democratic Presidential Prenomination Receipts, 2000

Item	Gore	Bradley	LaRouche[a]
$1,000 contributions	21,798,000	19,123,000	93,000
$500–$999 contributions	3,684,362	4,267,878	500,980
$200–$499 contributions	2,732,940	2,752,654	1,271,796
$199 and less contributions	5,655,904	3,127,057	1,453,262
Matching funds	15,317,872	12,462,045	1,184,372
Contributions and loans from the candidate	0	18,219	0
Political action committees	0	0	590

Source: Compiled from FEC data.
a. LaRouche is a right-wing fringe candidate who ran in Democratic presidential primaries, 1980–2000.

still had a network of senatorial supporters concentrated in the New York City area, and special links to the sports and entertainment worlds because of his basketball career. Although not as well connected as the vice president, he was well known enough in Democratic circles to adopt a similar financing strategy.[41]

The similarities between the Gore and Bradley fund-raising are shown in table 3-3. Gore obtained 20,600 donations of $1,000 from individuals, compared with 18,700 for Bradley. In both cases these maximum donations made up the lion's share of the private funds raised: 61 percent for Gore and 63 percent for Bradley, figures only slightly lower than for George W. Bush. Both Democratic candidates raised comparable amounts of donors in the $500 to $999 and the $200 to $499 ranges. However, Gore did better than Bradley with donations under $200 dollars (20 percent versus 12 percent), and consequently was able to receive more matching funds, $15.3 to $12.4 million. Bradley's smallest donations are a bit of a surprise because, like McCain, he invested in Internet fund-raising. Despite a few differences, the similarities among the candidates outweighed the differences.

The dynamics of Democratic fund-raising can be seen in figure 3-3, which plots Gore's and Bradley's weekly fund-raising over the election cycle. Although Gore began more strongly early in 1999, Bradley quickly followed, and his efforts largely tracked the vice president's. Gore enjoyed larger spikes, timed to show progress in the quarterly campaign finance reports: the weeks of April 1, June 30, and September 29. Bradley's best week was also September 29, somewhat after he formally announced his bid for the nomination. His weekly totals exceeded Gore's in the fourth quarter of 1999 but then declined steadily thereafter. Gore received an-

Figure 3-3. *Democratic Primary Fund-Raising, 1999–2000 (Gore and Bradley)*

Millions of dollars

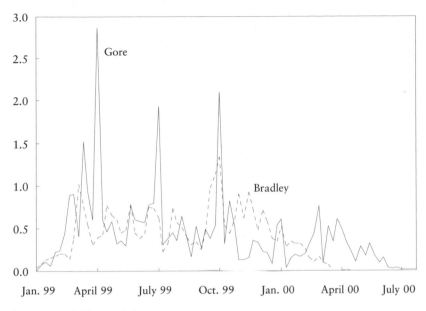

Source: Compiled from FEC data.

other fund-raising boost toward the end of February, as the nomination battle drew to a close.

Although Bradley raised somewhat less money than Gore throughout most of 1999, he stayed close enough for observers to conclude that contest could go either way, and by the fall he had amassed the $20 million recommended by conventional wisdom. As figure 3-4 shows, Gore and Bradley had about the same amount of cash on hand for most of 1999, with Bradley pulling ahead modestly at year's end. The principal reason for this pattern was the vice president's higher expenditure level. In a fashion reminiscent of George W. Bush, Gore set out to build a national organization, and this involved much higher overhead than that of the more frugal "Dollar Bill." These financial problems combined with weak poll numbers led Gore to reorganize his campaign, the symbol of which was moving his headquarters from Washington, D.C., to Nashville, Tennessee.[42] However, in some respects the damage had already been done; by the end of January 2000, the candidates had each raised some $29 mil-

Figure 3-4.   *Democratic Primary, Cash on Hand (Gore and Bradley)*

Millions of dollars

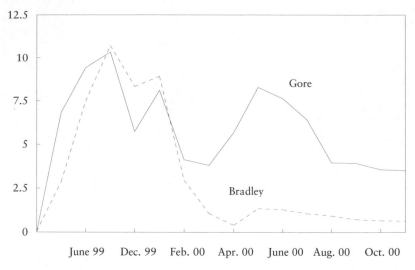

Source: Compiled from FEC data.

lion, and Bradley was in a position to spend $5 million more in the up-
coming contests.

In partial imitation of McCain, Bradley devoted considerable attention
to the New Hampshire primary. He was doing well in the polls, and one
of the staples of his campaign was campaign finance reform; he was critical of Gore's past involvement in questionable finance practices. But unlike McCain, Bradley made a point of contesting the Iowa caucuses,
believing that the press expected all serious candidates to compete in Iowa.
In retrospect, it was a serious mistake. Although Bradley was able to spend
more money in Iowa than Gore,[43] the vice president had a clear organizational advantage in the caucus environment. Many local Democratic officials rallied the troops for Gore, and more important, organized labor
and liberal interest groups spent heavily and worked hard on Gore's behalf.[44] The result was a decisive win for the frontrunner.

Bradley then scrambled to win New Hampshire. Here, too, he was
able to outspend Gore, but once again Gore benefited from the support of
key interest groups, especially labor and environmentalists.[45] Bradley faced
an unexpected foe as well—John McCain. Bradley and McCain each appealed to independent New Hampshire voters, and on election night, the
surging McCain won the "reform primary."[46] Although Bradley's 47 per-

cent of the vote was quite impressive against a sitting vice president, his campaign began to falter.

The political calendar then worked against Bradley: there were no delegate-electing events until March 7. Deprived of contests with which to right his listing campaign and overshadowed by the McCain-Bush fight in the GOP, Bradley sought unsuccessfully to invent opportunities to generate momentum. On Titanic Tuesday, Bradley outspent Gore in aggregate but lost every state to Gore and his interest group allies. Facing a string of southern primaries, including Gore's Tennessee primary, Bradley ended his campaign.

So, like Bush, Gore was able to use his financial resources and strong interest group spending to ward off a spirited challenge. But unlike the Republican race, the challenger had a modest spending advantage but was unable to convert it into victories at the polls. Gore secured the nomination with access to $11 million, slightly more than Bush, and enough to finance an adequate postprimary campaign. However, Gore soon reached the spending limits, while Bush was able to raise and spend additional funds. This disparity caused Gore some anxious moments on the way to the Democratic National Convention in August.

What were the lessons of the 2000 Democratic nomination campaign? In some respects, they mirrored the Republican experience. Gore's "insider" campaign was remarkably effective, and given the influence of reformers in Democratic politics, future Democratic frontrunners are unlikely to forgo public financing as Bush did among the Republicans. Instead, established Democrats will have incentives to "work within the system," exploiting every nuance in campaign law. The influence of party insiders is reflected in the role of outside money, especially the activities of labor unions. The Bradley campaign will give some hope to future insurgents, but it also suggests that mobilizing Democratic interest groups against frontrunners will be crucial.

The Costs of Innovation

In sum, fund-raising innovations sharply increased the costs of the 2000 presidential nomination campaigns over the 1996 election, gains that may well represent a modest real growth over time. George W. Bush's decision to forgo public financing was a principal cause of this increase, but other factors, such as the expansion of outside money and a close Democratic race, contributed as well. All these innovations reflected the confluence of rules, rivals, and resources in a highly dynamic nomination process. In some important respects, these innovations were peculiar to the 2000 campaign. For example, Bush's Pioneers may not be replicated any time soon. But in other respects, the 2000 fund-raising patterns reflected a broader increase in the influence of the party establishments.

While these increased costs had some positive aspects—after all, both major parties eventually had spirited contests—the negative elements were more numerous. Critics point to the use of early fund-raising to winnow the field of candidates, unnecessarily depriving voters of a wider range of choices—and in the case of late contests, any choice at all. Others note the increased influence of party insiders, from elected officials to high dollar solicitors, which biased the nomination process against challengers, reformers, and weaker interests. Still others complained about the rise of outside money, where vast sums can be quickly deployed in strategic races without limit or accountability. Although these criticisms are not new, the 2000 campaign gave them new force.

However, the biggest costs were to the legitimacy of the campaign finance system itself, further eroding the efficacy of the FECA. George W. Bush's forgoing of public funds was especially problematic, becoming a potent symbol of the "power of money" in contemporary politics. To many Americans, the public funding of presidential elections was a step toward a better finance system, one in which private money is regulated to foster a more democratic process. The Bush campaign not only disregarded such expectations, but it did so in a grand fashion. Although Bush suffered no serious backlash in the primaries, there may well be a more serious backlash against the legitimacy of the entire system.

In all fairness, it must be remembered that, unlike other recent innovations of more dubious legality, such as soft money, issue advocacy, and the aggressive exploitation of legal technicalities, Bush's decision to forgo public funds was entirely legal. And many other actors, from Al Gore to the National Right to Life Committee and the AFL-CIO, also contributed to undermining the campaign finance regime. In their assessment of the 1996 nomination campaign, Wesley Joe and Clyde Wilcox wondered if it would be "the last regulated campaign."[47] There is no question that the 2000 nomination campaign was another step away from the existing regulations. Although the innovations of the next campaign are hard to predict, there is every reason to expect that in the absence of fundamental reforms the increased importance of party notables and interest groups will continue to undermine campaign finance regulations. Indeed, campaign insiders were nearly unanimous in their views that the public financing regime, if not the FECA itself, has become increasingly irrelevant.

What, then, are the implications of the 2000 campaign for reform? Two readily come to mind. The first might be labeled the "limits of limits." The spending limits associated with the public financing system have long distorted the nomination process, creating strong incentives for candidates, parties, and interest groups to find ways around them—including bypassing the public financing system altogether. In most respects, the spending limits are arbitrary, bearing no resemblance to political reality. The state-by-state limits are clearly too low for the key state contests that come early in the front-loaded primary calendar, particularly if outside money and self-financed candidates are taken into account. In addition, the overall spending limits may be too low. After all, both McCain and Bradley nearly reached the overall limits before Titanic Tuesday. The frontloading of the primary calendar exacerbates these problems. If spending limits are to be an effective tool for reform, they must allow a wide variety of candidates to compete effectively during and after the primary season and not force otherwise reputable candidates to operate on the margins of the system.

One good feature of the current spending limits is that they are indexed for inflation. In contrast, the contribution limits are not. The steady erosion in the value of legal campaign contributions has also created strong incentives for candidates, parties, and interest groups to find ways around the system. Ironically, this erosion has tended to benefit well-established candidates who have the connections and organization to raise a large number of donations. Thus, if contribution limits are to remain an effective tool of reform, they must be adjusted for inflation. This change should apply especially to individual donations and the matching funds threshold, the key sources of primary funds under the FECA. This suggestion may appear counterintuitive to some observers, since it would seem to help established candidates like Bush and Gore over rivals such as McCain and Bradley. No set of contribution limits can fully prevent a massive fund-raising effort such as Bush's Pioneers, but it was the declining value of legal contributions that directly and indirectly provided the rationale for such an effort—otherwise there would have been no impetus for such an innovation. Of course, setting nonarbitrary limits is difficult because the nomination process is in a constant state of flux. But this difficulty is just another way of noting that there are limits to what limits can achieve.

The second reform implication might be called the "consequences of compromise." The seeds of the present campaign finance crisis were sown at the birth of the present legal regime, with the Supreme Court's compromise between controlling political money and protecting freedom of speech. The Court's uneasy distinction between "express" and "issue" advocacy has become the principal avenue by which innovation has undermined the campaign finance regime. All the most recent controversial innovations in campaign finance, including the voluntary nature of the public financing system and the unleashing of outside money, are based ultimately in this distinction. It may be time to revise this compromise to favor more regulation and less freedom. But even if such a revision takes place, additional incentives will be necessary to encourage candidates, parties, and interest groups to raise and spend funds within the campaign finance system rather than outside of it. Under such circumstances, innovations in campaign finance are likely to be less costly in all respects.

Notes

1. Anthony Corrado, "The Changing Environment of Presidential Campaign Finance," in William G. Mayer, ed., *In Pursuit of the White House* (Chatham House, 1996), pp. 220–53.

2. See Anthony Corrado and others, *Campaign Finance Reform: A Sourcebook* (Brookings, 1997).

3. See chapters 1 and 6 for discussion of express advocacy.

4. On this point see Jonathan S. Krasno and Daniel E. Seltz, *Buying Time: Television Advertising in the 1998 Congressional Elections* (New York University School of Law, Brennan Center for Justice, 2000).

5. For a good example of such manipulation in 2000, see Susan B. Glasser, "Over the Limit and through the Loophole," *Washington Post Weekly Edition,* December 13, 1999, p. 11.

6. Fund-raising and compliance funds must be raised according to hard dollar limits, but because these monies are segregated from campaign funds, donors can often double the maximum limit, by, for example, giving $1,000 to a candidate's campaign fund and $1,000 to the candidate's compliance fund.

7. See John H. Aldrich, *Before the Convention: Strategies and Choices in Presidential Nominating Campaigns* (University of Chicago Press, 1980).

8. On presidential fund-raising strategies, see Clifford W. Brown and others, *Serious Money: Fundraising and Contributing in Presidential Nomination Campaigns* (Cambridge University Press, 1995).

9. See Corrado, "The Changing Environment of Presidential Campaign Finance," pp. 245–46.

10. Paul West, "Year of the Invisible Primary," *Baltimore Sun,* August 8, 1999, p. 2A.

11. Emmett H. Buell Jr., "The Invisible Primary," in Mayer, *In Pursuit of the White House,* pp. 1–43. On the role of momentum in primary fund-raising, see Katherine A. Hinckley and John C. Green, "Fundraising in Presidential Primary

Campaigns: The Primary Lessons of 1988," *Political Research Quarterly*, vol. 49 (December 1996), pp. 693–718.

12. On 1996 nomination finance, see Wesley Joe and Clyde Wilcox, "Financing the 1996 Presidential Nominations: The Last Regulated Campaign?" in John C. Green, ed., *Financing the 1996 Election* (M.E. Sharpe, 1999), pp. 37–62. For an excellent overview of campaign finance in the entire 2000 cycle, see Anthony Corrado, "Financing the 2000 Election," in Gerald M. Pomper, ed., *The Election of 2000* (Chatham House, 2001), pp. 92–124.

13. David Magleby, ed., *Getting Inside the Outside Campaign* (Brigham Young University, Center for the Study of Elections and Democracy, 2000).

14. These comments are based on interviews by David Magleby and John Green with Richard Davis, McCain campaign, June 17, 2001; Benjamin Ginsberg, Bush campaign, July 6, 2001; and Bill Dal Col, Forbes campaign, July 9, 2001.

15. Linda L. Fowler and others, "The Role of Issue Advocacy Groups in the New Hampshire Primary," in Magleby, *Getting Inside the Outside Campaign*, pp. 30–39.

16. Susan B. Glasser, "George W. Bush's Dash for Cash," *Washington Post Weekly Edition*, April 19, 1999, p. 10.

17. Don Van Natta Jr., "Bush Uses Family Ties to Build Up Treasury," *New York Times*, January 30, 2000, p. A12; and Ginsburg, interview.

18. On past solicitors in nomination campaigns, see Corrado, "The Changing Environment of Presidential Campaign Finance," pp. 231–32.

19. Glasser, "George W. Bush's Dash for Cash," p. 10.

20. Much of this information on the Pioneers comes from Texans for Public Justice (www.tpj/org/pioneers June 1, 2001); for additional information, see Center for Responsive Politics, Washington (www.opensecrets.org. June 1, 2001).

21. Davis, interview.

22. On donor incentives, see Peter Francia and others, "Individual Donors in the 1996 Election," in John C. Green, ed., *Financing the 1996 Election* (M.E. Sharpe, 1999), pp. 127–54.

23. Davis, interview.

24. Dal Col, interview.

25. John Mintz, "McCain's Net Advantage," *Washington Post Weekly Edition*, February 21, 2000, p. 16.

26. Ruth Marcus, "Survival of the Fattest Purse," *Washington Post Weekly Edition*, October 25, 1999, p. 8.; and in 1999 numerous midwestern donors told the author that the Bush fund-raisers actively discouraged donors from giving to the campaigns of other GOP candidates.

27. Don Van Natta Jr., "Early Rush of Contributors Opened the Flood Gates for Bush," *New York Times*, January 20, 2000, p. A20.

28. James W. Ceaser and Andrew W. Busch, *The Perfect Tie* (Rowman and Littlefield, 2001), pp. 67–69.

29. John Mintz and Ruth Marcus, "Unlimited Spending, Limited Impact for Bush?" *Washington Post Weekly Edition*, February 26, 2000, p. A1.

30. Arthur Sanders and David Redlawsk, "Money and the Iowa Caucuses," in Magleby, *Getting Inside the Outside Campaign*, pp. 20–29.

31. Mark Z. Barabak, "McCain Swamps Bush as Gore Edges Bradley," *Los Angeles Times*, February 2, 2000, p. A1.

32. Susan Glasser, "Bush Raised $69 million, Spent $17 Million in '99," *Washington Post*, February 1, 2000, p. A4; and see Fowler and others, "The Role of Issue Advocacy Groups in the New Hampshire Primary."

33. David Magleby, "Issue Advocacy in the 2000 Presidential Primaries," in Magleby, *Getting Inside the Outside Campaign*, p. 14.

34. Susan B. Glasser and Dan Balz, "They Want Their Money's Worth," *Washington Post Weekly Edition*, February 21, 2000, p. 14.

35. Don Van Natta Jr. and John M. Broder, "With a Still-Ample Treasury, Bush Builds a Green 'Fire Wall' against McCain," *New York Times*, February 21, 2000. See also Bill Moore and Danielle Vinson, "The South Carolina Republican Primary," in Magleby, *Getting Inside the Outside Campaign*, pp. 40–48.

36. Ceaser and Busch, *The Perfect Tie*, pp. 89–91.

37. Terry M. Neal and Susan B. Glasser, "The Front-Runner Looks over His Shoulder," *Washington Post Weekly Edition*, February 28, 2000, p. 12.

38. Ceaser and Busch, *The Perfect Tie*, pp. 91–94.

39. David Magleby, "Issue Advocacy in the 2000 Presidential Primaries," in Magleby, *Getting Inside the Outside Campaign*, p. 14.

40. Ceci Connolly, "The $55 Million Man," *Washington Post Weekly Edition*, March 12, 1999, p. 8. The $55 million figure included the $45.6 million allowed under public financing, plus general election compliance funds. A change in the FEC rules required Gore to drop general election compliance fund-raising until after the nomination was secured. See also Ceci Connolly, "A Run for the Money," *Washington Post Weekly Edition*, March 8, 1999, p. 9.

41. Ceci Connolly, "Bradley's One-Woman Money Machine," *Washington Post Weekly Edition*, May 31, 1999, p. 18.

42. Don Van Natta Jr. and John M. Broder, "Advisers to Gore Are Concerned over Rapid Campaign Spending," *New York Times*, September 24, 1999, p. A18.

43. Sanders and Redlawsk, "Money and the Iowa Caucuses," in Magleby, *Getting Inside the Outside Campaign*, pp. 20–29.

44. Sanders and Redlawsk, "Money and the Iowa Caucuses," pp. 20–29.

45. Charles A. Radin, "Bradley Doubles His TV Presence in Final Week," *Boston Globe*, January 29, 2000, p. A6; and Fowler and others, "The Role of Issue Advocacy Groups in the New Hampshire Primary," in Magleby, *Getting Inside the Outside Campaign*, pp. 30–39.

46. Ceaser and Busch, *The Perfect Tie*, pp. 83–84.

47. Joe and Wilcox, "Financing the 1996 Presidential Nominations," pp. 61–62.

FOUR   *Financing the 2000*
          Presidential General
          Election

ANTHONY CORRADO

T HE 2000 PRESIDENTIAL general election was
one of the closest contests in the nation's history. It was also one of the
most expensive. Spurred by tight margins and a permissive regulatory environment, the candidates and their supporters took advantage of every
available opportunity to raise and spend money in the hope that additional resources would provide the narrow margin of votes needed to win.
When the race finally ended, after an extraordinary postelection recount
contest in Florida and a historic Supreme Court decision that was determined by a five-to-four vote, more than $300 million had been spent in
the general election alone.[1] This sum included more than $100 million in
expenditures that were made outside of the spending ceilings imposed on
presidential candidates and party committees by federal law.

While most of the funding in the presidential contest came from sources
regulated by the Federal Election Campaign Act (FECA), the steep rise in
the amount of unregulated money, especially party soft money funding,
characterized the financial activity in the race. As in 1996, the public monies
available to the candidates were supplemented by substantial party money
and significant issue advocacy and voter mobilization spending by interest groups.[2] The Democratic and Republican national party committees
aggressively solicited soft dollars on behalf of their respective presidential
nominees and spent tens of millions of these dollars on activities designed
to assist these candidates in their campaigns. A large share of these funds
was spent on broadcast advertising, especially issue advocacy advertisements with messages crafted to support one candidate or the other. These

ads, because they did not "expressly advocate" the election or defeat of a specific candidate, were exempt from the limits governing party expenditures made in coordination with a candidate and could be financed with combinations of hard and soft money. Organized groups mimicked these tactics, using their political funds, which in most cases were not subject to the FECA contribution restrictions, to sponsor issue ads of their own. Consequently, the public subsidies given to the candidates essentially served as a floor for campaign spending. The only ceiling on spending, for practical purposes, was the fund-raising capacity of parties and organized groups and their willingness to devote resources to the race at the top of the ticket.

The flow of money in the presidential contest reinforced the financial patterns established in 1996 and refined in the 1998 midterm elections.[3] So the strategies employed were not new. But in 1996, the use of party issue ads to supplement the public monies available to presidential candidates was considered a bold innovation; four years later, it had become the standard approach. This change was largely a response to Federal Election Commission (FEC) regulatory decisions issued in the aftermath of the 1996 election, which failed to restrain the new model of finance that emerged in that contest and thus effectively sanctioned the efforts of party committees to circumvent the FECA limits. Parties therefore operated as if there were no limits at all on their funding. In fact, with respect to the sources of money and amounts spent, the party activity in 2000 was more akin to the financial activity in the 1972 election, the last election before the adoption of the FECA contribution limits, than to any election conducted under the regulatory framework put in place after the 1972 election. The parties freely engaged in raising contributions of unlimited amounts from individuals, political action committees (PACs), corporations, and labor unions. They also spent unlimited amounts, and for the first time since the enactment of the FECA, the parties spent more on television advertising in the presidential race than the candidates did themselves.

The role of the parties was the most prominent but only one of the notable aspects of the financing of the presidential campaign. The contest also featured the first dispute between candidates within a party over the entitlement to general election public funding. It included the first instance of recount financing in a presidential race. Most important, it evidenced the further development of a new model of presidential campaign finance that signaled, in effect, the collapse of the FECA regulatory structure.

This chapter examines the major financial aspects of the presidential general election, highlighting the resource strategies now used in the presidential race. It also discusses the financing of the recount controversy in Florida, which stands as the first postelection contest in a presidential election in the FECA era. The chapter demonstrates how the FECA has failed and why reform is needed to achieve any meaningful regulation of money in the presidential election process.

The Regulatory and Strategic Environment

The regulations governing campaign funding and the strategic context of the race dictated the financing of the 2000 election. An increasingly lax regulatory structure gave candidates and their supporters ample opportunities to spend money on the presidential race, and the strategic context gave them the incentive to do so. Although the strategic factors ultimately determined the level of spending, the regulatory factors played the more important role in defining what types of financial activity paid for the campaign.

Under the FECA provisions, a major party presidential candidate who accepted public funding received a subsidy equal to the total amount of the general election expenditure ceiling, which was $67.6 million in 2000.[4] A minor party candidate could receive a proportional share of this subsidy if the party received 5 percent or more of the vote in the previous election.[5] A candidate who receives partial public funding is allowed to solicit private contributions to raise money to make up the balance between the amount received in public funding and the overall expenditure ceiling. Any private monies raised for this purpose must come from contributions of no more than $1,000 per individual or $5,000 per PAC.

To receive public funding, a candidate must agree to abide by the spending limit and refrain from soliciting additional private contributions. A candidate may, however, raise additional funds in amounts no greater than $1,000 from individuals to finance the legal and accounting costs incurred to comply with the law. These General Election Legal and Accounting Compliance funds (GELAC) are exempt from the spending ceiling. In addition, the Democratic and Republican national party committees are each allowed to spend a limited amount in coordination with, or on behalf of, their respective nominees. In 2000, the limit on such coordinated spending was $13.7 million for each party.[6] All of the monies used for coordinated expenditures must come from donations raised under federal contribution limits.

In recent elections, the FECA's relatively simple scheme for financing presidential campaigns has been replaced by increasingly complicated and sophisticated financial schemes that revolve around the parties' continuing efforts to exploit their ability to spend soft money in ways that benefit a presidential candidate. The most recent major innovation emerged in 1996, when first the Democratic Party and then the Republican Party supplemented the finances of their presidential nominees by spending millions of dollars on issue advertisements that featured President Bill Clinton and his opponent, Robert Dole. The parties claimed that these advertisements were not campaign expenditures subject to FECA restrictions because they did not use the "magic words," such as "vote for" or "vote against," which most previous court decisions had deemed necessary for the application of federal limits. The committees therefore paid for the advertising with a mixture of hard and soft money, mostly soft money, eventually spending a combined total of more than $65 million, not including the coordinated expenditures they were allowed to make under the law.[7]

These advertising campaigns pushed the borders of federal law and directly challenged the ability of federal regulators to control presidential campaign spending. If such actions were allowable, then the regulations were basically meaningless, since candidates could rely on party monies or other outside funding to assist their campaigns, regardless of any spending limits. Moreover, party committees could work with candidates to raise soft money that could be used to finance activities designed to benefit their campaigns. But whether such efforts were permissible under the FECA provisions was uncertain in 1996. While party lawyers claimed that these methods of subverting the rules were legal, they were based on gray areas in the law that needed further definition and regulatory interpretation.

Before the 2000 elections, the Federal Election Commission (FEC) took no action to prohibit or even deter the financial schemes used in 1996. In conducting the required audit of the 1996 presidential campaigns, the FEC Audit Division determined that the party ads should be considered campaign expenses and recommended that the Clinton and Dole campaigns be penalized for exceeding spending limits and receiving "excessive contributions" from the party committees.[8] But the commission voted 6 to 0 against the recommendation that the Clinton and Dole campaigns repay a total of $25 million to the federal treasury because they improperly benefited from party ads. The agency's Office of General Counsel also recommended an enforcement proceeding, based on its conclusion that the Democratic Party's ads were coordinated with the Clinton campaign and therefore constituted illegal soft money expenditures and campaign contributions.[9] The FEC, however, did not accept these recommendations. Instead, the commission deadlocked on a vote of 3 to 3 on the recommendations, and the investigation was closed.[10] In making this decision, the FEC did not set forth a position on whether soft money funded issue ads that featured a federal candidate or were coordinated with a candidate were permissible under the law. The FEC simply left the law in limbo, though in a lighter shade of gray, since with respect to future election activity, no decision was a decision.

The FEC also investigated the 1996 political activities of the AFL-CIO, one of the nation's largest labor unions. This enforcement case centered on the assistance that the AFL-CIO provided to Democratic candidates during the 1996 campaign. At issue was whether the union had improperly coordinated its activities with the Democrats and thus made improper contributions to the party and its candidates. The investigation, which produced 35,000 pages of documents, found that "national and state committees of the Democratic Party provided the AFL-CIO or its state affiliates nearly total access to their plans, projects, activities, and needs, at least with respect to a major voter mobilization program in each state known as the 'Coordinated Campaign.'"[11] The contact between the union and the Democrats included the labor federation's ability to "approve or disapprove" party political plans, but because the evidence did not show that the union had engaged in communications with the general public, as opposed to its own members, the FEC voted to dismiss the case. In other words, it did not attempt to enforce its own coordination rules and instead deferred to recent judicial interpretations that have provided independent groups with wide latitude to consult with parties and candidates in formulating their own plans without violating campaign finance laws.[12]

Congress and the Department of Justice also investigated the financial activities associated with the 1996 presidential campaign, but neither took actions that would prevent similar efforts in the future. The FEC considered making new rules on soft money coordination, but discussions in both 1998 and 2000 failed to produce any new guidelines or restrictions.[13] Thus, despite the major controversy sparked by soft money contributions in the 1996 election, no changes were made in the regulatory structure to stem the use of soft money before the start of the 2000 campaign. Instead, federal regulators essentially gave candidates and parties a green light to continue relying on soft money to subvert the contribution and spending limits.

The FEC did make some minor changes in its regulations to try to address one of the factors that stimulated the move to issue advertising: the problem of financing campaign activities during the period between the effective end of the presidential selection process and the national nominating conventions. Because of the increasingly compressed front-loading of the presidential primary calendar, the party nominations are being decided earlier and earlier in the process. In 1996 the battle for nomination in both parties was over by the end of March, which left the prospective victors, President Bill Clinton and Republican challenger Robert Dole, with a period of about four months to continue campaigning before the national conventions. But the spending limits imposed on prenomination campaigns, which were established more than twenty years ago, are not designed to accommodate the front-loaded primary process, especially in the case of a hotly contested contest. So Dole had already essentially reached the spending limit by the end of March. As a result, he was no longer able to spend monies to continue aggressive campaigning, even though two months remained before the official end of the state primaries in the first week of June. Clinton, however, had $20 million left to spend, largely because he was unopposed and had been the beneficiary of $34 million in Democratic Party issue advertising that promoted his reelection.[14] The Republican Party therefore financed issue ads supporting Dole to provide his campaign with a form of "bridge financing" to help him compete until the general election public funding was issued at the time of the convention.

The FEC eased some of its restrictions in recognition of the financial pressures created by the widening gap between the time when the nomination was essentially "wrapped up" and the formal decisions are made by the party conventions. The commission added flexibility to presidential campaign financing between June 1 of the election year and the date of a party convention. During this period, candidates who accept public funding can allocate salary and overhead expenditures equal to no more than 15 percent of the primary spending limit to the general election expenditure ceiling. The commission also eased the rules on party-coordinated expenditures by expressly granting party committees the option of making coordinated expenditures, which are limited to general election campaigns, before a presidential candidate has been formally nominated.[15]

These regulatory changes had no significant effect on the financing of the 2000 presidential campaign. While the revisions could assist limit-strapped candidates during the pregeneral election period, they offered little practical relief because any monies spent by candidates or parties under the new regulations would still count against the general election spending limits. The more practical alternative available to party committees was to rely on issue advertising financed by soft money, since such spending would not count against the FECA limits. Moreover, this option offered a potentially more effective approach to influencing voters than additional spending on salary or overhead, since the ads could be used to communicate with large blocs of voters in key battleground states.

Given the effects of the different financial strategies available to them, candidates and parties had sound reasons for following the new model of campaign finance that emerged in 1996. Their willingness to rely on soft money or any other means of increasing the resources poured into the White House contest was particularly strong given the strategic context of the race.

Competitive races spur campaign spending, and the presidential election was no exception. Throughout the general election period, most observers predicted a close contest between Governor Bush of Texas and Vice President Gore, but none could have anticipated the extraordinary final outcome. Expecting a hard fought battle, the major party nominees and their party supporters began expending resources on the general election campaign well before the conventions. Both candidates secured their party's nomination before the end of March, so they had a long period to campaign against each other. Neither candidate wanted to lose any momentum that might have been generated by his primary victory and neither wanted to cede any potential advantage to his opponent. So campaigning continued throughout the late spring and summer, blurring the line between the primary and general election campaigns so greatly that one election merged into the other.

The incentive to spend was especially high given the complicated electoral math Bush and Gore faced as a result of two minor party contenders, Reform Party nominee Patrick Buchanan and Green Party hopeful Ralph Nader. Buchanan, who contested the Republican Party presidential nomination in 1992 and 1996, pursued the Reform Party nomination instead of seeking an unlikely upset over George Bush in the Republican contest. The Reform Party standard was particularly valuable because it offered the nominee $12.6 million in general election public funding, which was earned by Ross Perot's share of the vote in 1996.[16] The major party aspirants thus faced the prospect of a well-funded third party candidate in the general election, one who was likely to criticize both of the major contenders and perhaps attract votes from conservatives who would otherwise select Bush.

Nader's candidacy was also noteworthy. As a nationally known consumer advocate with an established reputation as an opponent of major corporations and "politics as usual," Nader offered the prospect of a candidate who might be able to motivate independent voters and individuals alienated from the political process to rally around his Green Party platform. He thus presented the possibility of being the type of candidate, like Perot in 1992 or Jesse Ventura in the 1998 Minnesota gubernatorial race, who could scramble the electoral calculus and attract substantial support from traditional major party supporters. Nader's strong environmental positions, opposition to tax breaks and other forms of "corporate welfare," and advocacy of increased social spending was expected to be most attractive to voters who would otherwise prefer Gore.

By the beginning of the fall campaign, it was apparent that these challengers did not pose a threat to win the White House, nor was it likely that they were going to accrue any electoral votes, since their public support as measured in national polls remained in the low single digits. Yet they did have the potential to accumulate enough votes to affect the outcome between Bush and Gore in a number of battleground states. Both of the major candidates therefore had to give some regard to these minor party challengers.

By the final month of the campaign, it was clear that Buchanan would not have a material effect on the race—his candidacy failed to attract much support and barely registered in public opinion surveys. He ended up receiving less than 1 percent of the votes cast. But Nader's small share of public support in several states, including northern progressive states such as Washington, Oregon, Wisconsin, and Minnesota, which usually favor the Democrats, kept a large number of states in the category of "swing" states until the final days of the contest. Nader was also a minor factor in Florida, the state that decided the election's outcome. He eventually polled more than 97,000 votes in the Sunshine State, far surpassing the 930-vote plurality Bush held after the counting of absentee ballots or the 537-vote plurality he held at the time of the Supreme Court's historic ruling in December.[17] As a result, both major party candidates were spending significant sums in a larger number of states than is normally the case in the final stage of the general election. The relatively large number of close states and the closeness of the projected electoral college count exacerbated the demand for resources and set the stage for a free-spending race.

Candidate Finances

General election campaign financing reflected each of the basic approaches to presidential funding permitted under the FECA. Bush and Gore, the two major party nominees, received the full public subsidy available through the public financing program and supplemented these funds with additional private contributions raised to finance legal and accounting costs. Bush and Gore each accepted the general election subsidy of $67.6 million after being declared the nominee at their respective party nominating conventions. Though Bush did not accept public money and its accompanying restrictions during the primary season, he readily agreed to the subsidy for the general election, even though he had developed a remarkable donor base that had generated more than $94 million in donations by the time of the convention. His decision was a practical one. By taking the public money, Bush's campaign did not have to spend valuable time and effort attempting to raise money in the few months before the election. Even with his fund-raising base, this task would be difficult. Accepting public funding also sheltered Bush from the charge that he was "trying to buy the election" or "unwilling to play by the rules," and the risk that these charges might alienate some voters. It was also a more cost-efficient approach, since a privately financed general election campaign would have to spend great sums, perhaps as much as $10 million, on fund-raising costs. A privately funded presidential campaign would also elevate the already intense competition for dollars between candidates and party committees, which would have the likely effect of reducing the monies available to the party.

   Given the ability of party committees to use their unlimited resources to benefit a presidential candidate, the most logical approach to the financing of a campaign is for a nominee to take the public funding. Bush's decision to accept the subsidy in the general election thus highlights the value of public funding, as well as the failure of public funding in achieving its purposes. On the one hand, the availability of the subsidy frees candidates from the need to engage in constant fund-raising, reduces the demands on campaign budgets by eliminating fund-raising costs (except for those expenses associated with GELAC fund-raising), and reduces the role of private contributions. On the other hand, the changes in party finance have simply encouraged the financial activity that might be associated with a privately funded campaign to shift to the party-sponsored components of the campaign, thereby undermining the potential beneficial effects of the public subsidy.

In accepting the public subsidy, both Bush and Gore freed their fund-raisers to concentrate on raising money for the national party committees, thereby increasing the monies available to the party, which could in turn be spent on party efforts to promote Bush or Gore and turn out their voters. The nominees and their vice presidential running mates assisted these party efforts by appearing at party fund-raisers, and Bush engaged in an even more direct form of assistance: he transferred close to $5 million in excess funds from his primary campaign committee to party coffers for use in the general election. This included a shift of $2.9 million to the Republican National Committee hard money accounts and $1 million each to the National Republican Senatorial Committee and the National Republican Congressional Committee in the two weeks before the election.[18]

Bush and Gore supplemented the public monies they received with private monies raised to pay for the legal and accounting costs incurred to comply with the spending limits and other legal requirements. Both candidates began to raise these GELAC funds early in the general election campaign. By the end of 2000, Bush had reported $7.5 million in GELAC receipts, while Gore reported $11.1 million (table 4-1). The total amount, $18.6 million, was significantly higher than the $13.6 million in GELAC funds solicited by Clinton and Dole in 1996.[19] The aggregate amounts available to the candidates were thus far higher than the amount dictated by the public funding spending ceiling. In all, Gore had slightly more money than Bush, with total receipts of $78.7 million, compared with $75.1 million for his Republican opponent. When the contributions received for the recount battle in Florida are included, the total campaign budgets for each candidate are relatively equal, with each receiving about $82 million for the entire general election campaign (table 4-1).

The major party candidates placed great emphasis on the solicitation of GELAC contributions because these funds have proved a valuable means of supplementing the limited subsidies they receive from taxpayer funding. The basic purpose of these funds is to finance legal and accounting

Table 4-1.   *Presidential Candidates: General Election*
Millions of dollars

Source	Bush	Gore	Buchanan	Nader	Total
Public funding	67.6	67.6	12.6	0.0	147.8
Private funding	0.0	0.0	0.6	5.1	5.7
GELAC funds	7.5	11.1	0.0	0.0	18.6
Recount funds	7.5	3.7	0.0	0.0	11.2
Total	82.6	82.4	13.2	5.1	183.3

Sources: Federal Election Commission, Washington, as of 2000 year-end filings; Internal Revenue Service, Form 8872 Disclosure Reports for Gore-Lieberman Recount Committee; and Kenneth P. Doyle, "Democrats Complain to FEC about Nondisclosure by Bush Recount Fund," *BNA Money and Politics Report*, May 3, 2001, p. 1.

expenses, pay the costs of raising GELAC monies, cover the "winding down" expenses of the campaign (such as the maintenance of an office and small staff to handle the close-down of the campaign offices, postelection reports, and manage the audit process), and provide for any repayments imposed by the FEC for violations of public funding regulations. But the definition of compliance costs and the purposes for which GELAC funds can be used has been significantly broadened by FEC regulations over time, to the point where these funds can now be used to help defray the costs of a campaign. For example, a campaign can accept a reimbursement of 10 percent of payroll expenses (excluding taxes) and overhead expenditures for national and state campaign headquarters on the premise that this portion of salaries and overhead is related to compliance activities. Overhead costs include rent, utilities, office equipment, furniture, supplies, and telephone charges except for telephone calls related to special uses such as get-out-the-vote efforts. A candidate may also use GELAC money to pay for 50 percent of the costs associated with computer services, including the rental and maintenance of computer equipment, nonstaff data entry services, and related supplies. GELAC funds can thus be an important means of defraying campaign expenses and, in turn, freeing up limited public dollars for use on broadcast advertising and other campaign activities.

Major party contenders devoted most of the monies spent to broadcast advertising, as is usually true in a presidential election. According to an analysis conducted by the Brennan Center for Justice, candidate advertising expenditures in the top seventy-five media markets totaled at least $67 million during the period from June 1 to November 7, 2000. The Bush campaign spent $39.2 million on advertising in these markets, or about 58 percent of its public funding. Gore disbursed $27.9 million, or just over 40 percent of his public monies, in these markets.[20] These figures, however, are limited to the advertising broadcast on the national networks and twenty-five leading cable networks in a set number of markets. Although they include the estimated typical cost of broadcasting the ad, they do not include the related costs, such as the disbursements made for the production and placement of ads or the surcharge that stations often impose on parties and interest group, which can more than double the cost of running an ad in the rush before the election. The figures therefore significantly underestimate the emphasis placed on media spending by the two campaigns. For example, the Brennan Center reported comparable data for 1996, which indicated that Clinton spent $38 million on advertising in that year, as opposed to Dole's $33 million. Yet a more comprehensive analysis conducted by the Campaign Study Group of 1996 presidential general election spending found that Clinton devoted $46 million to advertising, which represented almost 63 percent of his campaign budget, including GELAC funds, while Dole disbursed $47 million on advertising, which represented about 61 percent of his total monies.[21]

Similarly, in 2000, according to tracking conducted by the Gore campaign, Gore devoted $36.7 million to media advertising, or almost $10 million more than the amount estimated by the Brennan Center, which represented about 47 percent of his total funding, including GELAC funds. Bush, according to Gore estimates, spent more than $46 million on advertising, or about $7 million more than the Brennan Center estimate.[22] Although Gore's share was lower than that of his predecessor, the proportion of campaign monies devoted to media costs followed the patterns established in previous elections. But the candidates were not the only participants financing broadcast advertising in the 2000 race. In fact, the relative role of candidate expenditures was smaller than in any previous election conducted under the FECA, owing to the unusually large sums spent by parties and interest groups.

Minor Party Candidates: Buchanan and Nader

The minor party presidential hopefuls, Buchanan and Nader, raised significant sums for their campaigns compared with other recent minor party contenders (with the notable exception of Ross Perot). Buchanan's money came mostly from public sources; only a small share of Nader's money was public. But neither Buchanan or Nader was financially competitive in the race. These two challengers managed to collect about $18 million, which was equivalent to about a quarter of the sum available to Bush or Gore, and most of this sum represents the funding available to Buchanan.

Buchanan received about $13 million for his White House bid, or more than twice the amount raised by Nader. Most of this money, $12.6 million, came from public funding as a result of the proportionate share of the full subsidy due to the Reform Party candidate by virtue of the 8.4 percent of the vote that Ross Perot received in 1996.[23] The existence of this financial award greatly enhanced the desirability of the 2000 Reform Party nomination and led to a dispute over which candidate should receive this money.

A factious Reform Party convention during the summer of 2000 produced no consensus on the choice of a candidate to bear the party standard in the absence of Ross Perot. The conservative former Republican Buchanan and the Natural Law Party's presidential nominee in 1992 and 1996, John Hagelin, both claimed the Reform Party mantle in the weeks after the convention. Buchanan and Hagelin each submitted formal requests to the FEC asking to be certified as the Reform Party nominee eligible for the subsidy. Commission rules required only that a minor party candidate be on the general election ballot in at least ten states in order to receive a party's financial entitlement. They do not specify the action to be taken if two candidates meet this minimum qualification and claim to be the nominee of the same party. The dispute was clouded further by the complications arising from ballot access laws. In some states, Buchanan had qualified for the ballot as the Reform Party nominee. In others, Hagelin had qualified. Hagelin had also been placed on the ballot as an independent in a few states. Other states automatically placed the Reform Party on the ballot but were waiting for the FEC decision to determine whose name should be placed on the line.[24]

In mid-September the FEC decided to grant the federal monies to Buchanan. The commission did not try to resolve the contentious issue of which candidate was the "legitimate" party nominee, nor did it establish guidelines for the future as to how to proceed when two competing candidates met the minimum qualification. It simply resolved the funding dispute by relying on its rules regarding ballot status. The commission determined that since Buchanan was officially listed as a Reform Party candidate in twelve states, while Hagelin was only listed in three, Buchanan should receive the entitlement.[25]

Under the law, Buchanan was allowed to raise private contributions up to the $67.6 million total that was permitted for presidential candidates. But he only managed to raise about $600,000 for a total of $13.2 million. The sum allowed Buchanan to mount a campaign and even buy television advertising, but his effort produced little support. His extreme views, combined with the closeness of the contest between the major party contenders, left him with little opportunity to attract a meaningful share of the vote. The major effect of his poor showing in the general election was to render the Reform Party ineligible for pre-election public funding in 2004, assuming the party were to endure and nominate a candidate in the presidential race.

Nader was not eligible for public money because the Green Party had not received the requisite 5 percent of the 1996 presidential vote needed to qualify for a share of the total subsidy, so he was allowed to raise private contributions subject to federal limits with no cap on spending. Nader formed a primary committee before the general election, which solicited close to $1 million. Most of this funding came in small contributions received through solicitations at campaign events, concerts, and other party fund-raising activities. The Nader primary committee also qualified for public matching funds, although only $44,000 had been awarded by the end of the campaign.

Nader's general election fund-raising effort was more successful, as his outsider image and appeal as a reformer led to a modicum of support that netted him about $5.1 million in individual donations. As an insurgent candidate, Nader relied on his volunteer support and grassroots fund-raising to generate the revenues needed for his campaign. His principal fund-raising vehicle during the general election was a series of "super rallies" held in major arenas that asked the thousands attending to contribute a modest $10 or $20 per head. These rallies often featured notable personalities such as television host Phil Donahue, actors Tim Robbins and Susan Sarandon, Texas populist Jim Hightower, and rock-and-roll entertainers. They proved to be some of the largest events in the entire 2000 election with crowds of 10,000 or more attending the rallies in Seattle, Minneapolis, Chicago, Boston, and New York's Madison Square Garden.[26]

The success of these rallies allowed Nader to build a base of an estimated 75,000 small donors who contributed a total of about $5 million to his general election effort.[27] This provided his campaign with the resources to develop a fairly extensive campaign organization focusing on grassroots support in progressive states including Washington, Oregon, Minnesota, and Wisconsin, and Nader hired staff in virtually every state, developed a network of 900 campus coordinators, and even purchased some television advertising.[28] But Nader was unable to gain much headway in the race, partly because he was increasingly cast by Democrats as a spoiler who was undermining Gore's chance for victory in a close race. Given the closeness of the contest between Gore and Bush, and the perceived stakes associated with control of the White House, few voters were willing to choose Nader. While his 3 percent showing was the best performance to date by a Green Party candidate in a national election, he did not reach the minimum vote total needed to qualify for public funding and left many observers wondering whether his foray into elective politics would have any long-term meaning in helping to build the party.[29]

Parties and Organized Groups: The Role of Soft Money Financing

While the candidates remained an important source of money spent in the general election, the more noteworthy phenomenon was the tens of millions of soft dollars poured into the contest from parties and organized groups. This spending began in the summer and continued throughout the general election campaign. Indeed, for the first time since the FECA was adopted, the party committees spent more on political advertising in the top seventy-five media markets than the presidential candidates did themselves. This change in financial patterns documented the changes taking place in the campaign finance system and demonstrated once and for all the minimal effect of the candidate spending ceilings.

Party committees followed the model established in 1996 and devoted generous resources to issue advocacy advertisements that featured their respective nominees. This tactic allowed them to spend much more in connection with the presidential contest than was permitted under the coordinated spending provisions of the FECA. Under these provisions, each national party was allowed to spend up to $13.7 million in support of the presidential ticket, all of which had to come from hard money funds. According to FEC filings at the end of 2000, the Republicans had spent $13.2 million on behalf of Bush, and the Democrats had spent $13.5 million in support of Gore.

The parties' coordinated advertising, which is financed exclusively with hard money and is limited by federal law, constituted only a minor share of the parties' total advertising for the presidential race. Exactly what percentage of total spending it represented is difficult to determine, given

Table 4-2. *Television Advertising in Presidential General Election*
Millions of dollars

Advertising for Bush		Adverstising for Gore	
Bush campaign	39.2	Gore campaign	27.9
Republican Party	44.7	Democratic Party	35.1
Political groups	2.1	Political groups	14.0
Total	86.0	Total	77.0

Source: Brennan Center for Justice, press release, New York, December 11, 2000. Figures reflect amounts spent in the seventy-five largest media markets.

the lack of adequate disclosure on party committee soft money spending. But it is clear from available data that parties spent much more on issue advertising in connection with the presidential race than they did in coordinated advertising.

According to the Brennan Center survey, the party committees spent a conservatively estimated $79.8 million on television advertising in the top seventy-five media markets, which was at least $12.7 million more than the candidates themselves spent in these markets (table 4-2). The Republicans disbursed an estimated $44.7 million on ads supporting Bush, as opposed to $35.1 million in Democratic expenditures in support of Gore. In contrast, the Brennan Center found that in 1996 the candidates spent $71 million in these markets, or $23 million more than the $48 million spent by the parties.[30] The 2000 election thus signaled a dramatic change in the relative role of candidates and party organizations in media campaign conduct; for the first time since the FECA was adopted, the parties took the lead.

Even if the assumption is made that all of the $21.2 million in coordinated spending that was devoted to advertising was done in these markets, which is not a safe assumption, that leaves more than $58 million in advertising unaccounted for. This $58 million was financed outside of the coordinated spending limits through a combination of hard and soft dollars. In most instances, these issue ads were sponsored by state party committees, so that a majority of the funding, as much as 65 percent in many cases, came from unrestricted soft money contributions. In other words, in the top advertising markets, the parties spent at least $2 on unrestricted issue ads for every $1 spent on limited coordinated ads. This estimate provides a strong indicator of the extent of soft money spending on advertising in the presidential race, and of the preference parties gave to issue ads over express advocacy ads in communicating messages to the electorate. Overall, the amount of soft money spent on issue ads was larger than the amount of hard money spent in the form of coordinated spending.

The Democrats were the first to resort to issue advocacy spending in advance of the general election, airing their first ad in early June, even though Gore had earlier said that Democrats would not run advertising financed by soft money unless the Republicans did so first. In announcing the advertising strategy, the Democrats cited what they estimated to be $2 million in anti-Gore advertising by political groups that favored Bush, including a group called "Shape the Debate" and a missile defense organization called the "Coalition to Protect America Now."[31] The Democratic ad, which touted Gore's commitment to fight for a prescription drug benefit for seniors, ran in fifteen states and was financed with a combination of hard and soft money.[32] Most of the funding was in the form of soft money that the national party transferred to state parties, since under FEC guidelines, parties were able to use a greater percentage of soft money when buying television time if it were purchased by state party committees (see chapter 6). In using this tactic, the Democrats were following the approach they had first used in 1996, which had become a basic method of operating by 2000. The Republicans also used this approach in paying for candidate-specific issue advertisements.

Once the Democrats had begun their assault, the Republicans were quick to follow. Only a few days after the Democrats launched their ads, the Republicans announced a campaign of their own. On June 10, the Republican National Committee unveiled a $2 million ad campaign targeted mainly at the same presidential battleground states. The only difference was that the Republicans also purchased time in Maine and Arkansas. This first commercial presented Bush's proposal to allow workers to invest part of their Social Security payroll taxes in the stock market.[33]

Although issue advertising represented the largest share of the programmatic expenditures made from soft money accounts (as opposed to administrative or fund-raising expenditures), they were not the only activity to be funded with soft money. Both parties also spent millions of soft dollars on voter identification, absentee ballot efforts, and voter turnout programs as part of their "coordinated campaigns" with state and local party committees to maximize their party's share of the vote.

As the Democrats' rationale for initiating the issue ad strategy indicates, the party committees were not the only political actors relying on the lax federal regulatory structure to channel money into the presidential contest. Organized groups also took advantage of their ability to raise unlimited monies to sponsor issue ads, besides spending millions of hard dollars on independent expenditures that expressly advocated the election or defeat of a presidential candidate. These efforts channeled tens of millions of dollars into the race and allowed some groups to play an especially meaningful role in the presidential contest.

Interest groups and individuals spent approximately $14.7 million on independent expenditures in support of presidential candidates between June 1 and December 31, 2000, according to the data reported to the Federal Election Commission. All of this money represented hard dollars that were used to pay for advertising, telephone banks, direct mail, and other forms of communication that were designed to persuade prospective voters to support one candidate or the other and get out to vote. Most of this amount, $14.2 million, was spent in support of the candidacies of Bush and Gore. The amounts spent on behalf of these candidates were fairly equal. About $7.2 million was spent in support of Bush, including $6.7 million in expenditures that advocated his election and $505,000 in expenditures in opposition to Gore. Almost $7.0 million was spent in support of Gore, including $4.6 million in expenditures that advocated his candidacy and $1.4 million in opposition to Bush.

Most of the monies spent on independent expenditures came from a few supporters of each of the major candidates. On the Republican side, the vast majority of spending came from three sources—the National Rifle Association Political Victory Fund, the National Right to Life PAC, and entrepreneur Stephen Adams. The National Rifle Association was responsible for almost a third of the expenditures made on Bush's behalf. The group spent close to $2.3 million on the White House race, including more than $2 million in support of Bush and about $213,000 on efforts against Gore. The National Right to Life Committee disbursed $2.2 million, all of which represented expenditures advocating Bush's election. The same was true for the funds spent by Adams, who disbursed a total of $2 million from his personal wealth.

On the Democratic side, the majority of the expenditures were made by the National Abortion Rights Action League PAC (NARAL). NARAL spent almost $4.2 million in support of Gore, which represented more than 60 percent of the total amount spent independently on his behalf. Additional support for Gore's candidacy was provided by Steven Kirsch, an entrepreneur and liberal philanthropist who made a personal fortune in high-technology ventures.[34] Kirsch spent $1.3 million on communications that advocated the defeat of George Bush.

The monies spent independently by groups and individuals were used to finance a variety of campaign communications, including broadcast advertising, newspaper ads, direct mail, and get-out-the-vote paraphernalia. Moreover, they represented only a portion of the amounts spent by organized groups to influence the outcome of the election. Many groups, especially those that did not have substantial hard money resources or those that are organized as tax-exempt entities and are restricted in their political activities, chose to participate in the presidential race in other ways. The most prominent option was to engage in issue advocacy advertising.

Although it is impossible to determine precisely the amounts spent by organized groups on the presidential contest, some sense of the scope of interest group activity, at least with respect to broadcast advertising, can be discerned from the data gathered by the Brennan Center on political advertising. According to their analysis, political groups spent an estimated $16.1 million in the top media markets alone on broadcast advertising related to the presidential election. This figure represents a conservative estimate of interest group activity, since it does not include newspaper advertising, direct mail, or other public communications. Even as an estimate of broadcast advertising, it is a relatively conservative figure, because stations are free to inflate the prices they charge organized groups for television and radio spot ads because these groups are not subject to the lowest unit rate restrictions that govern candidates, and many stations did raise their fees in 2000 in response to the heavy demand for broadcast airtime.[35]

Of the $16 million tracked by the Brennan Center, $14 million was spent in support of Gore. This group spending thus helped to reduce Bush's advantage. By the end of the general election period, the Bush campaign and the Republican Party had spent an estimated aggregate $84 million on television in the top markets, compared with an estimated $63 million by Gore and the Democrats. However, interest groups spent more heavily for Gore, reducing this $21 million margin in favor of Bush to only $9 million. But the Republican total included $10.8 million in spending by the Bush team in California. Ironically, Gore won in California by twelve points, even though his campaign did not spend a single dollar on television advertising in the state.[36] When California is excluded, the amounts spent in other states slightly favor Gore. So even though the

Table 4-3. *Presidential Election: Advertising Spending in Battleground States*
Millions of dollars

State	Bush	Gore	Total
Pennsylvania	12.9	15.4	28.3
Florida	14.5	10.1	24.6
Ohio	8.8	9.5	18.3
Michigan	7.5	9.7	17.2
California	10.8	0.1	10.9
Washington	5.4	5.4	10.8
Missouri	4.1	6	10.1
Wisconsin	3	3.7	6.7
Arkansas	1	1.1	2.1
Tennesse	1.1	0.9	2

Source: Brennan Center for Justice, press release, December 11, 2000. Figures reflect the combined spending of candidates, parties, and interest groups in the seventy-five largest media markets.

Bush team spent more, the advertising battle between the two sides (candidates, parties, allied groups) was fairly equal.

The key electoral battleground states received the heaviest concentrations of advertising dollars, as noted in table 4-3. Other than California, the only major states in which the Republicans outspent the Democrats in advertising dollars were Florida and Tennessee. In Florida, the state that proved to hold the key to the White House, the combined advertising by candidates, party committees, and political groups gave Bush a significant advantage with total spending of about $14.5 million, compared with $10.1 million on the Democratic side. In Tennessee, which Bush won even though it is Gore's home state, the Republican margin was $1.1 million to $869,000. But in most of the other major battlegrounds, including Pennsylvania, Ohio, and Michigan, the Democrats held the lead. In Pennsylvania, advertising on Gore's behalf totaled $15.4 million, compared with a total of $12.9 million for Bush. In Michigan, Gore advertising totaled $9.7 million versus $7.5 million for Bush. In Ohio, Gore's advantage was slimmer but still significant at $9.5 million to $8.8 million.[37]

The disparity in issue advertising by political groups, which favored Gore by a margin of seven-to-one, was striking. Americans for Job Security, a political committee organized under section 527 of the Internal Revenue Code, was the only group to spend a large sum on Bush's behalf. This committee purchased almost $1.8 million in advertising, which represented 90 percent of the total amount of group advertising supporting

Bush. The top markets in which these ads aired were in Washington, Oregon, Florida, and Tennessee.[38]

Of the $14 million in pro-Gore advertising done by political groups, about half can be attributed to advertisements sponsored by Planned Parenthood, which spent $7.2 million on Gore's behalf. Some have estimated as much as $10 million was spent in issue advocacy by the NAACP voter fund.[39] The AFL-CIO spent $3.1 million, the Sierra Club about $1 million, and Handgun Control, Inc., $1.7 million. As with the advertising done by Americans for Job Security, the television time was mostly bought in swing state media markets. Planned Parenthood spent the most in Pennsylvania, Florida, Washington, and Oregon. The AFL-CIO focused on Missouri, Ohio, Michigan, and Pennsylvania, as did Handgun Control. The Sierra Club targeted New Mexico, Oregon, and Colorado, as well as Missouri and Michigan.[40]

These advertising expenditures were only the tip of the iceberg of organized group efforts in the 2000 race. For example, politically active organizations, such as the National Education Association and the AFL-CIO, spent great sums on programs designed to educate and mobilize their large memberships in support of Vice President Gore. The vast majority of these "internal communications" expenditures are not specifically disclosed to the FEC or other disclosure agencies, so the exact amounts spent on such efforts are unreported. Other groups, such as the Christian Coalition, published and distributed millions of voter guides designed to educate followers on the candidates' records and thereby encourage them to support Governor Bush. Such activities suggest that interest groups channeled additional millions into the race beyond the amounts reported as independent expenditures to the FEC or the sums estimated by the Brennan Center and other sources. Further, they indicate the extent to which interest groups have become a major source of money in the overall financing of a presidential race.

Recount Financing

In the usual presidential election, the need to raise money basically ends on Election Day. But the 2000 election was not typical. The astonishing results of the voting, which ended in a virtual dead heat, left the electorate debating who had won, and led the candidates on a journey into unexplored territory. Victory hinged on the outcome of a recount and review of the ballots in a handful of Florida counties. The need for a "recount campaign" sent the major contenders scurrying for funds as they furiously sought to mount operations for a final battle over the counting of votes.[41]

Although recount funds had never before been necessary following a presidential race, they had been needed previously by candidates in contested congressional contests. The most recent case involved a fund established by U.S. Senator Mary Landrieu's campaign to finance the contest over her election in 1998. Landrieu, a Louisiana Democrat, created a special recount fund to pay for the expenses the campaign incurred following the election, an action which was sanctioned by the FEC in an advisory opinion issued that year.[42] The commission held that the recount fund was a separate entity from the campaign and that any contributions made to the recount fund would not be considered contributions to the campaign subject to FECA limits. The agency further declared that this fund would not be required to register and file reports with the commission but noted that Landrieu had already registered and begun filing reports voluntarily.

FEC regulations thus offered little guidance on the financing of recounts. For the most part, the commission exempted recount monies from federal campaign finance rules because recount activity does not represent an attempt to "influence" the outcome of an election. The regulations do, however, stipulate that unions and corporations cannot make contributions to recount funds.[43]

This lack of regulatory requirements gave the candidates leeway to decide on an approach for financing their recount activities. They selected very different methods. The Bush campaign established a fund and imposed a voluntary limit on contributions of no more than $5,000 per donor. These contributions were disclosed unofficially on the campaign's website, but the campaign chose not to disclose the expenditures made from these funds. The Gore campaign decided to establish a political committee, called the Gore/Lieberman Recount Committee, under section 527 of the Internal Revenue Code, which covers political organizations that are not required to report to the FEC. In accordance with the new rules governing section 527 committees, which were adopted in 2000 following the presidential primaries, the Gore committee was required to disclose its contributions and expenditures to the Internal Revenue Service. The agency made these reports available on its website along with the Form 8872 filings now required of all section 527 committees. But the Gore campaign decided against placing voluntary limits on its donors.

Instead, contributors could give any amount. The committee was even willing to accept PAC donations, even though Gore had refused to accept PAC gifts in raising money for his primary campaign.[44]

With the committees in place, both campaigns raised money at a frenetic pace. The time pressures were enormous and the costs of the recent effort substantial. Both campaigns began flying teams of attorneys, campaign staff, and political practitioners to Florida within twelve hours after the polls closed, to begin the myriad tasks involved in such a high-stakes enterprise. Eventually each side would have scores of staff and volunteers on the ground and teams of lawyers preparing and presenting court challenges in a number of venues, ranging from county courts to the highest court in the land. All of these costs had to be financed with new money raised by the candidates.

The fund-raising began immediately. Within hours after the contribution calls had begun, the Gore campaign had met its goal of $3 million. The Bush campaign, seeking limited donations, turned to urgent e-mail messages and its website to help bring in $2.4 million within a week of Election Day.[45] By the first week of December, the Bush campaign's fundraising prowess had given its candidate a substantial lead in the money chase, while maintaining a small lead in the votes, accruing more than $7.4 million from 34,000 contributions of $5,000 or less. Gore's campaign had received half as much, about $3.2 million by this time. Much of Gore's funding came from large contributions that were comparable to major soft money gifts. Some of his most generous donors included investor Steven Kirsch ($500,000), producer Steven Bing ($200,000), Slimfast company executive S. Daniel Abraham ($100,000), Jane Fonda ($100,000), and Tennessee developer Franklin Haney ($100,000).[46]

The amount spent by the campaigns in the recount battle is difficult to determine. The Gore recount committee disclosure reports indicate that his effort raised a total of $3.7 million and spent about $2.6 million, leaving a balance of $1 million in the fund as of March 31, 2001. The Bush committee's financial activity is more obscure owing to the lack of full disclosure of his funds. Because the campaign considered its recount committee an "affiliated committee" of the campaign, it did not feel that it was required to disclose its finances. The campaign did post donors on its website, and it is reported to have raised between $7 million and $8 million for its recount effort. But whether this amount covered all of the expenses incurred in the recount effort is unknown: no information was provided about the committee's expenditures.[47] As of May 2001, the amounts raised and spent by the committee continued to be a matter of controversy, and the Democratic National Committee had filed formal complaints with the IRS and the FEC in an attempt to force the committee to fully disclose its financial activity.[48]

Conclusion

The effect of all this spending on the eventual outcome of the race is hard to assess. What is clear is that candidate financing was only a part of a much broader funding pattern that, in essence, produced an almost indistinguishable flow of money that came from different sources but was put to similar purposes and delivered reinforcing messages to the electorate. Public money, party hard and soft money, and unregulated group money were all put to work toward common goals in a way that made the restrictions of the public funding program wholly ineffective. Indeed, the public money provided to candidates, while still important, played less of a role than in any other recent election, and the incentive to rely on soft money and the finances of independent groups became stronger and stronger.

The 2000 election reinforced the model of presidential finance that emerged in the 1996 election, a model based on a more extensive role for party organizations and the incorporation of their "nonfederal" soft money funds into the financing of federal elections. As such, it stands as a testament to the final collapse of the regulatory structure established by the FECA. The restrictions of the federal public funding program, which have been increasingly ineffective since at least 1988, have been rendered completely meaningless.

Presidential candidates now treat public financing as a floor, not a ceiling; they raise millions of additional dollars to supplement these funds either in the form of GELAC money, party hard and soft money, or, the new twist in 2000, recount money. The election thus demonstrated the continuing need for campaign finance reform, especially the need to address the problem of soft money funding and its use in financing candidate-specific issue advertising. It also highlighted a new problem in the law that should be a concern to reformers—the lack of effective regulations on recount funding and the need for disclosure requirements and contribution restrictions on such funding. Finally, the regulatory decisions made before the election provided a clear example of the inefficacy of the FEC, and its inability, or unwillingness, to stem the flow of unregulated monies in federal campaign financing. Indeed, the most ironic aspect of this election may be that the agency responsible for upholding the laws was ultimately responsible for their final collapse.

Notes

1. The $300 million figure is an estimate of the author. The text of *Bush* v. *Gore* and related documents can be found in E.J. Dionne Jr. and William Kristol, eds., *Bush* v. *Gore: The Court Cases and the Commentary* (Brookings, 2001).

2. On the financing of the 1996 presidential election, see Anthony Corrado, "Financing the 1996 Presidential General Election," in John C. Green, ed., *Financing the 1996 Election* (M E. Sharpe, 1999), pp. 63–93.

3. For a discussion of the financing of the 1998 congressional elections, see Paul S. Herrnson, *Congressional Elections: Campaigning at Home and in Washington*, 3d ed. (Washington: Congressional Quarterly Press, 2000), and David B. Magleby, ed., *Outside Money: Soft Money and Issue Advocacy in the 1998 Congressional Elections* (Rowman and Littlefield, 2000).

4. Federal Election Commission, "FEC Announces 2000 Presidential Spending Limits," press release, Washington, March 1, 2000, p. 1.

5. Minor party candidates can qualify for a proportional share of the general election subsidy based on the share of the vote they received in the previous election, compared with the average vote received by the major parties (defined under the FECA as parties that receive 25 percent or more of the vote in the general election). New parties and minor parties can also qualify for postelection subsidies on the same proportional basis, as long as they receive at least 5 percent of the vote.

6. See note 4.

7. For a discussion of these party advertisements, see Anthony Corrado, "Financing the 1996 Elections," in Gerald Pomper, and others, *The Election of 1996* (Chatham House, 1997), pp. 145–50.

8. See FEC, *Report of the Audit Division on Clinton/Gore '96 Primary Committee, Inc.*, Washington, November 19, 1998, and *Report of the Audit Division on the Dole for President Committee, Inc.*, Washington, November 19, 1998.

9. FEC, "Proposed Audit Report on the Clinton/Gore '96 Primary Committee, Inc.—Media Advertisements Paid for by the Democratic National Committee," memorandum to Robert J. Costa from Lawrence M. Noble and others, October 27, 1998.

10. Kenneth P. Doyle, "Fulani Filing Reveals FEC Rejected Staff Bid to Pursue Charges against Clinton Issue Ads," *BNA Money and Politics Report*, May 25, 2000, p. 1.

11. Kenneth P. Doyle, "FEC Votes to Drop 'Coordination' Case against AFL-CIO and Democratic Party," *BNA Money and Politics Report*, September 6, 2000, p. 1.

12. Ibid.

13. Kenneth P. Doyle, "Chairman Says FEC Will Again Consider Rulemakings on 'Soft Money' Coordination," *BNA Money and Politics Report*, September 22, 2000, p. 1.

14. Corrado, "Financing the 1996 Elections," pp. 145–47.

15. FEC, *Financial Control and Compliance Manual for Presidential Primary Candidates Receiving Public Financing* (Washington, July 1979; revised April 2000), pp. iv–v.

16. FEC, "Reform Party to Receive Public Funding for 2000 Convention," press release, Washington, November 22, 1999, p. 1.

17. Gerald M. Pomper, "The Presidential Election," in Gerald M. Pomper and others, *The Election of 2000* (Seven Bridges Press, 2001), p. 130.

18. These transfers are disclosed in the Bush for President filing with the FEC for the postelection period, which notes financial activity through November 27, 2000. The transfers are listed as "itemized disbursements" on Schedule B of the report at page 23 for line 29.

19. Corrado, "Financing the 1996 Presidential General Election," p. 75.

20. Brennan Center for Justice, "2000 Presidential Race First in Modern History Where Political Parties Spend More on TV Ads Than Candidates," press release, New York, December 11, 2000, p. 1.

21. The Campaign Study Group data are presented in Corrado, "Financing the 1996 Presidential General Election," pp. 84–85.

22. Telephone interview with Carl Smith, Gore Campaign, November 1, 2000.

23. See note 16.

24. Kenneth P. Doyle, "Buchanan, Hagelin Submit Rival Requests to FEC for $12.6 Million in Federal Funding," *BNA Money and Politics Report*, August 16, 2000, p. 1.

25. FEC, "FEC Certifies General Election Public Funds for Buchanan-Foster Ticket," press release, Washington, September 14, 2000; and Kenneth P. Doyle, "FEC Staff Says Buchanan's Ballot Status Entitles Him to Reform Party's $12.6 Million," *BNA Money and Politics Report*, September 11, 2000, p. 1.

26. Marc Cooper, "Duking It Out in the Naderhood," *The Nation*, October 30, 2000, p. 19; and David W. Chen, "The Green Party: In Nader Supporters' Math, Gore Equals Bush," *New York Times*, October 15, 2000, sec. 1, p. 28.

27. Marc Cooper, "Greens: Out of the Money," *The Nation*, November 27, 2000, p. 6.

28. John Nichols, "Nader: Fast in the Stretch," *The Nation*, November 20, 2000, p. 6.

29. Cooper, "Greens: Out of the Money," pp. 6–7.

30. Brennan Center for Justice, "2000 Presidential Race First in Modern History Where Political Parties Spend More," table 1.

31. Kenneth P. Doyle, "Democrats Justify Issue Ad Campaign Despite Gore's March Challenge to Bush," *BNA Money and Politics Report*, June 7, 2000, p. 1.

32. Kenneth P. Doyle, "First DNC 'Issue Ad' of 2000 Campaign Shows Gore Fighting for Drug Benefits," *BNA Money and Politics Report*, June 8, 2000, p. 1.

33. Kenneth P. Doyle, "GOP Responds to Democratic Ads with Ad on Bush Social Security Plan," *BNA Money and Politics Report*, June 13, 2000, p. 1.

34. Neil Munro, "The New High-Tech Benefactors," *National Journal*, March 31, 2001, p. 948.

35. Alliance for Better Campaigns, "Gouging Democracy: How the Television Industry Profiteered on Campaign 2000" (Washington, 2001), pp. 5–8.

36. Brennan Center for Justice, "2000 Presidential Race First in Modern History Where Political Parties Spend More."

37. Ibid.

38. Ibid.

39. The Brennan Center data do not include the ad run by the NAACP voter fund attacking Bush on hate crimes legislation.

40. Brennan Center for Justice, "2000 Presidential Race First in Modern History Where Political Parties Spend More."

41. For details on the events of the Florida recount, see The Political Staff of the *Washington Post, Deadlock: The Inside Story of America's Closest Election* (New York: Public Affairs, 2001).

42. FEC, Advisory Opinion 1998-26.

43. Kenneth P. Doyle, "Bush, Gore Camps Continue Raising Money after Election with Focus on Recount Effort," *BNA Money and Politics Report*, November 14, 2000, p. 1.

44. Ceci Connolly, "Bush Maintains Fundraising Advantage," *Washington Post*, December 8, 2000, p. A37.

45. "Florida Fracas Becomes a Boon for Campaign Coffers," *Wall Street Journal*, November 17, 2000, p. A1.

46. Connolly, "Bush Maintains Fundraising Advantage."

47. Kenneth P. Doyle, "Democrats Complain to FEC about Nondisclosure by Bush Recount Fund," *BNA Money and Politics Report*, May 3, 2001, p. 1.

48. Ibid.

FIVE   *Financing the 2000*
         Congressional Elections

PAUL S. HERRNSON
KELLY D. PATTERSON

T HE 2000 CONGRESSIONAL elections occurred
in the shadow of a tightly competitive presidential election. But while the
nation focused its attention on the very close contest between Vice President Al Gore and Governor George W. Bush, several congressional elections offered their fair share of drama. Democrats believed that they had
a genuine opportunity to recapture the House of Representatives and make
significant inroads into the Republican majority in the Senate. With so
many safe seats in the House and Senate, many of the financial players
focused their spending on the handful of competitive congressional races
that would determine who controlled the Congress.

While resources flowed into a few competitive races at an unprecedented
rate, other congressional races followed well-established patterns for
American politics. First, incumbents and members of the majority party
continued to raise and spend more money than challengers and members
of the congressional minority. Second, incumbents from both parties received more contributions from political action committees (PACs) than
challengers. Third, Democratic candidates collected most of the labor PAC
contributions and Republicans received most of the money given by corporate PACs, and finally, Republicans continued to raise more funds from
individual donors than their Democratic counterparts. All of these pat-

The authors wish to thank Peter Francia and Atiya Kai Stokes for their
research assistance and the Pew Charitable Trusts, which funded part of the
research.

terns reflect some of the long-standing habits and cleavages in American politics, but they take on greater meaning in the current political environment. For example, the fact that Republicans continued to raise more money than the Democrats helped the Republicans retain control of the House and Senate—though by the slimmest of margins—when the 107th Congress convened.[1] The surge in money in congressional elections displays the impact of a unique competitive environment on the 2000 congressional elections where Republicans sought to fight off strong Democratic challengers. Although several Democratic incumbents, including Rush Holt of New Jersey's Twelfth District and Joseph Hoeffel in Pennsylvania's Thirteenth District, fought to hold onto their seats against strong GOP challengers, 53 percent of incumbents who were involved in competitive races were Republicans.

The Setting for the 2000 Congressional Elections

The GOP's ascendance in the 104th Congress (1995–96) caught even the most veteran of Washington observers by surprise. The subsequent transition from Democratic to Republican control affected both policy and politics. On the policy side, the Republicans enacted much of the *Contract with America*, their 1994 election manifesto that promised both tax and congressional reform. On the political side, the abrupt change upset long-established routines for fund-raising in congressional elections, giving GOP candidates and party committees an opportunity to increase their campaign receipts. Over the two election cycles following the 1994 elections, Republicans exploited their advantages, setting new fund-raising records. Despite losing a few seats to the Democrats in both 1996 and 1998, the GOP managed to defend its slim House majority.[2] However, as the 2000 election approached, many politicians and pundits believed that the Republicans would lose their majority in the House. Republicans controlled 222 seats, the Democrats held 209, independents occupied 2, and 2 seats were vacant. The Republicans needed to defend 25 open House seats, 18 more than the Democrats. Some Republican members signed term-limit pledges in 1994, and others chose to retire rather than give up the chairmanships because of term limits imposed on committee chairs by Republican rules. The GOP had an eight-seat majority in the Senate, but it had to defend nineteen seats, whereas the Democrats only had to defend fifteen. Although defeating incumbents is extremely difficult, Senate campaigns generally attract higher-quality challengers that increase the odds of an upset. Furthermore, because nine Republican incumbents were facing their first re-election campaigns, they were more vulnerable.

This competitive environment virtually guaranteed that parties and interest groups would vigorously contest each race deemed to be close and pay less attention to other contests. Republicans wanted to hold on to the majority as strongly as Democrats wanted to regain it. Recognizing that a few open and incumbent-occupied seats would determine the control of Congress, the parties feverishly recruited highly qualified candidates to run in 2000. The respective party congressional campaign committee chairs, Representative Patrick Kennedy of Rhode Island, for the Democrats, and Representative Tom Davis of Virginia, for the Republicans, took primary responsibility for candidate recruitment. Their Senate counterparts, Democrat Robert Torricelli of New Jersey and Republican Mitchell McConnell of Kentucky, also recruited prospective contenders. All four party leaders sought to identify and encourage candidates who had the wherewithal to wage competitive congressional campaigns to run. The Democrats enjoyed notable success in candidate recruitment. Three of their Senate candidates— Jon Corzine in New Jersey, Mark Dayton in Minnesota, and Maria Cantwell in Washington—had significant personal fortunes, which they used to finance their own campaigns. These resources proved decisive in all three races and enabled the Democratic Senatorial Campaign Committee to spend its funds in other races.

Besides the competitive environment, structural features shape the way candidates contest elections. The United States has a candidate-centered system that places the burdens of raising money, assembling an organization, securing a party nomination, and waging a general election campaign on office seekers rather than party committees. Political parties and interest groups provide money and campaign assistance to many candidates, especially those in competitive districts, but they do not dominate campaigns. Only rarely, as with the Republicans in 1994, do parties set a national political agenda. But because of the high stakes in 2000, party committees and interest groups were eager to play supporting roles in the election.

In the final analysis, candidates must contest their elections under conditions that may or may not help their specific candidacy. In 2000, because economic conditions remained favorable, the environment strongly favored congressional incumbents.[3] Objective indicators such as low rates of unemployment, low rates of inflation, a high gross domestic product, and an impressive rise in the stock market provided the basis for public opinion polls favoring incumbents, and in foreign affairs, conditions seemed just as good. At the end of the summer, 70 percent of Americans gave the economy a rating of "good" or "excellent," and 59 percent said they were satisfied with "the way things are going in the U.S."[4] These conditions differed sharply from 1992 when only 14 percent rated the economy as "good" or "excellent," and a paltry 16 percent said they were satisfied with the direction the country was headed.[5]

The presidential election also influenced the congressional election environment. Presidential campaigns focus citizens' attention on certain issues, forcing other candidates to discuss them. The 2000 presidential campaign agenda prominently featured such issues as federal support for education, prescription drugs and reform of health maintenance organizations (HMOs), the economy, the environment, Social Security reform, and tax cuts. The attention brought to these issues helped congressional candidates who had strong records on them, and forced others to at least formulate responses to these issues. For example, when Governor Bush prominently featured a tax cut among his campaign promises, individual congressional candidates needed to decide whether or not they favored or opposed the cut. Presidential campaigns also influence the dynamics of congressional campaigns by increasing citizen interest in politics and by increasing voter turnout. On average, fewer than 40 percent of eligible individuals participate in off-year elections, while the number increases to almost 50 percent in presidential election years.[6]

Campaign Contributors

Individual and institutional motivations to donate money are of major consequence to congressional campaigns. Political parties, PACs, and individuals make campaign contributions for many reasons. Democratic and Republican party committees and some PACs and individuals contribute to influence the outcomes of elections, whereas some PACs and individuals view contributions mainly as investments that are useful in gaining access to influential members of Congress. Finally, some individuals contribute because they enjoy socializing with the politicians and participating with other individuals in the political process.

Political Parties

Current perceptions of polarization notwithstanding, American political parties act more pragmatically than ideologically. Party leaders, first and foremost, desire to win control of political institutions, not restructure society along some grand vision.[7] For the most part, national parties allow candidates to develop and run campaigns that appeal to their local constituencies. Because both national parties seek to win as many House and Senate seats as possible, they become heavily involved in competitive elections where they know their efforts have the potential to make the difference between victory and defeat and virtually ignore contests where the outcome seems a foregone conclusion.

The Democratic Congressional Campaign Committee (DCCC) and the National Republican Congressional Committee (NRCC) play the lead role in devising the parties' national strategies in House elections. They also advise House candidates on campaign strategy and provide campaign services, such as assistance in hiring campaign consultants, producing television ads, and encouraging contributions from PACs and individuals. The congressional campaign committees are especially helpful in assisting freshman lawmakers and competitive nonincumbents with fund-raising. In recent years, they have played a critical role in redistributing the wealth from party leaders and other safe incumbents to candidates involved in races that are too close to call. The Democratic Senatorial Campaign Committee (DSCC) and the National Republican Senatorial Committee (NRSC) perform similar roles in Senate elections.[8]

The competitiveness of the 2000 elections made it possible for all party committees to raise record sums of "hard" money. Hard money is regulated in terms of contributions and expenditures by the Federal Election Campaign Act of 1974 and its amendments (collectively referred to as the FECA); "soft" money largely escapes those limitations.[9] Hard money includes contributions to candidates, expenditures coordinated with them, and independent expenditures made without a campaign's knowledge or consent that expressly call for a specific candidate's election or defeat. The national, congressional, and state party committees can each contribute $5,000 to a House candidate in the general election. The parties' national and senatorial campaign committees can contribute a combined total of $17,500 in direct contributions to a Senate candidate, and state party committees can contribute an additional $5,000.[10] Parties also provide somewhat larger sums to candidates through coordinated expenditures. Coordinated expenditures pay for public opinion polls, television and radio ads, issue and opposition research, fund-raising activities, and other campaign services. In 2000 parties could contribute $33,800 in House elections and between $67,560 and $1,636,438 in Senate elections.[11] The limits for national party coordinated expenditures in Senate elections vary by state population and are indexed for inflation. State party committees are authorized to spend the same amounts in coordinated expenditures in House and Senate elections as the parties' national organizations. Parties can spend unlimited amounts on independent expenditures.

The national parties vigorously pursued the funds to sustain these various activities. Using the fund-raising prowess of President Bill Clinton, the Democratic National Committee (DNC) raised $124 million in hard money for the 2000 election season, roughly 14 percent more than it collected in 1996—the last presidential election cycle—and almost double the amount it raised in 1998. Other Democratic Party committees also raised more hard money for the 2000 elections than they had previously. The DCCC took in more than $48 million, an 82 percent increase from 1996 and a 92 percent increase from 1998. The DSCC amassed $40.5 million, which amounted to 32 percent and 14 percent increases over the previous two election cycles.

Republicans typically enjoy a fund-raising advantage over Democrats because they have a deeper pool of wealthy donors to draw from. This advantage generally continued in the 2000 elections. The Republican National Committee (RNC) accumulated more than $212 million, 10 percent more than it had collected in the previous presidential contest and 105 percent more than it had raised in the 1998 midterm elections. The NRCC raised more than $97 million, roughly one-third more than it had raised in either 1996 or 1998. The NRSC, which raised $51.5 million, was the only national organization of either major party to raise less hard money in 2000 than it did in the previous two elections. Overall, the 2000 elections continued the trend of growth in party hard money receipts. About half of this money is spent as direct contributions, coordinated expenditures, and on issue advocacy ads. The committees use the other half on voter lists, building maintenance, campaign equipment, fund-raising, staff salaries, and other forms of overhead.[12] Over time, the Republican Party has enjoyed a significant advantage in raising hard money. The Democratic Party has only raised on average 58 percent of what the Republican Party has raised over the past five election cycles in these types of funds.

Although the increase in hard money is notable, it does not tell the entire story; soft money also played a key role. Soft money is defined in detail in chapters 1 and 6. In congressional elections since 1996, parties have used soft money to produce so-called issue advocacy advertisements—

television, radio, and mail ads designed to influence the outcome of individual House and Senate elections without expressly advocating the election or defeat of specific candidates.[13] This use of soft money expanded in the 2000 elections, and both parties raised record amounts of soft money. Indeed, soft money accounted for more than 47 percent of all of the Democratic Party's campaign receipts and over 35 percent of those taken in by the Republican Party, and most of this money was spent on issue ads.

Candidates from both parties, but especially Senate Democrats, expanded on a fund-raising tactic called joint fund-raising committees or "Victory Funds." The most prominent example of joint fund-raising committees in 2000 was Hillary Clinton's in New York, but other candidates like John Ashcroft, Dianne Feinstein, Mel Carnahan, and Richard Gephardt also made use of Victory Funds. As discussed in chapter 1, joint fund-raising committees facilitate a single donor giving hard and soft money to a candidate and party at the same time. David Hansen of the NRSC concedes the Democrats made better use of this tactic in 2000 than did the Republicans.[14]

During the 2000 elections, Democratic Party organizations used hard money to directly contribute almost $1 million to their party's House candidates and spent more than $3 million in coordinated expenditures on behalf of their candidates. The Democrats also contributed almost $363,000 directly to their Senate candidates and spent more than $5 million on coordinated expenditures.[15] Parties prefer to distribute more in coordinated expenditures than direct contributions because the limits for coordinated expenditures are far higher and because they enable the party to exercise more influence over a candidate's campaign. In recent years, the national parties have distributed fewer hard money dollars on contributions and coordinated expenditures in order to spend more hard and soft money on issue advocacy ads.[16] This has enabled them to commit more of their resources to close elections and exercise even greater influence over the issues raised in connection with those elections.[17]

Reflecting their greater wealth, Republican Party committees spent significantly more hard money in 2000 than the Democrats. The GOP contributed almost $7 million to its House candidates; this sum included almost $1.8 million in contributions and $5.2 million in coordinated expenditures. The Republican Party also contributed slightly in excess of $11 million to Senate candidates, which included $500,000 in contributions and $10.8 million in coordinated expenditures. Although Republican candidates traditionally receive more party support than Democratic candidates, the gap has narrowed over the past few election cycles.

The parties strategically targeted their money in the 2000 House races. Both parties distributed most of their hard money to candidates in competitive contests. The Democrats distributed 82 percent of their funds to candidates in competitive races (competitive races are those decided by 20 percent or less of the two-party vote; see table 5-1). The Republicans delivered 91 percent of their funds to GOP candidates in these same contests. Republican Party spending favored House challengers (both competitive and noncompetitive), who received roughly 35 percent of all party funds. Incumbents of both parties received less, reflecting Democratic party leaders' desire to capture Republican-held seats, the GOP leaders' desire to expand their party's majority, and the beliefs of both parties that control of the House majority would be decided in a handful of close challenger and open-seat contests. The fact that most Democratic and Republican party decisionmakers believe that incumbents need little help with fund-raising also influenced the distribution of party funds.

The distribution of issue advocacy ads, which involves the expenditure of both hard and soft money, was even more concentrated on closely contested House elections than the distribution of party contributions and coordinated expenditures.[18] The parties also used soft money funds to finance voter mobilization drives and other campaign activities, in the most competitive congressional districts. The congressional campaign committees can place these ads themselves or transfer funds to state parties, allowing the states to do it. In the 2000 elections both parties' national, congressional, and senatorial campaign committees transferred considerable sums of hard and soft money to state party committees. Soft money must be used in conjunction with hard money, but at the state level, campaign finance regulations require fewer hard dollars per soft dollar than national regulations. Transferring funds to state parties allows national parties to maximize the impact of their hard and soft dollars.

Despite the rationality of the criteria the parties used to select candidates for support and the rigorousness of their research and decisionmaking processes, the distribution of party contributions, coordinated expenditures, issue advocacy ads, and grassroots efforts were not perfect. There were a number of elections where more party or interest group activity could have changed the outcome. In Wisconsin's Second District, for example, Democratic incumbent Tammy Baldwin defeated Republican chal-

Table 5-1.   *The Distribution of Party Contributions and Coordinated Expenditures in the 2000 House and Senate Elections*
Percent unless noted otherwise

Item	House Democrats	Republicans	Senate Democrats	Republicans
Competitive elections,	19	26	34	37
incumbents	(36)	(43)	(3)	(8)
Challengers	30	32	8	15
	(43)	(36)	(8)	(3)
Open seats	33	33	36	43
	(22)	(22)	(5)	(5)
Uncompetitive elections,	9	5	19	2
incumbents	(134)	(123)	(8)	(9)
Challengers	8	3	4	2
	(123)	(134)	(9)	(8)
Open seats	1	1	—	—
	(12)	(12)	—	—
Total (thousands of dollars)	4,034	5,905	5,405	10,368
N	(370.00)	(370.00)	(33.00)	(33.00)

Source: Compiled from Federal Election Commission data, Washington.
Note: Incumbents in competitive elections lost or won by 20 percent or less of the two-party vote. Challengers in competitive elections won or lost by 20 percent or less of the two-party vote. Open-seat candidates in competitive elections won or lost by 20 percent or less of the two-party vote. Incumbents in uncompetitive elections won by more than 20 percent of the two-party vote. Challengers in uncompetitive elections lost by more than 20 percent of the two-party vote. Open-seat candidates in uncompetitive elections won or lost by more than 20 percent of the two-party vote. Figures include contributions and coordinated expenditures by all party committees to general election candidates in major-party contested races, excluding a small number of atypical races that were decided in runoffs or won by independents. They do not include soft money expenditures. Some columns do not add to 100 percent because of rounding. The numbers of candidates are in parentheses. Dash means less than 0.5 percent.

lenger John Sharpless by a mere 3 percent of the vote. Republican Party committees made $66,500 (close to the legal maximum) in coordinated expenditures in the race but broadcast no issue ads in the race. Given the fact that Baldwin spent almost 2.6 times more campaigning than did Sharpless, the challenger was at a major communications disadvantage. Had the GOP or any conservative interest group broadcast any issue ads on his behalf, or provided him with additional fund-raising assistance, Sharpless might have been able to defeat Baldwin.

There also were a few instances in which the involvement of political parties appeared to hurt a candidate. For example, in Kentucky's Sixth Congressional District, the Democratic candidate and former representative Scotty Baesler suffered a public relations disaster when local television stations yanked a DCCC ad off the air because they believed it contained false accusations. The Republican candidate, Representative Ernie Fletcher, used the occasion to cry foul and undermine the already fragile credibility of his opponent. The DCCC had transferred more than $770,000 to the state party to fund these attack ads.[19]

The political environment also affected the allocation of party hard money contributions in the 2000 Senate races. Both parties spent well over a majority of their funds in competitive races, but the Republicans' targeting was superior. Republican incumbents and open-seat candidates in competitive elections received 80 percent of the party's funds. Challengers in close contests received 15 percent, whereas challengers in lopsided races received barely 2 percent. The Democratic Party followed a similar pattern. Vulnerable Democratic incumbents and open-seat candidates in close races garnered 70 percent of the Democratic funds. Democratic challengers in uncompetitive contests received only 4 percent. The distribution of party issue advocacy ads also follows this pattern.[20] The allocation patterns for hard money in Senate races clearly demonstrate that parties can and do act strategically. The distribution of party soft money follows a similar pattern. In hindsight, the Republican strategy might have been too aggressive with open-seat candidates receiving too large a share, and consequently five Republican incumbents lost their seats. Perhaps the Republicans' most glaring miscalculation occurred in the Delaware Senate race, where the Republicans spent only $250,000 to assist the incumbent William Roth, and the Democrats spent almost $4.3 million (including roughly $3 million in soft money) to help the challenger Tom Carper. Most of the blame for this miscalculation rests with Senator Roth, who explicitly asked the Republican Party not to spend any soft money in the race.

Political Action Committees

Political Action Committees contributed more than $257 million to congressional candidates in 2000.[21] Business interests, such as corporations; corporations without stock; cooperatives; and trade, membership, and health associations, sponsored almost 62 percent of all PACs. Labor PACs constituted less than 8 percent of the PAC community, and nonconnected PACs, sometimes called ideological committees, composed the final 30 percent. One would be hard-pressed to find a large and influential PAC sponsored by the homeless or dedicated exclusively to the interests of the poor.

A relatively small group of organizations account for most PAC contributions to congressional candidates. Less than 10 percent of all PACs made 74 percent of all contributions to congressional candidates in 2000. PACs sponsored by business interests contributed more money than any other group; in fact, more than one-in-three PAC dollars came from corporate PACs, and 64 percent of those contributions went to Republicans. Trade association PACs made another 28 percent of all PAC contributions, again largely to Republicans. PACs sponsored by corporations without stock and cooperatives accounted for another 3 percent. Labor PACs contributed 20 percent of all PAC dollars, and 93 percent went to Democrats. Ideological PACs gave 14 percent of all PAC dollars, 58 percent to Republicans.

Most PACs use ideological, access-oriented, or mixed strategies when contributing to House and Senate candidates.[22] PACs that use ideological strategies are similar to political parties in that they primarily seek to influence the political process through elections. Most ideological PACs contribute to maximize the number of House members in office who share their policy views, often on such salient issues as abortion rights and the environment. These PACs distribute most of their resources to candidates involved in competitive contests, but they occasionally make contributions to encourage the careers of promising politicians. Ideological PACs rarely make contributions for the purposes of gaining access to legislators because these PACs seek to advance issues that are linked to fundamental values that officeholders are rarely willing to compromise. Planned Parenthood and the Right to Life PAC are two prominent examples of these types of PACs.

Access-oriented PACs view elections pragmatically. They make contributions mainly to gain access to members of Congress who are in a position to influence regulations, appropriations, or treaties that affect the environment in which their industry or work force operates. These groups consider campaign contributions an important tool for reaffirming or strengthening their relationships with influential lawmakers. They recognize that contributions can create goodwill with representatives and senators, making it easier for the group's lobbyists to influence the legislative process.

PACs that follow access strategies are likely to contribute most of their money to incumbents, especially to members of the House and Senate who occupy party leadership posts, who chair or are members of important committees or subcommittees, or who are recognized leaders in specific policy areas. Because these PACs are interested in influencing congressional policy decisions more than election outcomes, they are not overly concerned with whether the incumbents to whom they contribute are involved in competitive elections. In fact, some recipients of PAC dollars do not even have election opponents. Businesses with dealings before Congress, such as AT&T and Microsoft, make up the largest share of this group.

The last group of PACs follows mixed strategies. These PACs, mostly trade associations and labor unions, give some contributions to candidates who share their group's views and other contributions to incumbents with whom they wish to maintain access. Most of the contributions that are motivated by the former goal are given to candidates in close races, and most of those motivated by the latter goal are given to powerful incumbents. In elections where PAC decisionmakers are cross-pressured because the incumbent is in a position to influence the group's legislative priorities and the challenger is more supportive of the group's interests, most PACs that follow mixed strategies contribute solely to the incumbent, but a few also contribute to the challenger. The National Association of Realtors' PAC is the largest PAC that utilizes a mixed strategy, followed by the Association of Trial Lawyers of America PAC.

In the 2000 elections, the overall distribution of PAC dollars did not change as dramatically as it did in the 1996 election cycle—the first election after the Republicans gained a majority in the House. During that election season, the partisan bias of corporate and trade association PAC contributions reversed itself to favor Republicans.[23] In 2000 expectations held true to form. Corporate PACs gave 64 percent of their House donations to Republican candidates. Similarly trade association and nonconnected PACs both gave nearly 59 percent of their House donations to Republicans. Labor union PACs, however, gave 93 percent of their House funds to Democrats. The overall distribution of PAC money was roughly evenly divided in House races: with Democrats raising 51 percent and Republicans collecting the remainder.

Despite the fact that many PACs began to favor Republican candidates over Democrats in the 1996 House elections, they did not totally abandon the Democrats, nor did they abandon their previous contribution strategies. During the 2000 elections, corporate PACs continued to support incumbents with a vast majority of their funds. They allocated 88 percent of their House contributions to incumbents, 9 percent to open-seat candidates, and a mere 3 percent to challengers. Moreover, corporate PACs gave little consideration to helping incumbents in close races. In fact, they distributed 62 percent of their House contributions to incumbents of both parties who won by more than 20 percent of the two-party vote. The

Table 5-2. *The Distribution of PAC Contributions in the 2000 House Elections*
Percent unless noted otherwise

Item	Corporate	Trade, membership, and health	Labor	Non-connected
Competitive elections				
Incumbents				
Democrats	9	10	19	11
Republicans	17	15	2	17
Challengers				
Democrats	1	3	14	9
Republicans	2	3	--	9
Open-seats				
Democrats	1	2	11	8
Republicans	6	7	—	14
Uncompetitive elections				
Incumbents				
Democrats	25	25	43	13
Republicans	37	32	6	15
Challengers				
Democrats	—	—	5	1
Republicans	—	—	—	1
Open seats				
Democrats	—	—	1	—
Republicans	2	2	—	2
Total (thousands of dollars)	54,241	48,621	39,139	25,106

Source: Compiled from FEC data.
Note: Figures are for general election candidates in major-party contested races, excluding a small number of atypical races that were decided in runoffs or won by independents. Dashes means less than 0.5 percent. The categories and numbers of candidates are the same as those in table 5-1. Some columns do not add to 100 percent because of rounding.

contribution patterns for trade association PACs are similar, except these committees invested slightly more money in challenger and open-seat contests.

Labor PAC contributions to 2000 House candidates continued to reflect their inclination to follow mixed strategies (table 5-2). They donated virtually all of their money to Democrats because of shared ideological goals. However, they gave 62 percent of their contributions to Democratic House incumbents who were best positioned to influence legislation important to the labor movement. Indeed, incumbents in uncompetitive elections received more labor dollars than any other group of Democratic candidates. Labor PACs even allocated 6 percent to Republican incumbents in lopsided contests. Labor's mixed strategy may have

Table 5-3. *The Distribution of PAC Contributions in the 2000 Senate Elections*
Percent unless noted otherwise

Item	Corporate	Trade, membership, and health	Labor	Non-connected
Competitive elections				
Incumbents				
Democrats	6%	6%	13%	7%
Republicans	35	31	1	29
Challengers				
Democrats	3	5	32	10
Republicans	4	3	—	5
Open-seats				
Democrats	5	6	21	8
Republicans	15	15	2	16
Uncompetitive elections				
Incumbents				
Democrats	10	12	21	9
Republicans	22	21	3	13
Challengers				
Democrats	—	—	7	1
Republicans	—	—	—	1
Open-seats				
Democrats	—	3	—	—
Republicans	—	—	—	—
Total (thousands of dollars)	21,107	12,771	6,104	8,153

Source: Complied from FEC data.

Note: Figures are for general election candidates in major-party contested races. Dashes means less than 0.5 percent. The categories and numbers of candidates are the same as those in table 5-2. Some columns do not add to 100 percent because of rounding.

enabled it to maintain good relations with some friendly Republican incumbents, but it slightly reduced the total amount that union PACs could contribute to Democratic candidates.

Nonconnected PACs also followed their usual pattern of giving most of their House contributions to candidates in close elections. They contributed 28 percent of their funds to Democrats involved in competitive contests and 40 percent to Republicans in similar races. These PACs also distributed 44 percent of their House contributions to challengers and candidates in open-seat contestants.

PAC contributions to Senate candidates followed predictable patterns and bear similarities to PAC activity in House elections (table 5-3). Corporate and trade PACs invested significant sums in pursuit of access, including giving large portions of their funds to safe and endangered incumbents. Both sets of PACs were more generous to candidates from the majority party. The only advantage enjoyed by the Democrats came from labor PACs, which overwhelmingly supported Democratic candidates, including many nonincumbents involved in close races.

PAC donations in Senate as well as House elections underscore the differences in the two parties' constituencies. Labor has been a faithful ally of the Democratic Party for more than five decades, whereas the Republican Party has been able to draw substantial support from corporations and trade association PACs, even when in the legislative minority. Both parties have strong supporters among nonconnected PACs, most of which contribute the vast majority of their funds to only one party's candidates.

As noted in chapter 7, interest group organizations besides PACs, including some organizations that sponsor or are affiliated with PACs, also participate in election financing. Some corporations, labor unions, trade associations, and other groups carry out issue advocacy ads, internal communications, and voter mobilization efforts intended to influence the outcome of congressional elections. Issue advocacy spending, unlike PAC contributions, is unlimited and undisclosed. In 2000 some groups spent millions of dollars on issue advocacy in a relatively small number of congressional contests. These efforts were similar to PAC contributions in 2000 in that business groups favored Republican incumbents; labor unions supported Democrats; and ideological groups focused principally on close races. As with party soft money expenditures, the distribution of interest group soft money was tightly focused on the most competitive races.[24]

Furthermore, the 2000 elections saw some groups seeking to bolster their influence by spending more funds on independent expenditures. Independent expenditures made by groups can directly urge voters to vote for or against a particular candidate, but interest groups cannot coordinate with the candidates. These independent expenditures must be reported to the FEC. Groups generally prefer "issue advocacy" ads because they can be paid for using hard and soft dollars. However, various groups, such as the NRA and NEA, spent more money on independent expenditures because they could attack candidates who opposed them or support candidates favorable to their issues and because they want their members to know about their involvement in the campaign. Groups poured $21.9 million in independent expenditures into various congressional races during the 2000 election cycle.

Individuals

Individuals constitute the largest source of campaign money in congressional elections, giving approximately $567.7 million dollars to all primary and general election candidates in the 2000 House and Senate elections. Individuals contribute for many reasons; therefore, it is more difficult to categorize their behavior than it is to categorize party and PAC behavior. Some individuals view campaign contributions as little more than a routine part of doing business. They consider them an investment that helps them gain access to the members of Congress who write legislation that affects their economic interests. Other individuals contribute because they are motivated by a few salient issues or some general beliefs about the structure of society or the role of government. A final group contributes for psychological reasons. Individuals in this category may know the candidates personally and want to help, or they may receive some psychological satisfaction from their involvement in the political process or from rubbing shoulders with important people at fundraisers.[25]

Regardless of their motives, the political environment affects the giving patterns of individuals. In the 2000 House elections, Republicans raised more money than Democrats from both large and small donors. The disparity between the parties was greatest for contributors who gave less than $200. Republicans received 57 percent of the contributions from those donors. The cause for this disparity probably emanates from the two parties' varying constituencies. Individuals who believe they have the disposable income to contribute to a campaign are often well educated and wealthy, two of the primary demographic groups of voters who identify with the Republican Party.

During the 2000 elections, individuals gave the majority of their contributions to incumbents and were particularly generous to Republicans. This generalization holds for contributions of all sizes, including those given in amounts of less than $200 and those ranging between $750 and $1,000 (table 5-4). Individuals also paid some attention to the competitiveness of the election when contributing to incumbents. But for the most part they gave more money to incumbents who had an easy road to victory.[26] On average 38 percent of the contributions went to Democratic or Republican House incumbents in noncompetitive campaigns, while on average only 25 percent went to incumbents in competitive elections. This

Table 5-4.   *The Distribution of Individual Contributions in the 2000 House Elections*

Percent unless noted otherwise

Item	Less than $200	$200–$499	$500–$749	$750–$1,000
Competitive elections				
Incumbents				
Democrats	8	10	10	10
Republicans	21	13	13	13
Challengers				
Democrats	10	11	10	9
Republicans	7	6	7	8
Open seats				
Democrats	6	7	6	5
Republicans	5	7	7	7
Uncompetitive elections				
Incumbents				
Democrats	14	17	19	20
Republicans	19	21	22	20
Challengers				
Democrats	3	3	3	2
Republicans	3	2	2	3
Open seats				
Democrats	1	1	1	1
Republicans	2	2	2	2
Total (thousands of dollars)	78,131	34,832	46,223	105,011

Source: Compiled from FEC data.

Note: Figures comprise individual contributions to general election candidates in two-party contested elections. The categories and numbers of candidates are the same as those in table 5-1. Some columns do not add to 100 percent because of rounding.

suggests that a plurality of individual donors follow the "investment" strategy, betting on candidates who have the highest chances of winning in order to maintain political access. In terms of the "demand side," it points to incumbents' fund-raising advantages. These include organizational advantages, such as employing professional fund-raisers on their campaigns and possessing lists of previous donors and the appeals that encouraged them to make contributions. Other fund-raising advantages relate to the relatively high levels of visibility incumbents enjoy among prospective donors and their ability to start raising money early in the election season—sometimes just weeks after their most recent election and a full year before their opponents have declared their candidacies.[27]

The disparity between Republicans and Democrats in individual contributions is even larger in Senate campaigns. Republican Senate candi-

Table 5-5.   *The Distribution of Individual Contributions in the 2000 Senate Elections*
Percent unless noted otherwise

Item	Less than $200	$200–$499	$500–$749	$750–$1,000
Competitive elections				
Incumbents				
Democrats	9	6	6	6
Republicans	17	21	18	16
Challengers				
Democrats	9	14	12	10
Republicans	5	5	6	8
Open seats				
Democrats	17	14	13	18
Republicans	29	23	25	24
Uncompetitive elections				
Incumbents				
Democrats	3	5	7	7
Republicans	9	10	10	9
Challengers				
Democrats	1	3	2	1
Republicans	1	1	1	1
Open seats				
Democrats	—	—	—	—
Republicans	—	—	—	—
Total (thousands of dollars)	63,594	15,930	27,068	96,819

Source: Compiled from FEC data.
Note: Figures comprise individual contributions to general election candidates in two-party contested elections. The categories and numbers of candidates are the same as those in table 5-1. Some columns do not add to 100 percent because of rounding.

dates received a much larger share of contributions from individuals than Democratic candidates (table 5-5). Incumbent Republican senators raised roughly twice as much as the Democrats. Republicans contesting open seats also raised more money from individuals than their opponents. Democratic challengers were the only group that raised more individual contributions than their Republican counterparts.

The Money Chase

Even though contributions are most often discussed in terms of donors, candidates are not passive spectators in financing congressional elections. Rather, many play active roles in the money chase, developing sophisticated fund-raising strategies. About one-fifth of all House candidates spend between 26 percent and 50 percent of their personal campaign schedule soliciting funds. Another 18 percent spend between 51 and 75 percent attending fund-raising events and dialing for dollars. Six percent spend more than 75 percent of their campaign schedule raising money. Candidates for the Senate and other statewide offices spend even more time raising funds.[28]

Congressional candidates target fund-raising appeals to individuals who are most likely to respond, including contributors who helped finance their previous campaigns. Incumbents and nonincumbents in competitive races often hire professional consultants to assist with fund-raising. They use direct mail, telemarketing, receptions, and other fund-raising events to collect money from individuals, parties, and PACs. Most candidates often hold backyard barbecues, coffee klatches, and cocktail parties to raise small and moderate contributions in their districts or states. Incumbents and the small number of competitive nonincumbents who have national fund-raising constituencies also hold "high-dollar" receptions in Washington, D.C., New York City, Hollywood, and other wealthy cities across the country.[29] These receptions often cost $250 or more per individual and $500 or more per PAC.

The fund-raising efforts of House and Senate primary and general election candidates resulted in record sums both raised and spent in the 2000 contests (table 5-6). Republican incumbents in both chambers raised and spent much more than their Democratic counterparts, reflecting their greater numbers and the fund-raising advantages associated with holding a congressional majority. Incumbents, especially House incumbents, because of their greater access to interested money were pressed by their party leaders to raise additional hard money for their parties in 2000. The close party balance in the House was used as a rallying call for their "teamwork" approach to fund-raising in 2000.

Democratic challengers in both chambers raised more money than Republican challengers. Democratic House challengers did especially well, raising about $21 million more than their GOP counterparts, while the average Democratic challenger raised $339,445, the average Republican challenger raised only $176,500.[30] However, in open-seat campaigns in the House, Republican candidates raised about $30 million more than the Democrats. The average Republican candidate in an open-seat contest had campaign receipts of $915,000, while the average Democratic opponent in the same kind of race raised over $1.3 million.

Table 5-6. *Campaign Receipts and Expenditures of All 2000 Major-Party Primary and General Election Candidates*
Millions of dollars

	Primary and general election candidates			
Item	House receipts	Expenditures	Senate receipts	Expenditures
Democrats				
Incumbents	169.7	151.8	43.7	40.3
Challengers	73.2	71.8	75.6	75.8
Open seats	45.8	43.2	111.0	110.2
Total	288.7	266.8	230.3	226.3
Republicans				
Incumbents	189.9	173.2	86.9	89.9
Challengers	52.3	51.8	21.9	21.4
Open seats	75.5	74.8	95.0	94.3
Total	317.7	299.8	203.8	205.6
All major-party candidates	606.4	566.6	434.1	431.9

Source: Compiled from FEC data.

In the 2000 Senate elections, which featured numerous hotly contested general election campaigns, several well-financed Republican incumbents lost to fairly well-financed Democratic challengers. Even though Republican incumbents raised close to $87 million, Democratic challengers raised and spent almost $76 million. The average Republican incumbent in a Senate campaign had receipts of almost $5 million, and the average Democratic challenger raised almost $3.3 million. The average Republican challenger amassed receipts of almost $1.8 million, but the average Democratic incumbent raised almost $4 million. However, it is difficult to discuss average spending in the Senate open-seat contests because some candidates, most notably Jon Corzine, spent so much more than the average candidate. Nevertheless, the median spending level for open-seat candidates in both parties was relatively even: for the Democrats it was $6.6 million, as opposed to $6.4 million for the Republicans.[31]

The fund-raising advantages that incumbents enjoy over their general election opponents were glaringly apparent during the 2000 contests. The typical House incumbent collected 3.1 times more money than the typical challenger (table 5-7). This advantage was not a historical abnormality, as incumbents have raised about three times more than challengers in previous years.[32] Incumbents and challengers raise their money from a differ-

Table 5-7.   *The Sources of House Candidates' Campaign Resources*

Item	Incumbents	Challengers	Open seats
Individual contributions under $200	15% ($146,846)	18% ($54,558)	13% ($154,154)
Individual contributions from $200 to $1,000	36% ($346,658)	39% ($122,021)	35% ($420,450)
Political action committee	41% ($395,444)	17% ($52,465)	26% ($317,430)
Parties	1% ($8,833)	3% ($10,672)	4% ($49,792)
Candidates	1% ($8,740)	18% ($57,175)	18% ($216,059)
Miscellaneous	6% ($55,288)	4% ($12,805)	4% ($46,090)
Total resources	$961,807	$309,697	$1,203,973

Source: Compiled from FEC data.

Note: Party figures include contributions and coordinated expenditures. Candidate contributions include contributions and loans from the candidates. Miscellaneous includes interest from savings accounts and revenues from investments. The categories and numbers of candidates are the same as those in Table 5-1. Some columns do not add to 100 percent because of rounding.

ent mix of sources. Incumbents depend more on PAC money, whereas challengers depend more on individual and party committees and money that they donate or loan their own campaigns.

Open-seat House candidates' receipts are yet another story. In 2000 these candidates raised, on average, significantly more money than incumbents and almost four times more than challengers, reflecting the fact that open-seat races tend to be among the most competitive. Open-seat campaigns resemble challenger campaigns in that they rely heavily on candidate self-financing and individual contributions. Nevertheless, they also collect substantial PAC contributions.

Senators also enjoy important fund-raising advantages over challengers, but these are not nearly as substantial as those enjoyed by House members. During the 2000 elections, the typical Senate incumbent raised approximately 70 percent more funds than his or her opponent (table 5-8). Senators depended more heavily on PAC contributions than their challengers, but members of the upper chamber did not rely on PACs nearly as much as their House counterparts. Another major difference between Senate incumbents and Senate challengers is that the former contribute relatively little to their own campaigns, whereas the latter dig relatively deeply into their own pockets. Finally, open-seat Senate candidates raised far more than challengers and incumbents in 2000. This was largely be-

Table 5-8.   *The Sources of Senate Candidates' Campaign Resources*

Item	Incumbents	Challengers	Open seats
Individual contributions under $200	18% ($869,571)	13% ($367,973)	16% ($2,894,322)
Individual contributions from $200 to $1,000	41% ($1,943,904)	37% ($1,014,278)	31% ($5,698,740)
Political action committees	24% ($1,162,516)	8% ($229,783)	6% ($1,050,500)
Parties	5% ($248,609)	3% ($83,895)	4% ($646,261)
Candidates	5% ($257,728)	30% ($840,137)	33% ($6,137,887)
Miscellaneous	6% ($311,326)	8% ($223,672)	10% ($1,908,063)
Total resources	$4,793,655	$2,759,738	$18,335,772

Source: Compiled from FEC data.

Note: Party figures include contributions and coordinated expenditures. Candidate contributions include contributions and loans from the candidates. Miscellaneous includes interest from savings accounts and revenues from investments. The categories and numbers of candidates are the same as those in table 5-1. Some columns do not add to 100 percent because of rounding.

cause a few open-seat candidates invested heavily in their own campaigns. Democrat Jon Corzine spent a record $60 million of his own money to win a Senate seat in New Jersey.

Winners and Losers

What impact did campaign spending have on the outcomes of the 2000 congressional elections? As is usually the case, most of the candidates who raised and spent the most money won, and most of these candidates were incumbents. Because most members of Congress have political clout and a high probability of electoral success, they are able to amass huge war chests, which they use to deter strong challenges and defeat their opponents. Nevertheless, not every incumbent was successful in 2000. Three House incumbents, Republican Merrill Cook of Utah and Democrats Michael Forbes of New York and Matthew Martinez of California, were defeated in primaries. Another six House incumbents lost their general elections. No senators lost their nomination bids, but six were defeated in November.

Was money the major determinant of the outcomes of these contests? Probably not. In the cases of Cook, Forbes, and Martinez, for example, other forces were at work. During the 106th Congress, Cook exhibited strange behavior that led many politicians and the media to publicly question the soundness of his judgment. Forbes, who was first elected to Congress in 1994 as a Republican, switched to the Democratic Party in 1999 and was attacked by Republican Party committees as well as activists of both parties. He ultimately lost by forty-four votes in the Democratic primary to Regina Seltzer, a retired librarian, who had little political experience. Martinez's defeat was largely the result of casting congressional votes at odds with his constituents' views on labor issues, abortion rights, and gun control. Although two of these incumbents—Cook and Martinez— were outspent by their primary opponents, other aspects of their candidacies were important in determining the outcomes of their primaries. Money clearly did not play a decisive role in Forbes's defeat, as he spent over $1 million more than Seltzer.

In the six heavily contested House general elections, money was only one of several important factors that helped challengers defeat incumbents. The challengers spent an average of $1.98 million in these contests, about $550,000 less than their opponents. However, three of the challengers who won spent more than their opponents, but the differences were relatively small, ranging from $9,800 to $80,000. The results demonstrate that not every congressional challenger needs to outspend the incumbent in order to win. Once a challenger's spending reaches a visibility threshold, that candidate has the possibility of mounting a viable campaign. A competitive challenger helps publicize issues, holds the incumbent accountable, and increases voter interest in the election. Outside spending, whether in the form of independent expenditures or issue advocacy ads, can also help challengers gain name recognition and win votes. However, these expenditures can pose some risks for a challenger in that they can introduce issues that are not part of the challenger's message and distract voters from the challenger's major campaign themes. In some cases, outside spending by parties and interest groups can overwhelm a candidate's message.[33] Of course other aspects of the elections, including the partisanship of the district, the candidates' policy positions, and campaign tactics also influenced outcomes.

In some Senate elections, money also played a significant role. Half of the successful challengers outspent their opponents. Two challengers, Democrats Maria Cantwell of Washington and Mark Dayton of Minnesota, each outspent their opponents by more than $5 million; this monetary advantage was amplified by the fact that both largely financed their own campaigns and therefore avoided fund-raising costs. Money probably played a significant role in their victories. Nevertheless, their spending advantages paled next to Corzine's $56.8 million advantage over former House member Bob Franks. Corzine's largely self-financed campaign enabled this newcomer to politics to raise his name recognition to a level that made it possible for him to defeat Franks, who was much better known before the start of the campaign.

Conclusion

The financing of the 2000 congressional elections has many similarities to the financing of the elections that preceded it. The 2000 elections took place in a political environment that dates back to the enactment of the FECA of 1974 but that has also greatly evolved as a result of the prominent role now played by soft money and was substantially altered by the Republicans' historic takeover of Congress. Party committees and ideological PACs, which are strongly committed to electing candidates who share their partisan affiliations or policy views, continued to focus most of their resources in close elections in 2000. Access-oriented PACs and individuals continued to favor congressional incumbents, especially members of the majority party, because of the incumbents' influence over policymaking and their excellent re-election prospects. The Republicans were the major beneficiaries of these donation patterns because they controlled the House and Senate.

Money played a significant role in influencing the 2000 congressional election outcomes. Most incumbents enjoyed huge financial advantages and were victorious. Nevertheless, not every incumbent outspent his or her challenger, and some incumbents were defeated. Indeed, several challengers were able to spend sufficient funds, often their own money, to successfully deliver their message and win a congressional seat.

The growth of both hard and soft money spending by parties and interest groups continued unabated in 2000. Given that control of Congress was at stake, it came as little surprise that most political organizations would raise and spend record sums in their efforts to influence election outcomes. However, when the courts gave their assent to party independent expenditures and party and interest group issue advocacy spending, they effectively removed the ceilings on these organizations' political expenditures, encouraging them to raise and spend record sums on campaign-related activities. Many party committees and several interest groups spent more on issue advocacy than they did on direct contributions during the 2000 elections—a pattern that will probably be repeated in future elections because only issue advocacy ads can be financed with soft money. The introduction of these new vehicles for campaign spending has the potential to greatly increase the roles of organized groups in congressional elections and challenge the abilities of candidates to dominate the political communications that are intended to influence their elections.

Notes

1. The Republicans lost control of the Senate on June 6, 2001 when Senator James Jeffords of Vermont quit the GOP to become an independent but caucus with the Democrats.

2. The GOP's loss of five seats in 1998 bucked a sixty-year trend in which the president's party (the Democrats in 1998) had always lost House seats in the midterm elections.

3. On the impact of economic conditions on congressional elections, see Gerald Kramer, "Short-Term Fluctuations in U.S. Voting Behavior," *American Political Science Review,* vol. 65 (March 1971), pp.131–43; Gary C. Jacobson, "Does the Economy Matter in Midterm Elections?" *American Journal of Political Science* vol. 34 (May 1990), pp. 400–04; and Robert S. Erikson, "Economic Conditions and the Vote: A Review of the Macro Level Evidence," *American Journal of Political Science,* vol. 34 (May 1990), pp. 373–99.

4. The economic evaluations are from a Gallup Poll taken in August 2000, and the figures for the state of the nation are from a Gallup Poll taken September 2000 (www.gallup.com [July 28, 2001]).

5. The 1992 figures are from a Gallup poll taken in June of 1992.

6. To review the differences in dynamics between congressional and presidential elections, see M. Margaret Conway, "Political Participation in Mid-Term Congressional Elections," *American Politics Quarterly,* vol. 9 (April 1981), pp. 221–44.

7. Leon Epstein, *Political Parties in the American Mold* (University of Wisconsin Press, 1986), chap. 1.

8. Paul S. Herrnson, *Congressional Elections: Campaigning at Home and in Washington* (Washington: Congressional Quarterly, 2000), pp. 88–90.

9. The term *soft money* was coined by Elizabeth Drew in *Politics and Money: The New Road to Corruption* (Macmillan, 1983), p. 15. See also Herbert E. Alexander and Anthony Corrado, *Financing the 1994 Election* (M. E. Sharpe, 1995); and Robert Biersack, "The Nationalization of Party Finance," in John C. Green and Daniel M. Shea, eds., *The State of the Parties,* 2d ed. (Rowman and Littlefield,1996).

10. Party committees can also contribute $5,000 to candidates in primaries and runoff elections. However, they rarely make financial contributions until the

general election. This changed somewhat in 2000 as both parties sought to nominate the most electable candidates in a few races.

11. Parties can only make coordinated expenditures for general election candidates. The limits for coordinated expenditures in states that have only one House member are twice the level as those for states with two or more House members.

12. Herrnson, *Congressional Elections*, pp. 89–90.

13. According to *Campaign Finance Reform: A Sourcebook* "issue advocacy has come to mean political speech that may mention specific candidates or political parties but does not 'expressly advocate' the election or defeat of a clearly identified federal candidate through the use of words such as 'vote for,' 'oppose,' 'support,' and the like." Anthony Corrado and others, eds., *Campaign Finance Reform: A Sourcebook* (Brookings, 1997), p. 227.

14. David Hansen, National Republican Senatorial Committee (NRSC), interview by David B. Magleby, 8 December 2000, Washington.

15. FEC, "FEC Reports Increase in Party Fundraising for 2000," press release, Washington, Washington, May 15, 2001.

16. The NRSC is an exception to this generalization, having spent less in contributions and coordinated expenditures in 2000 than 1998.

17. Herrnson, *Congressional Elections*, p. 94.

18. For a discussion of the role of issue advocacy in congressional elections see David B. Magleby, ed., *Election Advocacy: Soft Money and Issue Advocacy in the 2000 Congressional Elections* (Center for Study of Elections and Democracy, Brigham Young University, 2000); Herrnson, *Congressional Elections*, pp. 111–15, 140–46, 230—31, 236–37, 239; and Paul S. Herrnson, "Political Party and Interest Group Television Advertising in the 2000 Congressional Elections," in Kenneth M. Goldstein, ed., *Television Advertising and American Elections* (Prentice-Hall, forthcoming).

19. Penny M. Miller and Donald A. Goss, "The 2000 Kentucky Sixth Congressional District," pp. 174–92, in Magleby, *Election Advocacy: Soft Money and Issue Advocacy in the 2000 Congressional Elections*.

20. Herrnson, "Political Party and Interest Group Television Advertising in the 2000 Congressional Elections."

21. Figures include $11.9 million contributed to candidates not up for election in 2000.

22. For a discussion of PAC giving strategies, see Theodore J. Eismeier and Philip H. Pollock III, *Business, Money, and the Rise of Corporate PACs in American Elections* (Quorum Books, 1988); Craig Humphries, "Corporations, PACs, and the Strategic Link between Contributions and Lobbying Activities," *Western Political Quarterly*, vol. 44 (June 1991), pp. 357–72; and Frank J. Sorauf, *Inside Campaign Finance: Myths and Realities* (Yale University Press, 1992).

23. Paul S. Herrnson, "Money and Motives: Spending in House Elections," in Lawrence C. Dodd and Bruce I. Oppenheimer, eds., *Congress Reconsidered,* 6th ed. (Washington: Congressional Quarterly, 1996), pp. 122–24; Thomas J. Rudolph, "Corporate and Labor PAC Contributions in House Elections: Measuring the Effects of Majority Party Status," *Journal of Politics,* vol. 61 (February

1999), pp. 195–206; Gary W. Cox and Eric Mager, "How Much Is Majority Status in the U.S. Congress Worth?" *American Political Science Review,* vol. 93 (June 1999), pp. 299–309.

24. Magleby, *Election Advocacy;* and Herrnson, "Political Party and Interest Group Television Advertising."

25. Peter L. Francia, Rachel Goldberg, John C. Green, and Clyde Wilcox, "Money Matters: Individual Donors in Federal Elections," in Green, *Financing the 1996 Elections,* pp. 127–53.

26. The exception to this generalization is that competitive Republican incumbents received slightly more than GOP incumbents in uncompetitive races.

27. Herrnson, *Congressional Elections,* pp. 156–60.

28. Paul S. Herrnson, "Candidates Devote Substantial Time and Effort to Fundraising" (www.bsos.umd.edu/gvpt/herrnson/reporttime.html [July 7, 2000]).

29. See, for example, Herrnson, *Congressional Elections,* chap. 6.

30. These averages for the House and the Senate are computed from receipts for general election candidates in major-party contest races. They include candidate receipts and party coordinated expenditures.

31. Averages once again include candidate spending and party-coordinated expenditures.

32. In 1998 incumbents raised three times more than the typical challenger, and in 1996, they raised 2.5 times more. For the 1998 number see Herrnson, *Congressional Elections,* 3d ed., p. 151, and for the 1996 number see Herrnson, *Congressional Elections,* 2d ed., p. 120.

33. Herrnson, *Congressional Elections,* pp. 231–37.

SIX

Throwing Out the Rule Book: Party Financing of the 2000 Elections

DIANA DWYRE

ROBIN KOLODNY

AFTER THE 1996 ELECTION, the political parties' campaign finance activities were characterized as "spitting on the umpire" because of the major parties' "contempt" for the Federal Election Commission's (FEC) attempts to enforce the rules governing campaign finance.[1] The parties got around many of those rules and stretched the limits of the law. In 2000 the parties went even further. The major parties threw out the rule book altogether by conducting a good deal of campaign finance activities outside of the campaign finance laws. This marked a turning point in party campaign finance, characterized not by a real change in the parties' limited, regulated, and disclosed campaign finance activities but by tremendous growth in party activities conducted often under the radar of the Federal Election Campaign Act's (FECA) disclosure provisions.[2] Soft money and issue advocacy were the primary vehicles for these activities, and recent changes in the parties' campaign finance role in federal elections, as well as changes in the political and regulatory environments, help us understand this shift toward unregulated activities. This chapter documents the parties' campaign finance activities during the 2000 presidential and congressional elections and evaluates the dramatic shift to a system in which parties and other campaign actors conduct many activities outside the law's reach.

The Parties' Growing Financial Role

Long noted for their lack of strength and influence, the political parties now play an important role in financing federal elections. Since the 1980s the parties have expanded as service providers, and during the 1990s the parties took on a more active role in campaigns.[3] For example, parties now engage in voter identification and mobilization, fund-raising, candidate training, opposition research, issue development, polling, and media advertising both in coordination with and independently of their candidates. These activities often put parties at the center of exchanges between candidates, contributors, and consultants as well as in direct contact with voters.[4]

Yet the parties have taken on this new role only because their candidates find it useful. Like John Aldrich and Joseph Schlesinger, we argue that politicians only turn to their parties in the presence of true competition.[5] Absent electoral competition, incumbent officeholders have little trouble winning their own elections and therefore have little reason to pool their resources under the party label. But when majority control of Congress or occupancy of the White House is truly up for grabs, politicians are motivated to give their parties more control over the allocation of resources, candidate recruitment, and determination of national election themes. Additionally, politicians must believe that the political parties have something to contribute to their potential victories. In 2000 the nature and magnitude of party activity suggest that the parties had a lot to offer candidates in competitive contests.

Since 1994, races to control the House and Senate have been legitimately competitive. The new viability of the Republican Party at the congressional level not only encouraged the GOP to increase its electoral activities but also forced the Democrats to retool their campaigns and reconsider their assumptions about electoral politics. With close margins in both the House and Senate, the parties aggressively pursued majorities in both chambers. Consequently, the parties have changed their campaign finance strategies to adapt to changes in the political environment as well as to the regulations that govern party financing of federal elections. In 2000 true competition for the White House also invigorated the parties, fueling record fund-raising and new spending strategies.

The financial activities of political parties in federal elections are governed by the 1971 Federal Election Campaign Act, its amendments of 1974, 1976, and 1979, various regulations and decisions issued by the Federal Election Commission, and a number of court decisions. This regulatory patchwork defines how much parties may raise, from whom they may raise funds, how much they may give directly to candidates or spend on a candidate's behalf, and how they can spend independently of their candidates. In federal elections, regulations prohibit contributions from corporations, labor unions, federal contractors, and foreign nationals, and individuals and political action committees (PACs) have strict limits on what they may give to candidates and political committees. This regulatory framework governs the raising and spending of party federal funds, or "hard money." Party hard money activity must be fully disclosed to the public through reporting to the FEC, which posts the reports and summaries of party receipts and expenditures on its website. Conversely, party "soft money" may not be used for expenses associated with a direct role in the outcome of an election for national office, but it is not limited and it is not subject to the same disclosure requirements as hard money. A full list of the FECA hard money contribution limits is presented in table 6-1.

Party Hard Money

For the 1999–2000 election cycle, the major party committees raised more hard money than they had for the last presidential election cycle. The FEC reports that the Democrats raised $221.6 million in 1995–96 and $275.2 million in 1999–2000, and the Republicans raised $416.5 million in 1995–96 and $465.8 million in 1999–2000. Yet when controlled for inflation by standardizing all amounts in 2000 dollars, the recent increases in party hard money fund-raising are not very significant. The Democratic and Republican national, state, and local party committees combined raised $741 million in hard money for federal elections, which is only a 6 percent increase over 1996 when controlled for inflation.[6] Most of the increase was by the Democratic committees (13 percent), with the Republican committees increasing only 2 percent over their 1996 fundraising levels. Yet the Democrats' stepped-up fund-raising in 2000 did not eliminate the Republicans' seemingly permanent financial edge.

As in past elections, the major party committees raised most of their hard money from individual contributors. The Republican National Committee (RNC) and the Democratic National Committee (DNC) raised the vast majority of their hard money from individuals (around 90 percent in 2000), while the congressional campaign committees raised only between 40 percent and 70 percent of their funds this way.[7] The congressional campaign committees generally raise more of their hard money from PACs than the national committees because of the PACs' interest in gaining access to members of Congress for purposes of lobbying.[8]

Table 6-1. *Federal Contribution Limits*

			Recipients			
Donors	*Candidate committees*	*Political action committees*	*Local party committees*[a]	*State party committees*[a]	*National party committees*[b]	*Special limits*
Individuals	$1,000 per election	$5,000 per year	$5,000 per year combined limit		$20,000 per year	$25,000 per year overall limit
Local and state party committees (multicandidate)[a]	$5,000 per election combined limit	$5,000 per election combined limit	Unlimited transfers to other party committees		...	...
National party committees (multicandidate)[b]	$5,000 per election	$5,000 per year	Unlimited transfers to other party committees		...	$17,500 to Senate candidate per campaign[c]
Political action committee (multicandidate)	$5,000 per election	$5,000 per election	$5,000 per year combined limit		$15,000 per year	...
Political action committee (not multicandidate)	$1,000 per election	$5,000 per year	$5,000 per year combined limit		$20,000 per year	...

Source: Federal Election Commission, "Campaign Guide for Political Party Committees" (Washington, August 1996).

a. Local and state party committees share limits unless the local party committee can prove its independence.

b. A party's national committee, Senate campaign committee, and House campaign committee are commonly called the national party committees, and each has a separate limit. See the "special limits" column for the exception.

c. The Senate campaign committee and the national committee share this limit.

For all federal election candidates, overall Democratic Party hard money *spending* was up 13 percent in 2000 over 1996 when adjusted for inflation, but the Republicans actually spent 5 percent less hard money in 2000 than they did in 1996.[9] Once again, however, even with their increased hard money spending and the GOP's decreased spending, the Democrats were still outspent by the Republicans and only slightly chipped away at the GOP's long-standing financial advantage. The interesting development is the decrease in Republican hard money spending. In the following paragraphs we discuss how this decreased party hard money spending is a consequence of increased party soft money spending.

Table 6-2 shows the variety of ways each of the party committees spent their hard money in 1996 and 2000. There are differences between party financing of presidential and congressional candidates, and we consider the presidential race first.

Party Hard Money in the 2000 Presidential Election

Besides the public funds given directly to the presidential candidates, the national political parties receive public funds to sponsor nominating conventions. Each of the major political parties received $13,512,000 for their 2000 presidential nominating conventions, and the Reform Party received $2,522,690.[10] According to FECA regulations, in exchange for public funds, the parties must agree to spending limits, disclosure requirements, and detailed audits.

However, as Candice J. Nelson points out in chapter 2, the federal grant does not preclude the host committees from raising and spending money on the conventions. *Philadelphia 2000* raised more than $66 million to host the GOP convention, and *LA Convention 2000* raised $31 million to host the Democrats' convention.[11] These funds essentially supplemented the normal public money allowance. Because the host committees for the two convention cities are technically nonpartisan, nonprofit organizations, no federal contribution limits apply. Consequently, major corporations donated enormous sums to both parties. For example, Microsoft Corporation donated $1 million to each organizing committee to assist with Internet needs. AT&T and Lockheed Martin were also among the most generous donors.[12]

Besides their convention spending, parties may work with a candidate's campaign to determine how the party should spend money on the candidate's behalf. These are called coordinated expenditures, and the amount the parties may spend is limited but indexed to inflation so that

Table 6-2. *How Party Hard Money Was Spent*
Constant 2000 dollars

Party committee[a]	1996				2000			
	Direct contributions	Coordinated expenditures	Independent expenditures	Transfers to states (hard and soft)	Direct contributions	Coordinated expenditures	Independent expenditures	Transfers to states (hard and soft)
DNC	32,143	7,348,212	0	81,598,662	10,215	13,548,520	0	114,647,819
DSCC	592,658	9,215,969	1,521,179	11,540,977	290,530	127,157	133,000	62,975,797
DCCC	1,136,754	6,244,465	0	9,629,741	574,765	2,593,614	1,933,246	50,008,554
Democratic state and local	672,562	1,968,835	119,704		485,089	4,720,581	243,929	
Total Democrats	2,434,117	24,777,482	1,640,884	102,769,380	1,360,599	20,989,872	2,310,175	227,632,170
RNC	533,835	24,986,139	0	72,761,890	400,000	23,670,006	0	129,060,394
NRSC	764,419	338,385	10,683,692	2,236,761	382,334	172	267,600	31,489,360
NRCC	1,382,680	8,044,648	0	422,543	698,769	3,696,877	548,800	26,810,663
Republican state and local	1,394,980	608,938	320,580		812,647	2,231,910	740,402	
Total Republicans	4,075,914	33,978,110	11,004,272	75,421,194	2,293,750	29,598,965	1,556,802	187,360,417

Source: Compiled from FEC, "FEC Reports Increase in Party Fundraising for 2000," news release, Washington, May 15, 2001.
a. Democratic National Committee (DNC); Democratic Senate Campaign Committee (DSCC); Democratic Congressional Campaign Committee (DCCC); Republican National Committee (RNC); National Republican Senatorial Committee (NRSC); and National Republican Congressional Committee (NRCC).

the limit increases each election cycle. The parties report this spending to the FEC. For the 2000 presidential election, the Democratic National Committee (DNC) and the Republican National Committee (RNC) were each limited to $13,680,292 in coordinated spending for their presidential nominees.[13] Coordinated expenditures were designed to be the primary way for the parties to participate in their nominees' presidential campaigns. For the 2000 presidential election, both parties came close to spending the maximum in coordinated expenditures: the DNC spent $13.5 million of the allowed $13.7 million on behalf of Al Gore and Joe Lieberman, and the RNC spent $13.6 million on behalf of George W. Bush and Dick Cheney. We expect that when final audits of FEC data are complete, we will find that both the DNC and RNC spent the maximum allowable coordinated expenditure. Most coordinated expenditure money was spent on media advertising.[14]

Party Hard Money in the 2000 Congressional Elections

One way that party committees assist their congressional candidates is by giving them direct cash contributions. These party hard money contributions are limited: the national party may contribute up to $5,000 per election (primary, general, runoff, and special) to a House candidate and $17,500 to each Senate candidate per campaign along with an additional $5,000 from the state party (table 6-1). As table 6-2 shows, five of the six national party committees (all except the DNC) gave less in direct contributions to candidates in 2000 than they had in 1996.[15]

Political parties may also spend money independently of their candidates. The 1996 decision in *Colorado Republican Federal Campaign Committee* v. *Federal Election Commission* allowed parties to make unlimited independent expenditures for or against a candidate for federal office.[16] Independent expenditures are hard money dollars spent to conduct express advocacy for the election or defeat of a candidate but without the candidate's knowledge or consent. The advantage of such expenditures is that the parties may spend as much as they like to advocate directly the election or defeat of a candidate, allowing parties to send loud and clear messages to help their candidates win.

However, independent expenditures must be paid for with hard money, which is difficult to raise because it must be raised in small, limited increments (table 6-1). Independent expenditures must also be reported to the FEC, so large party expenditures are quite transparent and may reflect badly on the candidate they are intended to help. Moreover, the parties cannot coordinate such spending with their candidates, making it difficult to separate independent spending from other party efforts. Indeed, the authors of the original FECA did not believe that political parties were capable of true *independence* from the candidates they nominated (even if such a nomination was obtained despite or apart from the party establishment such as through a primary election).

Whether or not a party can act independently of its candidates was brought to court when the Colorado Republican Party began broadcasting ads against an incumbent Democratic senator before the Republican nominee was known. Although the court decided the parties were capable of such independence and allowed parties to spend unlimited amounts on independent expenditures, the parties have not embraced this form of spending. While the DSCC, NRSC, and state and local party committees experimented with significant independent spending in 1996, the practice was largely abandoned in 1998 (table 6-2). The reason party operatives gave was that it was too difficult to establish separate offices to meet the "independent" requirements for these expenditures.

In 2000 some party committees made an effort to try independent expenditures again, but only the Democratic Congressional Campaign Committee (DCCC) did so in a substantial way. A detailed examination of the DCCC's independent expenditures for 1999–2000 reveals that the entire $1.9 million was spent on phone banks averaging $50,000 each in thirty-eight close House races in the last few days before the election.[17] Phone banking is an ideal way to spend independent money, as it requires no direct strategizing with a candidate or his or her campaign to be useful and therefore can be implemented without having to establish a separate party operation. Yet, although independent expenditures offer the potential to significantly enhance a party's presence in a particular race, the prohibition against coordination isolates this party activity from the candidate's campaign efforts.

Finally, parties may also make hard money coordinated expenditures on behalf of their congressional candidates. As with presidential candidates, the amount parties may spend in coordinated expenditures on congressional candidates is limited but indexed to inflation. The 1974 FECA amendments set the amount of coordinated expenditures for U.S. House candidates at $10,000, plus an adjustment pegged to the Consumer Price Index for the national party and the relevant state party. By 2000 the coordinated expenditure limit had increased to $33,780, for a total of $67,560 from both party organizations (the national committee and the state committee).[18] As is usually the case, the national party committees did not spend the maximum allowable coordinated expenditure for each race possible, or even for every competitive race. Hard dollars are so difficult to raise that the committees cannot fully fund all races this way.

However, table 6-2 reveals an interesting trend in party coordinated expenditures from 1996 to 2000. As with direct contributions, both parties' congressional campaign committees, the Democratic Senatorial Campaign Committee (DSCC), the Democratic Congressional Campaign Committee (DCCC), the National Republican Senatorial Committee (NRSC), and the National Republican Congressional Committee (NRCC), spent significantly less on coordinated expenditures in 2000 than they did in 1996. In the next section, we explain that increased party soft money spending has caused the parties to spend less hard money directly on candidates. The NRSC spent only $172 in 2000 on coordinated expenditures after having spent $338,385 in 1996. Meanwhile, both parties' state and local committees spent significantly more on coordinated expenditures in 2000 than they had in 1996 (table 6-2). Despite this reduction in coordinated spending by the national party committees in 2000, the national and state parties went to the Supreme Court to try to get the limits on coordinated spending eliminated. In a 5–4 decision handed down on June 24, 2001, the court found such spending limits constitutional and upheld them.[19] This ruling will not have much effect on the parties' current financing practices because it pertains only to how the parties spend their hard money.

Soft Money in the 2000 Elections

The more significant change in party campaign finance activity during 1999–2000 was the parties' tremendous increase in soft money receipts and expenditures. Elizabeth Drew first coined the term "soft money" in 1983.[20] The term denotes largely unregulated and unlimited nonfederal funds raised by political parties that fall outside FECA limitations. Soft money was originally permitted to strengthen party campaign finance activities at the state and local levels that are aimed not at federal elections but at general party building. These funds are called soft money because they are "not subject to the 'hard' limits of the law," and they are often collected from sources that are barred from participation in federal elections, such as corporations and labor unions.[21]

Soft money first came into the picture in the 1970s, when the FEC issued two Advisory Opinions that released the parties from having to use the more difficult-to-raise hard money for all of their campaign activities. The intent of party soft money was to enable political parties to fund volunteer-based, party-building activities, such as voter registration and get-out-the-vote (GOTV) drives and allow parties to reserve hard money for direct election expenses that must be paid for with hard money. Permitting the use of soft money for these indirect election activities was seen as important to the maintenance of viable political parties and to promote democratic ends that candidates alone would overlook. However, soft money spending skirts the FECA's intent to regulate and make public all federal election campaign finance activity because it may be raised from otherwise prohibited sources, such as corporations and labor union treasury funds.[22] Moreover, soft money skirts the FECA's intent because it often is difficult to trace how soft money is actually spent since party committees at the national, state, and local levels are allowed to transfer soft money funds between one another in unlimited amounts.

Before 1992, soft money spending was not reported to the FEC. Since then, national parties must report soft money spending, but they have avoided full disclosure by transferring soft money funds to the state parties. Since the state parties do not spend the money in direct support of federal candidates, that spending is not reported to the FEC and is instead regulated by the various states' disclosure requirements.[23]

The national parties' success at raising soft money is shown in figure 6-1. The graph presents each party's national organizations' soft money receipts, including the congressional campaign committees, in constant 2000 dollars. In 2000, for the first time since soft money receipts were first reported in 1992, the Democratic Senate and House campaign committees (the DSCC and DCCC) raised more soft money than their GOP counterparts (the NRSC and NRCC). The Republicans lost their soft money fund-raising edge to the Democrats in large part because of soft money contributions to the Democrats from labor unions.

Union support for Democrats is not a new story, but the fact that seven of the Democrats' top ten soft money donors in 2000 were unions with contributions of well over a million dollars each is new (only four of the top ten soft money donors to the Democratic Party were labor unions in 1996) (table 6-3) . Labor union soft money contributions to the Democratic Party jumped significantly from 1996 to 2000. According to figures compiled by Common Cause, union soft money contributions to the Democrats rose from $9.1 million during the 1995–96 election cycle to $32.6 million during the 1999–2000 cycle, while labor unions

Figure 6-1.   *Party Soft Money Receipts in 2000 Dollars*

Millions of dollars

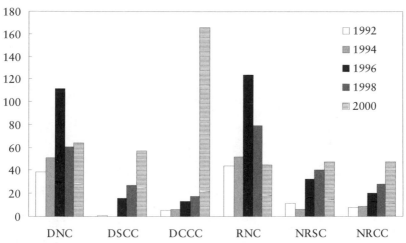

Source: FEC, "FEC Reports Increase in Party Fundraising for 2000."
Note: Democratic National Committee (DNC); Democratic Senate Campaign Committee (DSCC); Democratic Congressional Campaign Committee (DCCC); Republican National Committee (RNC); National Republican Senatorial Committee (NRSC); and National Republican Congressional Committee (NRCC).

gave only $208,335 in 1995–96 and $391,194 in 1999–2000 to Republican Party committees.[74]

This significant increase in labor's soft money contributions to the Democratic Party is because control of both the House and Senate as well as the White House were all truly in play for the first time in decades. This heightened competition and the realistic chance that either party could take unified control compelled the parties to raise soft money more aggressively. It also motivated interested groups and individuals who have a strong preference for which party controls the government, such as labor unions and business interests, to do more to help their favored party win. For instance, the AFL-CIO announced in 1999 that it planned to spend almost $50 million to return the House and Senate to Democratic control in 2000. In response, business groups acted to maintain GOP control of Congress by assisting Republican candidates and educating workers on "how a pro-business agenda benefits workers. In this way, business tried to cut in on the influence labor [had] on employees."[25]

Also important in 2000 is the revelation that both parties show another political committee as one of their largest soft money donors (New

Table 6-3.   *Top Soft Money Donors to the Major Political Parties*
Dollars

Top donors to Democrats	
1. New York Senate 2000	8,585,961
2. AFSCME	5,949,000
3. Service Employees International Union	4,257,696
4. Carpenters & Joiners Union	2,873,500
5. Communications Workers of America	2,405,000
6. United Food & Commercial Workers Union	2,146,450
7. International Brotherhood of Electrical Workers	1,730,000
8. American Federation of Teachers	1,657,000
9. Slim-Fast Foods/Thompson Medical	1,543,000
10. Saban Entertainment	1,496,000
23 donors gave the Democrats 1 million or more dollars each.	
Top donors to Republicans	
1. AT&T	2,423,151
2. Philip Morris	2,086,812
3. Bristol-Myers Squibb	1,527,701
4. National Rifle Association	1,489,222
5. Pfizer Inc.	1,398,817
6. Freddie Mac	1,373,250
7. Republican Party of California	1,325,000
8. Microsoft Corp.	1,313,384
9. Enron Corp.	1,138,990
10. Amway/Alticor Inc.	1,138,500
11 donors gave the Republicans 1 million or more dollars each.	

Source: Center for Responsive Politics, "Top Soft Money Donors: 2000 Election Cycle," Washington, 2001.

York Senate 2000 for the Democrats and the Republican Party of California for the Republicans). These committees suggest how great the party committees' innovation for maximizing soft money truly is. The New York Senate 2000 committee is an example of a new and controversial development in soft money fund-raising. Several of the most competitive Senate candidates in 2000 created new "joint committees" that linked their candidacies to the political parties. Usually called "victory committees," these entities raise both hard and soft money, but the soft money generally is transferred to the national party committees, since it cannot be used to directly advocate for a candidate's election or defeat. The national committees in turn send the money to appropriate state parties, which sometimes turn out to be the Senate candidate's home state party.[26] Though the candidates deny they are involved in money laundering, which is prohibited by the FECA, it is a curious arrangement that will probably play a role in future elections.

Soft Money Spending and Transfers to State Parties

As figure 6-1 and table 6-3 illustrate, raising soft money is not difficult for the political parties. Spending soft money, however, is more of a challenge because soft money generally must be spent in combination with hard money. Party activities that affect only state or local elections may be paid for exclusively with soft money if the relevant state's law permits. Yet party activities that affect both federal and state/local elections (for example, overhead expenses for running the party, GOTV drives that support both federal and state/local candidates, or generic party communications that support the party generally, such as "Vote Republican, For a Change") and party issue advocacy ads must be paid for with a combination of hard and soft money according to ratios set by the FEC and the respective state's campaign finance regulations. This need to combine soft money with hard money in order to spend it on federal campaign activities has been the real motivating factor behind the recent changes in national and state party spending patterns. The national parties are spending less hard money, and consequently the state parties have increased their hard money spending, in order to comply with the matching requirements that allow the parties to spend soft money on federal election activities.

During presidential election years, the national parties (when spending money themselves instead of through state parties) must pay for these activities with 65 percent hard money and 35 percent soft money. In nonpresidential years, the ratio is 60 percent hard and 40 percent soft money. Depending on the mix of federal and nonfederal activity, different hard and soft money ratios apply to other party activities such as soft money fundraising.[27] The national party committees are required to report disbursements they make with a mixture of hard and soft money. They must declare the total amount spent, the amount for federal activity, the amount for nonfederal activity, whom the money was paid to, and the purpose of the expenditure. As there currently is no uniform list of purpose codes, the parties give as much or little information as they wish. A recent examination of Democratic Senatorial Campaign Committee expenditures of this sort for the 2000 year-end report found numerous entries for "salary." Some individuals received 70 percent of their salary from federal accounts, some only 50 percent. No explanation was given on the forms for the difference beyond the word "salary" for the expenditure's purpose.

The proportion of federal races on a state's general election ballot combined with state campaign finance laws governing the raising and spending of soft money determines the hard/soft money ratios for state political parties.[28] Typically a state's ratio will allow for more soft money spending than the national party's ratio, so the national parties often transfer hard and soft money to a state party in amounts proportionate to those required by the more favorable state ratio. The state party may in turn pay a media consultant selected by the national party to help with issue ads to be run in that state. Since party committees are permitted to transfer unlimited amounts of money to other party committees, these spending arrangements do not violate FECA contribution limits.

Yet these national party transfers to state parties have come under a great deal of criticism and are seen by many as a loophole in the federal law that should be closed. Indeed, once national party soft money is transferred to a state party committee, it is extremely difficult to trace exactly how that money is eventually spent. The national committees disclose this money to the FEC as transfers to state parties, but each state has different reporting requirements and different rules for soft money use, making expenditures difficult to track.[29]

The national parties have come to spend their hard money quite differently in part because of the more favorable environment for spending soft money in many states. The national parties are spending less hard money directly on federal candidates and are transferring much more hard money to the states than previously. Because of the need for hard money in order to take advantage of the more favorable ratios in some states, party committees often are willing to pay a 10- to 15-percent premium to "swap" soft money for hard money.[30]

In the 2000 election cycle, all the national party committees increased their soft money transfers to state parties from the last presidential election (table 6-4). Note how much more the Democratic Senate and House campaign committees (the DSCC and the DCCC) transferred in hard and soft money than the Republican congressional campaign committees (the NRSC and the NRCC). Although the national committees clearly have significant fund-raising peaks in presidential years, the four congressional campaign committees have shown a steady increase in hard and soft money transfers over all of the past three election cycles. This trend is not likely to slow unless comprehensive reform legislation is enacted that either bans soft money or somehow discourages the parties from spending hard and soft money in this way.

Table 6-4. *National Party Committee Hard and Soft Money Transfers to State Party Committees*
Constant 2000 dollars

Party committee[a]	1996		1998		2000	
	Hard money	Soft money	Hard money	Soft money	Hard money	Soft money
DNC	22,120,526	59,478,136	3,489,780	12,973,600	38,250,048	76,397,771
DSCC	5,109,796	6,431,181	12,837,000	16,478,000	24,160,093	38,815,704
DCCC	4,641,320	4,988,421	3,682,400	7,276,790	15,381,305	34,627,249
Total	31,871,642	70,897,737	20,009,180	36,728,390	77,791,446	149,840,724
RNC	19,841,171	52,920,719	7,398,730	21,869,600	35,810,935	93,249,459
NRSC	434,862	1,801,899	3,123,620	12,287,400	10,734,700	20,754,660
NRCC	0	422,543	2,786,690	2,100,730	10,957,743	15,852,920
Total	20,276,033	55,145,161	13,309,040	36,257,730	57,503,378	129,857,039

Source: Compiled from FEC, "FEC Reports Major Increase in Party Activity for 1995-96," news release, Washington, March 19, 1997; and FEC, "FEC Reports Increase in Party Fundraising for 2000."

a. See table 6-2.

Issue Advocacy Advertisements

In recent elections, the most common, and also the most controversial, use of soft money has been to pay for issue advocacy advertisements. The FECA requires national parties to use hard money for campaign communications that expressly advocate the election or defeat of a candidate for federal office. As David Magleby explains in chapter 1, the test for candidate or express advocacy is the language of the ad, including "vote for," "vote against," "elect," and "defeat." Any communication that does not include such words of express advocacy, no matter how much it appears to be a campaign ad, is not considered a campaign communication. Therefore, the ad may be paid for partially with soft money, and the expenditure does not count against the spending limits for a presidential campaign. Such ads are called issue advocacy ads, and they are supposed to advocate some position on an issue.

Yet the parties, as well as interest groups and wealthy individuals, fund issue advocacy ads that in every respect, except for the lack of words of express advocacy, look and sound like express advocacy campaign ads. Issue ads allow parties to communicate directly with voters about candidates for federal office without having to fully face the limits and constraints of party hard money fund-raising and with less complete disclosure.

Here are some national party issue advocacy ads that were broadcast during the 2000 presidential election. These ads were paid for in part with soft money:

DNC Ad: "Oil & Water" (aired mid-September 2000)

ANNOUNCER: They say that oil and water don't mix. Nowhere is that more true than in Texas. After seventeen years in the oil business, George W. Bush ran for governor. Then passed laws to let big polluters regulate themselves.

(On screen: Source: *New York Times*, 11/9/99, *Tacoma News Tribune* 7/9/00)

Today, Texas is number three in water pollution, number one in air pollution.

(On screen: EPA, "1998 Toxics Release Inventory," 5/00)

For over 20 years, Al Gore has fought against polluters and helped pass laws to clean up our air and water. America's environment is cleaner now. Do we really want it to look like Texas?

(On screen: 1800thefacts.com; Paid for by the Democratic National Committee)

RNC Ad: "Agenda" (aired early August 2000)

(On screen: Paid for by the Republican National Committee)

ANNOUNCER: While George Bush offers a positive issue agenda, more negative attacks from Al Gore. The truth? George Bush is cleaning up Texas. The Environmental Protection Agency reports that Texas leads America in reducing toxic pollution.

(On screen: *Toxics Release Inventory*, Environmental Protection Agency, 1995–1998)

And Al Gore? Gore has allowed mining companies to mine zinc from his property.

(On screen: Bill Turque, *Inventing Al Gore*, 2000, p. 106)

They've been cited for polluting the source of local drinking water . . .

(On screen: Tennessee Department of Environment and Conservation, Notice of Violation, May 16, 2000)

. . . all while Gore's made half a million dollars in mining royalties.

(On screen: Al Gore's 1999 Executive Branch Personnel Public Financial Disclosure, filed May 15, 2000)

Even on the environment, Al Gore says one thing but does another.

(On screen: www.gorepollution.com)

Clearly it is not difficult to make a hard-hitting and effective advertisement that benefits a favored candidate without using express advocacy words. Most voters in the television audience would interpret these ads as campaign ads designed to suggest a vote for or against a particular candidate because they look and sound just like ads that are considered campaign ads under the court's definition. Indeed, Magleby found in his report *Dictum without Data* that voters tested in focus groups "saw election issue ads as more about the election or defeat of a candidate than the candidates' own commercials."[31] Also, negative issue advocacy ads run during campaigns often feature ominous background music, code words such as "liberal" and "radical," and grainy, unflattering black-and-white pictures common in campaign attack ads. Positive issue ads use cheery music, code words such as "trust," and family-values pictures, all while praising some policy position of a candidate or party.[32] These are the same techniques used in conventional campaign television ads, making issue advocacy ads paid for in part with soft money virtually indistinguishable from campaign ads that must be paid for with hard money.[33] It is not surprising that the parties and interest groups that use issue advocacy advertising hire the same consultants that they hire to produce regulated campaign advertisements.[34]

Although the national parties aired soft-money issue ads as early as 1980, the use of issue advocacy advertising by parties and interest groups exploded during the 1996 election.[35] Yet the use of issue ads in the 1996 elections pales in comparison to the 2000 elections. The 2000 presidential election marked the first time in modern campaign history that political parties spent more on television advertising than the presidential candidates themselves, most of it issue advocacy advertising.[36] Even though the parties spent $48.8 million on television advertising for their presidential nominees in 1996, that amount was still less than the candidates themselves spent on TV advertising that year, $67.3 million.[37] The Brennan Center for Justice reports that for their presidential nominees in 2000 the DNC and the RNC spent an estimated $79.9 million—most of which was soft money—for television advertisements in the seventy-five largest media markets, or $13 million more than the candidates spent.[38] The gap may be much larger, however, since the researchers did not include ads sponsored by state party committees, nor did they include the cost of production and placement of the ads.[39] Add to this amount the more than $16 million spent by interest groups on behalf of the presidential candidates, and it becomes clear that the candidates' own spending on advertising ($67.1 million) was significantly overshadowed by party and interest group advertising spending in 2000.

Furthermore, parties and interest groups spent millions in soft money on issue advocacy messages sent through the mail, run in newspapers, delivered in person, or conveyed over the phone or through e-mail. In a study of seventeen targeted House and Senate races in 2000, Magleby and a team of scholars found that parties and interest groups waged extensive ground wars to elect their favored candidates.[40] For instance, political party committees sent more than 400 unique pieces of mail in the seventeen monitored races, an average of twenty-seven mail pieces per race.[41] The NRCC alone mailed sixty-seven different pieces to voters in the twelve House races in the study.

Most of the national parties' presidential issue advocacy ads stuck to a few common themes. The number one issue was health care.[42] Other topics included education, the environment, Social Security, and taxes. The national party committees targeted most of their presidential issue advocacy advertising in just seventeen battleground states: Arkansas, Florida, Georgia, Illinois, Iowa, Kentucky, Louisiana, Maine, Maryland (for broadcast to Delaware viewers), Michigan, Missouri, New Mexico, Ohio, Oregon, Pennsylvania, Washington, and Wisconsin.[43] Other states saw considerable issue advocacy advertising by state political party committees.

The national political parties did not wait until their nominees were selected at their summer nominating conventions to start their ad campaigns. The RNC hit the airwaves as early as mid-January with a spot that attacked the Democratic front-runner Al Gore. The ad accused Gore of wanting to require a "political litmus test" regarding gays in the military that neither Generals Colin Powell nor Norman Schwartzkopf—"the heroes of Desert Storm"—could pass.[44] The RNC also began running ads targeted at Hispanic voters in January 2000. By election day, the RNC had spent more than $5 million on Spanish-language ads supporting Bush or the GOP in general.[45]

The DNC waited a bit longer before airing ads designed to help Gore win, with the first issue advocacy ad sponsored by the DNC debuting in early June.[46] The GOP's early spending is much like the strategy used by the Democrats in 1996, when the DNC spent almost $50 million on issue advocacy ads that promoted incumbent president Clinton's accomplishments and criticized the "Gingrich-Dole" agenda before the general election began.[47] In 2000, while the presidential candidates were still in the throes of the primary season, the Republican Party was already waging the general election. The new trend is for the national parties to begin their issue ad campaigns against each other well before the general election begins. Such a tactic violates the parties' norm against prenomination campaigning, but as John C. Green and Nathan S. Bigelow explain in chapter 3, the Clinton soft money strategy in 1996 has made abiding by that norm impossible.

The parties also ran issue ads for their congressional candidates. Magleby and his team of scholars found that the typical ad conveyed a candidate's position in a specific way (favorable or unfavorable) and asked the viewer (or reader in the case of direct mail) to contact the candidate to tell him or her that you agree or disagree with that position.[48] Although staying away from express advocacy, congressional party issue ads often end with an appeal for citizens to respond to the candidate's position, usually with the candidate projected in an unfavorable way. Some of the more hotly contested congressional races featured particularly incendiary appeals. In the open-seat contest for Michigan's Eighth Congressional District, the NRCC attacked the ultimately unsuccessful Democratic candidate, Dianne Byrum, for missing votes in the state senate and voting to borrow from the state's Veterans' Trust Fund. In an ad called "Failed for Lack of Attendance," Byrum was accused of missing an important vote while attending a fundraiser "held at a casino." The tag line encouraged citizens to "Call and ask her why she turned her back on Michigan schools to go to a casino."[49] The Democrats' ads could be equally hard-hitting. In New Jersey's Twelfth Congressional District, the DCCC was accused of distorting Republican Dick Zimmer's voting record in Congress in a cable television ad and of downright cruelty in a mailer sent to constituents' homes. The DCCC mailer accused Zimmer of turning his back on funding for women's health issues, asking citizens to "Tell Dick Zimmer to quit voting against women's health." When the media disclosed that Zimmer's mother had died of lymphoma and all three of his sisters were breast cancer survivors, the mailer became a subject of great controversy.[50] Both of these races witnessed an extraordinary amount of issue advocacy advertising by the parties, and both were virtual dead heats, requiring recounts after election day (the parties split the outcome with a Republican victory in Michigan and a Democratic victory in New Jersey).

Spending Soft Money Instead of Hard Money

The national party committees decreased their hard money contributions and coordinated spending, and state and local parties increased their hard money coordinated spending in 2000 primarily because the national parties needed to reserve their hard money to match with their larger pots of soft money. The national parties are mixing their hard money with soft money for spending on issue ads and other activities, and they are transferring money to states where there are more favorable soft money spending rules. These transfers help explain why the national party committees have decreased their hard money spending on coordinated expenditures and direct contributions. This strategy permits parties to concentrate resources in states with competitive races, but it also makes direct hard money contributions and coordinated spending on behalf of specific candidates less important.

This change in hard money spending has prompted the national party committees to ask the state parties to take responsibility for direct contributions and coordinated expenditures. Thus the increase in state and local party coordinated spending indicates an abandonment of the agency agreements, which were the backbone of party committee strategy in the 1980s. Agency agreements allowed each party's national congressional campaign committee to spend both the national party's and the state party's coordinated expenditure limit on a candidate. Now because the national parties are reserving their hard money for matching with soft money, the parties have returned to the original agreement whereby the state party committees and national party committees may each spend their own maximum allowed in coordinated expenditures, though some states receive funds through congressional campaign committee transfers for this purpose rather than having to raise these hard dollars on their own.

House and Senate candidates often do not receive the maximum party coordinated expenditure allowed, since the national party committees are reserving hard money to combine with soft money for issue ads and other activities. Table 6-5 shows the percentage of the maximum allowable coordinated expenditures the parties spent on their congressional candidates categorized by chamber, incumbency status, and competitiveness of the race. Coordinated expenditures and direct contributions were low enough that a number of House and Senate candidates begged their parties to send hard money their way, but instead their parties aired issue ads.

Candidates generally prefer to spend the money themselves, so they can control how the money is spent. Indeed, on several occasions the parties have aired issue advocacy ads that have actually hurt their candidates because the ads contained inaccurate information or were not targeted well. For example, in 1996, the NRCC ran an anti-union issue ad in Pennsylvania's Twenty-First District intended to help Republican incumbent Phil English win reelection. The ad featured a heavy-set "union boss" in a smoke-filled room reaching into a briefcase and handing stacks of cash across the table. The announcer stated, "The big labor bosses in Washington, D.C. have a big scheme to buy the Congress . . . They've spent $150,000 here on ads favoring Ron DiNicola," the Democratic challenger for the seat.[51] Congressman English did not appreciate the party's help: "If they had asked me, I would have told those guys that attacking big labor is not a particularly effective strategy in Erie."[52] In 2000 the

Table 6-5. *Party-Coordinated Expenditures by Chamber, Status, and Competitiveness*

Chamber, status, and competitiveness of election[a]	Democrats		Republicans	
	Number of candidates	Percent of maximum allowed	Number of candidates	Percent of maximum allowed
Senate incumbents				
High	1	0	5	66
Medium	2	65	3	98
Low	8	0	10	14
Senate challengers				
High	5	22	1	99
Medium	3	46	0	. . .
Low	9	8	9	6
Senate open seats				
High	4	33	3	67
Medium	0	. . .	2	92
Low	1	0	0	. . .
House incumbents				
High	21	32	20	70
Medium	20	12	30	15
Low	163	3	147	1
House challengers				
High	11	60	8	97
Medium	27	25	21	73
Low	103	5	109	1
House open seats				
High	14	88	12	100
Medium	5	63	8	74
Low	13	6	12	8

Source: Compiled from FEC, "FEC Reports Increase in Party Fundraising for 2000," and "FEC Announces 2000 Party Spending Limits," Washington, March 1, 2000.

a. High competition, 54 to 46 percent of the general election vote; medium competition, 55 to 59 percent and 45 to 40 percent of the general election vote; low competition, 60+ or less than 40 percent of the general election vote.

Democrats ran an issue ad in Kentucky's Sixth Congressional District against incumbent Republican Ernie Fletcher that accused him of voting to decrease funding for education when in fact Fletcher had voted for an increase in education funding, though a smaller increase than President Bill Clinton had proposed. Though the Democratic candidate, Scotty Baesler, at first defended the ad, four television stations in Lexington pulled the ad, creating a serious credibility issue that ultimately hurt Baesler badly.[53]

Although their parties' soft money spending may direct more resources to their races, candidates still prefer to control the spending themselves, and moreover, the parties' shift away from hard money spending is increasing the overall cost of the most competitive congressional campaigns. Even if they advocate a larger role for parties in contemporary elections, many scholars and other observers believe that this is a negative development.[54]

If we consider the party's direct spending of hard money on candidates, it would seem that the Republican Party knows how to target their money in competitive races, while the Democrats do not (table 6-5). The Democrats seem especially guilty of such hard money abrogation: when you take away the 88 percent of maximum coordinated money spent in House open-seat races, the level of Democratic hard money support seems nominal at best, even in the highly contested Senate races. The Republicans seem to fare much better, investing more heavily in medium and highly competitive races. Of course, the GOP's large hard money advantage over the Democrats gives them more hard money to spend.

However, the soft money spending tells a very different story. Because the parties do not have to report precisely how soft money is spent, we can only rely on aggregate transfer figures to states to get a rough idea of the importance that parties place on particular contests. In a presidential election year, we can only guess how much money was spent on presidential, senatorial, and congressional races. Fortunately, Magleby's studies in 1998 and 2000 used designated observers in select races to help discover the approximate (or sometimes precise) amounts of soft money spent in these competitive contests. Their findings give us a much different view of party spending.

One good example is the Senate race in Delaware between five-term incumbent Republican William (Bill) V. Roth and two-term Democratic incumbent governor Thomas (Tom) Carper. The hard money story shows Republicans virtually "maxing out" to Roth, contributing $24,500 directly, and spending $130,600 in coordinated expenditures, 97 percent of Delaware's coordinated expenditure allowance. Democrats, however, sent $16,500 in direct contributions and $50,000 in coordinated expenditures (or 37 percent of the maximum). In total, Republicans sent Roth $155,100 in hard money while Democrats sent Carper only $66,500. But the soft money picture is vastly different. Roth's campaign forbade the national Republican Party from spending soft money in the state, fearing it would hurt him in the election. The NRSC transferred only $250,000 in soft money to the state party, and even this was to be earmarked for the coordinated campaign and not Roth directly. Carper had no such reservations, and the DSCC sent more than $4.3 million—$2.95 million in soft money and $1.4 million in hard money—to Delaware on his behalf.

Joseph Pika finds that in this race at least $1.6 million was spent on airtime alone.[55] Carper won the race with 56 percent of the vote.

A similar story is found in the U.S. House race for Pennsylvania's Thirteenth Congressional District. One-term Democratic incumbent Joe Hoeffel faced what was thought to be a stiff challenge from Republican state senator Stewart Greenleaf. The district had a Republican registration advantage, and Greenleaf was well known, well liked, and had moderate politics that fit the district's general trends. Hoeffel, a former county executive and a moderate himself, ran for the seat twice before defeating a Republican incumbent in 1998. The national Republican committees spent $14,747 in direct contributions and $62,577 in coordinated expenditures (93 percent of the legal maximum) for Greenleaf. However, according to Greenleaf's campaign, they sent no soft money to Pennsylvania earmarked for Greenleaf. The NRCC transferred $1.66 million ($864,000 in hard money and $792,000 in soft money), but that money seems to have been spent for the coordinated campaign as well as for two other contested House races clearly of greater interest to the NRCC. Hoeffel, by contrast, received only $4,997 in direct contributions and $10,765 in coordinated expenditures (16 percent of the maximum) from the Democratic Party. However, the DCCC reported sending almost $1.4 million for Hoeffel's campaign, $1.2 million for the production and airing of issue ads alone. Hoeffel received 52 percent of the vote to Greenleaf's disappointing 45 percent.[56]

The Magleby study includes many similar case studies, demonstrating that parties can keep their soft money strategy well hidden unless trained observers are willing to dig and uncover it. In these two cases, Democrats spent soft money earlier in the election cycle (in September in both cases) than campaigns typically do, building early momentum for both candidates. The Republicans spent soft money strategically in other races, but they did more to maximize their hard money commitment to candidates first, saving soft money for late in the races. With the Democrats' pickup of four in the Senate and two in the House, their early and aggressive use of soft money at the expense of maximizing hard money contributions may have been the wisest route.

Implications

The 2000 elections solidified a remarkable trend first noticed in 1996: political parties are using soft money to put themselves in a central role in competitive elections. Though the number of competitive elections is declining, so is the number of seats needed to win control of the legislative chambers, making each competitive race more important. Through the 1980s and 1990s, parties mastered a number of clever techniques (such as steering PAC giving, encouraging member to member giving, and sending "star quality" elected officials on fund-raising tours) to devote maximal hard money resources to the most competitive races. Yet all of these methods depended on cajoling and good feelings, and the FECA contribution limits meant that raising hard money was very time consuming and expensive. With the innovation of soft money spending for issue ads, parties had a more efficient means to raise and spend money in targeted races— soft money, making their hard money activities less urgent, though still present. It must be stressed that soft money is one of many tools employed by the parties, and the amounts raised have certainly made the political parties more important actors in electoral politics. However, the fact that interest groups engage in issue advocacy with funds raised "off the books" and that candidates must now respond to party and group activity with even more funds raised on their own, often mitigate the effects of increased party activity.

In presidential elections, the parties' increased use of soft money and issue advocacy advertising have fundamentally altered the presidential campaign finance system. The presidential public funding system itself has shaped this development, in that the candidates are limited in the amounts they may raise and spend if they accept public funding. Thus while the presidential public funding system has accomplished one of its goals by slowing the growth of campaign spending by candidates, at least in comparison to the growth in congressional campaigns, the public funding rules have encouraged spending outside of the regulated system.[57] And the tremendous growth in party soft money spending has all but nullified the public funding system's intent to control the cost of running for president and guard against corruption by removing a candidate's need to raise huge amounts of money. The presidential public funding system may have already outlived its usefulness.

Although presidential nominees may welcome their parties' assistance, the parties' increasing role takes some control out of the candidates' hands. Moreover, unlike ads run by candidates, party issue advocacy advertisements are more inclined to be attack ads.[58] Indeed, the overwhelming majority of party issue ads run during the 2000 presidential election featured an attack on the other candidate or his or her positions on relevant issues.[59] Thus the more ads that the parties run relative to the number of ads that the candidates run, the more negative the tone of the campaign is likely to be. Yet the parties are not held responsible for the negative ads because the candidates are the only ones on the ballot, and they can often distance themselves from the negative campaigning conducted by their parties. Indeed, presidential nominee George W. Bush asked that the RNC pull a controversial attack ad criticizing Gore's prescription drug proposal. The ad flashed the word "rats" subliminally across the screen. Bush had the ad pulled so that his campaign would not suffer because of the negative fallout from the ad. However, some candidates might leave it to their parties to do the dirty campaigning and not personally suffer the consequences on election day.

Finally, while it is clear that top party leaders and elected officials derive great benefits within their political party community from the amount of funds they bring to the table, it is less clear what the implications of party soft money are for the conduct of elections in the United States and the access soft money donors gain to lawmakers. What does this trend mean for the quality of our democracy? Although it is clear that many observers of politics lament the increased money in the political system, we are not in a position to make a candid assessment of its effects since full disclosure of spending is not available. The political parties in the 2000 election have almost flaunted their disregard for the regulatory system enacted by the FECA more than twenty years ago, and it seems that the time is now ripe for comprehensive reform of the campaign finance system.

In the summer of 2001, there had been renewed interest in achieving real campaign finance reform. Much of the momentum for reform in the Senate was the result of Senator John McCain's (R-Ariz.) presidential run and the positive public response to his calls for campaign finance reform with a ban on party soft money and limits on the use of issue ads by parties and interest groups. Although a reform bill did pass the Senate on April 2, 2001, the House sponsors of the measure chose to withdraw the bill in the summer (through a defeat of the rule) rather than watch it face almost certain doom on the House floor. As this book goes to press and the Enron scandal has put campaign finance reform back on the agenda, the House is expected to consider the reform bill again. If the bill passes and is not vetoed by the president, we will see significant changes in party campaign finance. If the bill does not become law, we are likely to see that even more campaign finance activity will be conducted outside of the confines of the law and hidden from public scrutiny.

Notes

1. Robert Biersack and Melanie Haskell, "Spitting on the Umpire: Political Parties, the Federal Election Campaign Act, and the 1996 Campaigns," in John C. Green, ed., *Financing the 1996 Election* (M.E. Sharpe, 1999), p. 156.

2. See later in this chapter a discussion of how full disclosure of soft money is avoided through the use of state parties to conduct the actual expenditures of soft money. Such disclosures are subject to state regulations and not the FECA's.

3. John H. Aldrich, *Why Parties? The Origin and Transformation of Political Parties in America* (University of Chicago Press, 1995); see also Paul S. Herrnson, *Party Campaigning in the 1980s* (Harvard University Press, 1988); and Paul S. Herrnson, *Congressional Elections: Campaigning at Home and in Washington,* 3d ed. (Washington: Congressional Quarterly, 2000).

4. Robin Kolodny and Diana Dwyre, "Party-Orchestrated Activities for Legislative Party Goals: Campaigns for Majorities in the U.S. House of Representatives in the 1990s," *Party Politics,* vol. 4 (July 1998), p. 278.

5. Aldrich, *Why Parties?*; see also Joseph Schlesinger, *Political Parties and the Winning of Office* (University of Michigan Press, 1991).

6. State and local party committees that raise funds for the direct benefit of candidates for federal office must report their hard money activities to the Federal Election Commission (FEC).

7. Percentages compiled by authors from FEC, "FEC Reports Increase in Party Fundraising for 2000," news release, Washington, May 15, 2001.

8. See chapter 7 for further discussion of PAC giving strategies and chapter 5 for the effect of PAC activity on congressional candidates.

9. When disbursement figures are converted to constant 2000 dollars, the Democrats spent $235 million in 1996 and $266 million in 2000. The Republicans spent $448 million in 1996 and $427 million in 2000. These figures are compiled by the authors from FEC, "FEC Reports Increase in Party Fundraising for 2000."

10. FEC, "Reform Party to Receive Additional Funds for Nominating Convention," Washington, news release (www.fec.gov/press/addrefconv.htm [May 25, 2000]).

11. Jane M. Von Bergen, "Costs for a National Party Add Up: Philadelphia 2000's Report on the Republican Convention Tells a $66 Million Story," *Philadelphia Inquirer,* October 22, 2000, p. E1; and Jim Newton, "Major Firms Give Heavily to Political Conventions," *Los Angeles Times,* May 29, 2000, A1.

12. Josh Goldstein and Jane M. Von Bergen, "Conventions Rake in Business Donations: Some Firms Give to Both Democrats and the GOP. The Support Is Driven by Civic Pride or Political Strategy?" *Philadelphia Inquirer,* April 26, 2000, A1; and Newton, "Major Firms Give Heavily," p. A1.

13. FEC, "FEC Certifies Public Funds for Bush-Cheney Ticket," news release, Washington, August 4, 2000; and FEC, "FEC Certifies Public Funds for Gore-Lieberman Ticket," news release, August 18, 2000.

14. Robin Kolodny, "Towards a Theory of Political Party Institutional Capacity, or Why Parties Need Political Consultants to Remain Viable in the C20th," annual conference of the Elections, Parties and Opinion Polls (EPOP) division of

the Political Studies Association, University of Edinburgh, Edinburgh, Scotland, September 2000. This assessment is based on party coordinated spending in past presidential elections. Exact figures that break down how the parties spent their coordinated expenditure funds are not yet available for 2000. Full audits of the presidential campaigns are usually completed two years after the election.

15. All numbers adjusted for inflation to 2000 dollars.

16. *Colorado Republican Federal Campaign Committee* v. *Federal Election Commission* (95-489) 518 U.S. 604 (1996).

17. Robin Kolodny and David A. Dulio, "Where the Money Goes: Party Spending in Congressional Elections," annual meeting of the Midwestern Political Science Association, Chicago, Illinois, April 2001.

18. FEC, "FEC Announces 2000 Party Spending Limits," news release, Washington, March 1, 2000.

19. *Federal Election Commission* v. *Colorado Republican Federal Campaign Committee* (00-191) 213 F. 3d 1221, reversed.

20. Elizabeth Drew, *Politics and Money: The New Road to Corruption* (Macmillan, 1983).

21. Anthony Corrado, "Party Soft Money," in Anthony Corrado and others, eds., *Campaign Finance Reform: A Sourcebook* (Brookings, 1997), p. 172.

22. Corporations and labor unions may establish political action committees (PACs) to spend money to influence the outcome of elections, but they must raise this money in separate, segregated funds and not from their general operating budgets. The receipts and disbursements of PAC funds are very tightly regulated by the FECA.

23. Anthony Gierzynski discusses the extensive variation among state regulations in chapter 8.

24. Common Cause, "Soft Money Laundromat" (www.commoncause.org/laundromat/industry.cfm [July 5, 2001]).

25. *Inside the New Congress,* newsletter, Washington, February 26, 1999, as cited in Roger H. Davidson and Walter J. Oleszek, *Congress and Its Members* (Washington: Congressional Quarterly, 2000), p. 344.

26. Greg Gordon, "Donations to Joint Committees Getting around Soft Money Laws," *Star Tribune* (Minneapolis), October 27, 2000, p. 18A.

27. Biersack and Haskell, "Spitting on the Umpire," p. 177.

28. In all states except Connecticut and Alaska, which ban soft money, party activities that affect both federal and state/local elections and party issue advocacy ads must be paid for with a combination of hard and soft money according to ratios set by the FEC. See chapter 8.

29. Diana Dwyre, "Spinning Straw into Gold: Soft Money and U.S. House Elections," *Legislative Studies Quarterly,* vol. 21 (August 1996), 409–24; see also Sarah M. Morehouse, "State Parties: Independent Partners: The Money Relationship," American Political Science Association annual meeting, 2000.

30. Morehouse, "State Parties: Independent Partners—The Money Relationship"; see also Common Cause, "Party Soft Money" (Washington, 1998). An example from 1996 makes the point well: "The Florida state Democratic Committee transferred $10,000 in hard money to the Nebraska state Democratic Committee on

May 2, 1996. On the same date, the Nebraska State Democratic Committee transferred $12,000 in soft money back to the committee in Florida. In essence, Nebraska was paying extra for hard money that could be used either to directly support federal candidates or as the federal share of some activity that permitted both hard and soft funding sources." Biersack and Haskell, "Spitting on the Umpire," p. 179.

31. David Magleby, "Dictum without Data: The Myth of Issue Advocacy and Party Building," report produced and distributed by Brigham Young University, Center for the Study of Elections and Democracy, November 13, 2000 (www.byu.edu/outsidemoney/dictum, p. 13 [July 8, 2001]).

32. Paul S. Herrnson and Diana Dwyre, "Party Issue Advocacy in Congressional Elections," in John C. Green and Daniel M. Shea, eds., *State of the Parties*, 3d ed. (Rowman and Littlefield, 1999), pp. 86–104.

33. Darrell M. West, *Air Wars: Television Advertising in Election Campaigns, 1952–1996*, 2d ed. (Washington: Congressional Quarterly, 1997), pp. 4–9; and see also Kathleen Hall Jamieson, *Dirty Politics: Deception, Distraction and Democracy* (Oxford University Press, 1992).

34. David A. Dulio and Robin Kolodny, "Political Parties and Political Consultants: Creating Alliances for Electoral Success," paper presented at the Western Political Science Association annual meeting, March 2001.

35. Biersack and Haskell, "Spitting on the Umpire"; see also Diana Dwyre, "Interest Groups and Issue Advocacy in 1996," in John C. Green, ed. *Financing the 1996 Election* (M. E. Sharpe, 1999).

36. Brennan Center for Justice at New York University School of Law, "2000 Presidential Race First in Modern History Where Political Parties Spend More on TV Ads Than Candidates," news release, December 11, 2000.

37. Ibid., p. 1.

38. Ibid., pp. 1–2.

39. Ibid., p. 2.

40. David B. Magleby, ed., *Election Advocacy: Soft Money and Issue Advocacy in the 2000 Congressional Elections* (Brigham Young University, Center for the Study of Elections and Democracy, 2001).

41. Ibid., p. 3.

42. Annenberg Public Policy Center, "Issue Advertising in the 1999–2000 Election Cycle," University of Pennsylvania, 2001 (www.appcpenn.org/issueads [March 3, 2001]).

43. "DNC Turns Bush's New Slogan against Him," in *Ad Spotlight* (www.nationaljournal.com [September 19, 2000]).

44. "RNC Attacks Gore's Gay Litmus Test," in *Ad Spotlight* (www.nationaljournal.com [January 11, 2000]). There actually was a Republican Party issue ad that ran even earlier, but it was not focused solely on a particular candidate. During the summer of 1999, the Republicans appealed to President Bill Clinton, Senate Democratic Leader Tom Daschle, and "Hillary and Al" to support the Social Security "lock box" idea. See Annenberg Public Policy Center, "Issue Advertising in the 1999–2000 Election Cycle."

45. "This *Familia* Likes Bush," in *Ad Spotlight* (www.nationaljournal.com [November 1, 2000]).

46. "Dems Fire First with Health Care Spot," in *Ad Spotlight* (www. nationaljournal.com [June 8, 2000]).

47. Anthony Corrado, "Financing the 1996 Presidential General Election," in Green, *Financing the 1996 Elections*, p. 80.

48. Magleby, ed., *Election Advocacy.*

49. Eric Freedman and Sue Carter, "The 2000 Michigan Eighth Congressional District Race," in Magleby, *Election Advocacy.* p. 198.

50. Adam Berinsky and Susan Lederman, "The New Jersey Twelfth Congressional District Race," in Magleby, *Election Advocacy,* p. 221.

51. Guy Gugliotta and Ira Chinoy, "Money Machine: The Fund-Raising Frenzy of Campaign '96," *Washington Post,* February 10, 1997, sec. A; and National Republican Congressional Committee, "Chapter Two," NRCC-sponsored issue advocacy ad, produced by Sipple Strategic Communications, 1996.

52. Gugliotta and Chinoy, "Money Machine."

53. Penny Miller and Donald Gross, "The 2000 Kentucky Sixth Congressional District Race," in Magleby, *Election Advocacy,* p. 180.

54. See the Campaign Finance Institute's cyber-forum at www.cfinst.org; various reports by the Alliance for Better Campaigns at www.bettercampaigns.org; and Paul Taylor's editorial "Free and Fair TV Spots," *Washington Post,* July 8, 2001, p. B7.

55. Joseph A. Pika, "The 2000 Delaware Senate Race," in Magleby, *Election Advocacy.*

56. Robin Kolodny, Sandra L. Suarez, and Kyle Kreider, "The 2000 Pennsylvania Thirteenth Congressional District Race," in Magleby, *Election Advocacy.*

57. Frank Sorauf, *Inside Campaign Finance: Myths and Realities* (Yale University Press, 1992), p. 158.

58. Herrnson and Dwyre, "Party Issue Advocacy in Congressional Elections."

59. Annenberg Public Policy Center, "Issue Advertising in the 1999–2000 Election Cycle," p. 19.

SEVEN   *Interest Groups*
and Financing
the 2000 Elections

ALLAN J. CIGLER

O RGANIZED INTERESTS have long played a role
in American elections; their activities range from simple endorsement of
candidates to mobilizing voters and supplying candidates and campaigns
with money and other necessities. During the past four decades, however,
a spectacular increase in the number and types of organized interests seeking
to influence elections and in the breadth of their involvement has taken
place.[1] Many factors have contributed to this upsurge in activity. Foremost has been the virtual explosion of government lawmaking and government regulatory activity since the early 1960s that has raised the stakes
in politics for both established interests and the many newly created interests. Drawn to the fray have not only been large numbers of occupation-
based groups and corporate interests but also interests that previously
had eschewed involvement in electoral politics, such as nonprofit and tax
exempt organizations and many "cause" and single-issue organizations.
The expansion of organized interest involvement in elections has been
aided by changes in party nomination rules and the campaign finance
laws adopted since the early 1970s, coupled with favorable court decisions, which together have made it far easier for such interests to participate in almost all aspects of electoral politics, from early in the party
nomination process to helping pay for the presidential inauguration.[2]

The common denominator of contemporary federal election politics,
with its premium on high-tech information gathering and timely communication with the electorate, is the ever-increasing need for resources that
must be purchased with cash. As candidates and parties have sought funds,

organized interests have proved quite willing to contribute to candidates who share their public policy perspectives. But in the contemporary era, interest groups are more than mere resources to be tapped by parties and candidates in an ad hoc manner during election years. Some believe that the nation has entered an era characterized by the "permanent campaign," where political fund-raising is continual and there is a blurring of electoral and policymaking activity.[3] In such an environment it is sometimes difficult for observers of interest group and electoral politics to distinguish between organizational lobbying efforts and activity meant to influence elections.[4] In competitive races it is often difficult to distinguish the parties, various interests, and candidate organizations.[5]

For some organized interests, one of the consequences of the permanent campaign is that they must be involved in electoral politics on a continual basis. Groups such as the National Rifle Association, the Christian Coalition, and the AFL-CIO, for example, have emerged as semipermanent, full-service electoral organizations, at times operating on their own without the cooperation or collaboration of either parties or candidates. Several groups operate in a manner not unlike traditional political parties: it is not unusual to see groups recruiting and training candidates to run for public office, serving as advisers to their campaigns in primary as well as general elections (typically in an "unofficial" capacity), and communicating with voters on a candidate's behalf or against his or her opponent. Often the involvement is effectively indistinguishable from that of the candidate's own campaign or that of party electioneering.[6]

The role of organized interests in the 1999–2000 election cycle represented a continuation of the upward spiral of interest group involvement in federal elections. There were several new twists, more in degree than in kind, but important nevertheless. Sometimes a lot more of the same is simply no longer the same. The huge escalation of organized interest money found in our most recent elections continued, much of it raised and spent outside of the Federal Election Campaign Act's (FECA) provisions. A large proportion of group activity was shielded from public view, as more and more groups learned to take advantage of opportunities to influence electoral politics through such devices as soft money contributions to the political parties (covered primarily in chapters 1, 4, and 6) and "issue-advocacy" advertising.[7] A greater contingent of groups than ever before seemed involved earlier in the election cycle than previously, a number playing a key role in the spring 2000 primaries, especially in the Republican Party, rather than waiting until the general election. One study, for example, found that more than a hundred groups, often spending huge sums, were active in issue advocacy efforts during the period leading up to the 2000 mid-March Super Tuesday primaries.[8]

Groups and institutions interested in the direction of public policy viewed the 2000 elections as pivotal. Organized interests ranging from pharmaceutical companies, who feared a Democratic regime that would add prescription drug coverage to Medicare along with price controls, to pro-choice activists, who believed Republican control of both Congress and the presidency would mean an antiabortion Supreme Court ready to overturn *Roe* v. *Wade,* appeared to mobilize far earlier than in previous electoral cycles. Not only was a close presidential contest in the offing but also narrow Republican majorities in the House and Senate going into the election raised hope among Democrats and their allied groups of recapturing one or both houses of Congress, while Republicans and their allies understood the tenuous nature of their congressional majorities. In the end, far more money was raised and spent by candidates and parties for the 2000 elections than any other in the nation's history.

Although the huge increase in party spending attracted much attention in 2000, we should not forget that a large portion of this money came from organized interests or individuals with direct ties to such interests.

Contemporary Groups and Electoral Politics

As political scientist Anthony Corrado has argued, campaign finance in the 2000 elections "bore a greater resemblance to campaign finance prior to the passage of FECA than to the patterns that were supposed to occur after it."[9] This was certainly true for organized interests, which were only modestly constrained by law in terms of their activities for or against those running for federal office.

The FECA and its 1974 amendments established a private system for funding congressional campaigns, limiting individuals, parties, candidates, and interest groups by imposing ceilings on contributions. Provisions creating public funding for presidential elections were also included. At the core of campaign finance law was the need for full disclosure of financial activity as it concerns federal elections. Ideally, meaningful disclosure of the various interests supporting or opposing a candidate and the degree of their financial commitment can be taken as a shorthand indicator of the values and policy orientations of the candidate, potentially enabling voters to make informed choices linking their preferences with those running for public office.

However, the FECA regulations were never fully implemented; in *Buckley* v. *Valeo* the Supreme Court greatly limited the scope of the sweeping reform legislation, creating opportunities for interested individuals and groups to skirt the intention of the law. The Court, concerned about government infringement upon the right of free speech, ruled that the government-imposed contribution and spending ceiling could only apply to expenditures that "in express terms advocate the election or defeat of a clearly identified candidate for federal office."[10] Later in the decision, buried in a footnote, the Court spelled out what has come to be called its "express advocacy" guidelines, noting that any legal limitations on independent spending to influence elections would only apply to communications expressly advocating election or defeat of a candidate, such as "vote for," "elect," "support," "cast your ballot for," "Smith for Congress," "vote against," "defeat," "reject."[11] In practical terms, these so-called magic words have come to mean that any federal election communication with voters that does not use these or similar words is beyond the scope of government regulation; disclosure of donors or amounts expended is not required.

Despite the 1976 court decision, the use of issue advocacy campaigning outside of the confines of FEC regulations is a relatively recent intruder on the electoral scene. Individuals, parties, and groups did not quickly realize and exploit the opening created by the standards outlined in the decision. Groups continued to rely on a variety of FEC-disclosed activities, including hard money contributions to candidates, independent spending, or various internal organizational means to activate the membership to vote for preferred candidates.

The first group to engage in issue advocacy on a truly massive scale was the AFL-CIO and its affiliated unions. Historically, unions had relied on mobilizing their membership through grassroots get-out-the-vote (GOTV) efforts. But in 1996, under the leadership of its new president, John Sweeny, the AFL-CIO changed its political tactics. The group spent roughly $35 million in 1996 in an attempt to reverse the 1994 Democratic loss of Congress. Some of the funds went to train union activists to organize efforts in targeted congressional districts and to increase voter registration, but the bulk went to buy air time for 27,000 television ads in forty congressional districts (an average of nearly 800 spots per district, at a cost of nearly $25 million dollars.[12] In twenty-one of the most competitive districts, the AFL-CIO spent roughly $10 million on advertising during the last few weeks of the campaign.[13] Seeing an opportunity to spend beyond the hard money limits, other groups, including such diverse interests as the Business Roundtable, Americans for Tax Reform, Americans for Limited Terms, and the Sierra Club, engaged in unregulated issue advocacy, although on a smaller scale. By the 1998 elections, issue advocacy campaigning was part of the standard electoral arsenal of a large proportion of the major interest groups active in elections.[14]

Interest group activities in the 2000 elections were limited more by imagination than by constraints of federal law. Both hard money contributions directly to candidates and soft money activities such as issue advertising had their place. Many groups, particularly the larger and better-financed ones, engaged in both kinds of election strategies.

Traceable Hard Money: Interest Group PAC Contributions in 2000

From the early 1970s to the mid-1990s observers of American political life would have been hard-pressed to name a feature of electoral politics that had attracted more negative attention and aroused more suspicion than political action committees (PACs). But the rise in importance of interest group influence through nonregulated or undisclosed avenues in the most recent decade has made PACs seem less "evil" than previously, probably because PAC contributions are typically modest in size and must be open to public scrutiny, at least compared with soft money activity.

The 1971 Federal Election Campaign Act, its amendments enacted in 1974, 1976, 1979, and a number of federal court and FEC rulings, constitute the rules under which registered federal PACs operate. A few PACs did exist before the FECA. The Congress of Industrial Organizations (CIO) is usually credited with creating the first PAC in 1943. This PAC, the Committee on Political Education (COPE), was a way around then-existing campaign finance laws. When the union merged with the American Federation of Labor (AFL) in 1955, it quickly became the largest interest group contributor in elections before the FECA reforms.

With the FECA's legal sanctioning of the PAC concept, PACs became the vehicle of choice for all kinds of organized interests to contribute to candidates and political parties. PACs may raise unlimited money for electoral purposes, but they face spending constraints on direct contributions. Besides disclosing their donors and recipients of their contributions and regularly required reporting of their activities to the FEC, they must also abide by contribution limits to congressional candidates; no more than $5,000 in a primary, $5,000 if a runoff primary is required, and $5,000 for the general election contest. Contributions of up to $5,000 to a candidate in presidential nomination contests are permitted, as is another $5,000 for the presidential nominee in the general election but only if that candidate elects not to accept presidential matching funds. Registered PACs may also contribute up to $15,000 per year to national party committees. However, spending limits do not apply to all PAC behavior. Registered committees may also engage in so-called independent expenditures, financially unlimited efforts on behalf of or against a candidate as long as such efforts are not coordinated in any way with the preferred candidate or their representatives. Such campaigning falls under the category of "express advocacy."

Growth in the number of registered PACs took place quickly after the enactment of the FECA. In 1974, 608 PACs registered with the FEC—a decade later there were more than 4,000. The greatest growth took place among corporate PACs, which went from under 100 in 1974 to nearly 1,700 a decade later. The number of registered PACs has leveled off since the mid-1980s, with each election cycle having roughly between 4,000 and 4,500 committees reporting donor contributions or distributing funds.[15] In the 1999–2000 election cycle, 4,499 registered PACs were on the FEC books for at least part of the cycle.[16]

But the growth in PAC contributions has not leveled off. The growth of aggregate PAC contributions during the past two decades is presented in figure 7-1. In the 2000 election cycle PACs made $259.8 million in direct contributions, a 19 percent increase over the previous presidential year election, and a 17 percent increase over contributions in the 1997–98 cycle (after controlling for inflation, the increase was 9 percent from 1996 and 12 percent from 1998). This is a large increase to be sure, but it pales when compared with the rates of increase of soft money contributions to the parties and the amounts spent by issue advocacy campaign efforts.

Overall, it seems safe to say that the PAC funding universe reflects an overall business bias (not necessarily a partisan bias) in the system. The category of organized interests that contributed the most to candidates in 2000 was corporate PACs, with more than $91.5 million in contributions, followed by trade association PACs that contributed nearly $72 million. Labor PACs were next with nearly $51.6 million, followed by

Figure 7-1. *PAC Candidate Contributions, 1979–80 to 1999–2000*

Total in millions

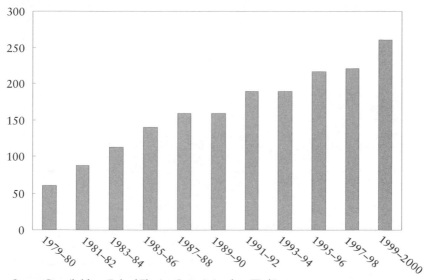

Source: Compiled from Federal Election Commission data, Washington.

nonconnected PACs, typically issue or ideologically oriented organizations set up solely to influence elections, which contributed more than $37 million. PACs representing corporations without stock registered nearly $5.3 million in contributions, and PACs representing cooperatives contributed nearly $2.4 million. Not all registered PACs were active during the cycle; only 3,064 out of the nearly 4,500 PACs contributed to at least one candidate for federal office; 1,365 of these were registered corporate PACs.

The pattern of PAC contributions to Republican and Democratic candidates in 1999–2000 largely mirrored that of the previous two election cycles, when Republican control of Congress after the 1994 election started to translate into major contribution gains to the party's candidates, especially incumbents. PAC contributions to candidates and parties in the 1999–2000 election cycle are presented in table 7-1. For both parties, PAC giving remained incumbent oriented in the House and Senate. Republican senatorial candidates retained a relatively large advantage over Democrats in Senate races, while PAC congressional contributions were roughly equal between Republicans and Democrats. Overall, contributions to House races

Table 7-1. *Political Action Committee (PAC) Contributions to Candidates and Parties, 1999–2000 Election Cycle*
Millions of dollars

Item	Democratic	Republican	Total
Senate candidates	18.7	33.2	51.9
Incumbents	9.5	24	33.5
Challengers	5.2	1.9	7.1
Open seat	4	7.3	11.3
House candidates	98.1	94.7	192.8
Incumbents	76	74.1	150.1
Challengers	12.9	7	18.9
Open seat	9.2	13.6	22.8
Presidential candidates	0	2	2
Political parties	30.7	28.9	59.6

Source: Federal Election Commission data, Washington, May 2001.

rose the most compared with the previous election cycle, a substantial 21 percent; Senate contributions rose only 6 percent.

As table 7-1 indicates, presidential candidates receive little if any PAC money. During the nomination season, federal matching funds are not available for PAC contributions, and campaign organizations spend their fund-raising time pursuing individual donations. Presidential candidates would have to forgo federal funding during the general election if they accepted PAC funds, clearly an unlikely possibility.

The pro-incumbent bias among PACs remains one of the constants among PAC givers, but even here there are major distinctions depending on the type of PAC. As has been the case in the past, corporate PACs are the most incumbent-oriented giving category, with nearly 88 percent of contributions going to individuals already holding office, and a little less than 4 percent to challengers: open-seat candidates received the remaining 8 percent of contributions. Association/trade PACs behaved similarly, with more than 83 percent of their contributions going to incumbents and only 6 percent targeted for challengers. Labor PACs continued to demonstrate a willingness to invest in nonincumbents; more than 18 percent of labor contributions were given to challengers, while 12 percent targeted candidates contesting open seats. The nonconnected PACs were the ones most likely to fund challengers (21 percent) or to invest in open-seat races (23 percent).

As has been true since the 1970s, PAC giving remained highly concentrated among a relatively small number of PACs, though some emerging patterns are evident. In the 1999–2000 election cycle, less than 1 percent of registered PACs contributed nearly 24 percent of all the money given to candidates. Of the thirty-seven PACs that made contributions of more than $1 million dollars each, only four were corporate PACs, while fifteen were connected to associations or trade groups; seventeen labor groups each contributed more than $1 million in the most recent cycle. Given the great growth of soft money contributions to political parties in the last election, especially contributions from large corporations or individuals connected to such institutions, it seems that business contributions to political parties are given increasingly in the form of soft money.[17] In the case of corporations, contributions come directly from company treasuries, rather than through more scrutinized political action committees. The number of PACs contributing huge sums of money through the regulated process is relatively small. Overall, the 222 PACs that each contributed $250,000 or more in the 1999–2000 election cycle represented just under 5 percent of all of the participating PACs but accounted for 59 percent of all direct PAC contributions. Nonconnected PACs, which are so important to congressional challengers and open-seat candidates, tended to be less active; more than 50 percent made no contributions in the recent election cycle, and less than 2 percent of such PACs contributed $250,000 or more. Unlike union, industrial, or association PACs, which typically fund their PAC overhead from other organizational funds, nonconnected PACs must fund their total operation from their PAC receipts, leaving far less money that can be given directly to candidates.

The top twenty PAC contributors to candidates in the 1999–2000 election cycle are presented in table 7-2. Groups at the top of the list are familiar to those that have followed PAC giving historically. The Realtors Political Action Committee, typically at the top of the list, was the leading giver again, contributing more than $3.4 million to candidates, mostly Republican incumbents. The second ranking group, the Association of Trial Lawyers of America Political Action Committee, emerged during the Clinton years as a major Democratically aligned PAC, with levels of partisan PAC giving approximating that of organized labor. Both blue-collar and white-collar union PACs are well represented among the leading contributors to Democratic campaigns.

For some PACs, looking at contributions may greatly understate their role in electoral politics. Besides being sources for hard money contributions, PACs can make "in-kind" contributions in a variety of forms such as sharing poll results or letting candidates use their phone bank facilities

Table 7-2. *Top Twenty PAC Contributors to Candidates,*
1999–2000 Election Cycle

Rank	Name	Contribution to candidates (thousands of dollars)
1	Realtors Political Action Committee	3,423
2	Association of Trial Lawyers of America Political Action Committee	2,656
3	American Federation of State County & Municipal Employees—P E O P L E, Qualified	2,590
4	Dealers Election Action Committee of the National Automobile Dealers Association (NADA)	2,498
5	Democrat Republican Independent Voter Education	2,455
6	International Brotherhood of Electrical Workers Committee on Political Education	2,181
7	Machinists Non-Partisan Political League	2,181
8	UAW-V-CAP (UAW Voluntary Community Action Program)	2,155
9	American Medical Association Political Action Committee	1,942
10	Service Employees International Union Political Action Committee	1,887
11	National Beer Wholesalers' Association Political Action Committee (NBWA PAC)	1,871
12	Build Political Action Committee of the National Association of Home Builders	1,822
13	Laborers' Political League-Laborers' International Union of NA	1,792
14	United Parcel Service Inc. Political Action Committee	1,755
15	United Food & Commercial Workers, Active Ballot Club	1,734
16	NEA Fund for Children and Public Education (FKA NEAPAC)	1,716
17	Carpenters Legislative Improvement Committee, United Brotherhood of Carpenters & Joiners of AME	1,714
18	NRA Political Victory Fund	1,583
19	American Federation of Teachers Committee on Political Education	1,580
20	Committee on Letter Carriers Political Education (Letter Carriers Political Action Fund)	1,530

Source: FEC data, Washington, June 2001.

at far below what it is likely to cost on the open market. The FEC also
requires PACs to report their receipts and disbursements for each electoral cycle, and sometimes PAC disbursements are a better indicator of
their electoral activity than contributions. For example, consider the role

of EMILY's List ("Early Money Is Like Yeast—It Makes Dough Rise"), a PAC founded in 1985 to fund prochoice Democratic women candidates. Although the group was not officially among the top direct contributors to federal candidates in the last election cycle, it spent more than $14.7 million in federally disclosed expenditures, the second largest amount of any PAC. The group has made its reputation for its skill at "bundling," collecting individual contributions made out to specific candidates and presenting them directly to those candidates. For FEC compliance purposes, these contributions are considered individual donations, not EMILY's List contributions.

The National Rifle Association Victory PAC ranked eighteenth among contributions to candidates in 2000, contributing $1.6 million, but the group ranked first in terms of disbursements, which totaled more than $16.8 million. The NRA's PAC relies a lot on in-kind contributions to candidates, such as sponsoring fund-raising and meet-and-greet events for candidates, as well as helping with candidates' research needs. As discussed shortly, the NRA also relies heavily on independent expenditures to help candidates it supports or those it opposes, spending more than four times as much on such expenditures compared with direct campaign contributions in the 1999–2000 election cycle.

Even though PAC contributions seemed not to garner as much attention in 2000 as in previous elections, it would be wrong to dismiss their importance. Hard money is especially important to candidates early in a political cycle, and it still represents a core financial component of a congressional campaign war chest. In the 1999–2000 election cycle, PAC contributions continued to be important for House incumbents of both parties and, one could argue, a major hurdle for challengers to overcome. Forty-four percent of Democratic congressional campaign receipts came from PACs, and Republican House members received 39 percent of their funds from such sources. PAC contributions were less important to senatorial incumbents; Democrats and Republicans had PAC receipts that represented 21 and 27 percent of their budgets respectively.

Political parties benefit from PAC contributions as well. Democratic Party committees received nearly $30.7 million from PACs in the last election cycle, 11 percent of their total receipts; Republicans received more than $28.9 million, or 6 percent of their total receipts. In the 1995–96 presidential election cycle, Democrats received 9 percent of their funds from PACs, while Republicans received only 3 percent.

Traceable Hard Money—Independent Expenditures and Internal Communications

As a consequence of the *Buckley* v. *Valeo* case, both individuals and groups were permitted to spend unlimited sums of money expressly advocating the election or defeat of a candidate as long as such efforts were made without consultation or coordination with a candidate or a representing agent. By the late 1970s and early 1980s several independent PACs, the National Conservative Political Action Committee (NCPAC) being the most prominent, became notorious for spending huge sums on independent advertising against a number of senators, some of whom were defeated in close votes. In 1982 NCPAC was the leading fund-raiser among all PACs and spent more than $3 million in independent expenditures against six incumbent liberal senators.[18] Besides greatly irritating the targeted candidate, the typical negative focus of these early independent spending efforts received strident criticism from the media and even from the candidates who were the supposed benefactors of the advertising. Favored candidates worried whether or not the electorate would be confused about the sources of such ads, and that they might be blamed for the negative campaigning. In recent years, independent advertising has lost its appeal for groups because financial donors have to be reported to the FEC. Issue advocacy advertising, in particular, can accomplish virtually the same goal of supporting or opposing a candidate, without making group contributors visible and associated with negative advertising.

According to FEC records, 125 PACs combined made a little more than $21 million in independent expenditures in the 1999–2000 election cycle. Those making independent expenditures classify whether their spending was for or against a candidate. Surprisingly, given conventional wisdom, roughly three-fourths of expenditures argued "for" rather than "against" a candidate. This was particularly true in the presidential race, where PACs spent more than $5.7 million in favor of a candidate, while spending only $416,000 against candidates. Independent spending in congressional races was similarly unbalanced. In Senate races $4.5 million represented positive spending in favor of candidates, while $2.3 million represented spending against candidates; House contestants were the recipients of $6.1 million in positive PAC independent spending, while $1.6 million was spent against individuals seeking a congressional seat.

Despite the relatively small amounts of independent expenditures, such expenditures still represent a major component of PAC strategy for some groups, especially ideologically oriented groups. Two PACs stood out in 2000 for their reliance on such spending. The League of Conservation Voters (LCV) spent $2.1 million on such expenditures, typically through direct mail. The amount represented virtually the total of all of its disbursements reported to the FEC. The NRA Political Victory Fund reported nearly $6.5 million in independent expenditures during the 1999–2000 election cycle, as the group took an aggressive stance for and against candidates.

Political action committees also have to report any money spent on internal communications advocating the defeat or endorsement of any candidate, providing communication costs are more than $2,000 per election. But there is a very large loophole. If the primary reason for the communication was not the election endorsement, no reporting is necessary. In 2000 a reported $17.9 million was spent on internal communications.[19] No doubt this type of reported spending is likely understated because of the loophole. Examples of groups who use internal communications include organized labor, the teachers' unions, business associations, and the NRA.

Although the total amount of independent expenditures and internal communication costs are dwarfed by other forms of group expenditures, they can still be crucial in certain situations. For example, Magleby and associates, studying seventeen of the most competitive congressional races and senatorial races in 2000, found that nearly 40 percent of all independent and internal communications expenditures reported to the FEC occurred in these intense electoral contests. In the Virginia Senate race between Democrat Charles Robb and Republican George Allen, an estimated $2.2 million in such expenditures was recorded. In the hotly contested Michigan Senate race between Republican Spencer Abraham and Democratic challenger Deborah Stabenow, more than $1 million was spent on independent and internal communications for and against the candidates.[20]

Interest-Group Issue Advocacy Activity in 2000

Large numbers of opportunistic interests engaged in issue advocacy campaigning throughout the 2000 election season in what some observers believed were unabashed attempts to argue for their favored candidate or to denigrate those they opposed, despite not using the magic words of express advocacy. Activities were directed at congressional candidates and the presidential contenders. One of the more vivid and highly criticized examples were the ads sponsored by the NAACP National Voter Fund, a tax-exempt 501 (C)(4) organization, whose donor identities are not public information. During the last week of October, a few days before the election, the group ran two ads, which criticized Republican presidential candidate George W. Bush for his veto of a hate crimes bill while he served as governor of Texas.

> *Video*: A chain being dragged from the back of a pickup truck with a Texas license plate.
>
> *Audio*: I'm Renee Mullins, James Byrd's daughter. On June 7, 1998, in Texas, my father was killed. He was beaten, chained, and then dragged three miles to his death, all because he was black. So when Governor George Bush refused to support hate crimes legislation, it was like my father was killed all over again. Call George W. Bush and tell him to support hate crimes legislation. We won't be dragged away from our future.

Not all election issue ads are so negative. Indeed, some were quite positive, so-called thank you ads. One such group that preferred positive issue ads was the 750,000-member National Association of Realtors. In a California congressional race, the group named Democratic congressman Cal Dooley "a leader in helping Americans buy their very first home," going on to ask viewers to call his office and thank him "for his hard work."[21] Neither the negative NAACP nor the positive National Association of Realtors' ads are seen as "express advocacy."

It is extremely difficult to put a precise figure on the amount of money invested on issue advocacy campaigns, but estimates can be made. All indications are that, compared with hard money expenditures, issue advocacy campaigning by groups is growing at a far faster rate. Particular attention has focused on radio and television broadcast advertising, where it is possible to put a dollar figure on the activity. It has been estimated by the Annenberg Public Policy Center researchers, who track issue advertisements during election cycles, that political parties and interest groups combined spent roughly $135 million to $150 million on broadcast issue advocacy advertising in the mass media in the 1996 election. In the 2000 election cycle, it was estimated that parties and groups spent $509 million on broadcast issue advertising, more than three times the amount spent in the previous presidential year.[22]

Although the biggest gain in expenditures may have been by political parties, interest group expenditures increased substantially too. The Brennan Center, which tracks both interest group radio and television ads in seventy-five of the nation's largest media markets, covering only a small portion of Senate and House races, found that interest groups spent $57 million on issue advocacy ads to influence their monitored races in 2000. While this figure represented roughly 10 percent of all candidate-centered advertising that was uncovered, the percentage of group spending was much higher in competitive Senate and House races.[23] In the research conducted by David Magleby and associates focusing on five competitive U.S. Senate and twelve House races in 2000, the researchers estimated that interest groups spent $20 million out of the $95 million spent on radio and television ads in the sample races.[24]

Issue advocacy campaigning through radio and television is only one form of issue advocacy, however, and often not the most preferred influence tactic even if it gets the most media attention. The 2000 election saw an escalation as well in the so-called ground war campaign conducted by organized interests, as a number of groups invested in heavily targeted GOTV (get-out-the-vote) efforts, direct mail, and telephone banks. If such efforts avoid express advocacy and are not coordinated with either political party or candidate campaigns, they remain undisclosed and outside the confines of federal regulations.

Some groups, however, find it in their public relations interest to take credit for their extensive efforts and publicize their activities while others behave in a clandestine manner. For example, in February 1999 the AFL-CIO announced that for the first time it had made a decision to keep its political operatives in the field on an ongoing basis and to concentrate on its field operations; roughly three-quarters of the $46 million that was to be allocated to helping Democrats win back the House was to be spent on GOTV and direct mail voter education efforts, with the balance used for mass media campaigns, a reversal of the organization's 1996 proportional allocations. The aim was to be in personal contact with workers and their families through workplace contacts, home visits, phone calls, and direct mail. Labor had not been happy with the results of its television and radio investments in 1996 and began to gravitate back toward its traditional grassroots activity by 1998. Labor leaders had formed the impression that union ads were not cost effective because they were just as effective in activating opponents as they were in getting union supporters to the polls.[25]

After the 2000 election, the AFL-CIO claimed it had made a significant contribution to the Democratic effort by registering 2.3 million new union household members, had made 8 million phone calls to union households, distributed more than 14 million leaflets at union worksites, and e-mailed some 60,000 e-vote cards urging people to vote.[26] Union GOTV efforts on Election Day were crucial in swing states such as Michigan and Pennsylvania. Republican Governor John Engler, attempting to explain the Gore victory in Michigan, pointed to the fact that the United Auto Workers had negotiated a paid holiday for Election Day in their contract, calling it "the largest-soft-money contribution in history."[27]

The NAACP, using its National Voter Fund as a vehicle, organized a massive GOTV drive in forty targeted congressional districts and several key swing states like Michigan, Ohio, and Pennsylvania. An estimated $9 million was spent in an effort to boost African-American turnout.[28] The primary effort focused on registering voters at public facilities such as supermarkets, shopping centers, transit centers, and especially churches. In some areas the effort went far beyond normal registration activity. In Philadelphia, where African-American turnout was viewed as essential for Gore to carry the state, an extra effort was made to reach out to voters "through phone banks, direct mail, community forums, a motorcade, and extensive use of well-known African-American performers and radio personalities."[29] The NAACP coordinated efforts with the American Federation of Teachers (AFT) to reach out to young voters in Philadelphia, arranging to speak at high school assemblies and compiling lists of students eligible to vote.

The number of groups involved in substantial issue advocacy campaigns, especially those relying on GOTV efforts, is difficult to pinpoint. Some groups were active only in one congressional district, while others were involved throughout the country in both the congressional and presidential contests. Magleby and associates were able to identify 211 interest groups that communicated in some way with the electorate in the seventeen races they monitored, 159 of which "made extensive use of telephone contacts and targeted direct mail."[30]

During the 2000 election season a number of other groups stood out because of the breadth of their involvement and the extensiveness of their financial investment.[31] Some had been involved in issue advocacy advertising for at least the previous two election cycles, such as League of Conservation Voters, the Business Roundtable, Planned Parenthood, and the Sierra Club. Some, such as EMILY's List and the NAACP National Voter

Fund, were involved for the first time. Others, like Christian Right organizations, seemed less involved than previously on a broad basis but were still a major force in selected races, such as the South Carolina Republican presidential primary.[32]

The National Rifle Association (NRA) was one of the more broadly active interests in the 2000 election. The NRA focused on a number of high-profile Senate races, such as those in Michigan and Virginia, running negative ads against the Democratic contenders.[33] The presidential contest was important to the group as well. The group's president, Charlton Heston, upon his re-election to a second term, proclaimed, "I intend to dedicate my remaining time as president to ensure that the Second Amendment is safe from Al Gore and all those who threaten it."[34] He and the group did everything they could to deliver on such a promise. One of the group's more intriguing strategies was to run "infomercials" in the fall of 2000 encouraging sportsmen to join the organization and register to vote. Gun owners were told the necessity of avoiding what had happened in Canada, where the government was portrayed as aggressively discouraging weapons ownership. The ads usually appeared during the weekend on various sportsman channels on cable television. Without endorsing Bush with any magic words, the ads did strongly imply that the NRA believed Democratic candidate Al Gore was a threat to law abiding gun owners.

Sometimes interest groups advertised to counteract another group. Although underfunded compared with the NRA, Handgun Control, the liberal antigun lobby, ran issue ads reflecting its hostility toward both the Republican presidential candidate and the NRA. One ad attacked Bush's progun voting record in Texas, showing footage of an NRA representative claiming that with Bush in the White House the NRA "would work out of their office."[35] The NRA's and Bush's support for "concealed carry" drew the special wrath of Handgun Control in an ad which ended with the narrator saying, "Say no to the gun lobby. Tell George Bush handguns don't belong in our nursing homes and churches."[36] Opposition to "concealed carry" drew Handgun Control to a number of Senate and House races such as in Virginia, where the group spent an estimated $165,000 in an effort to defeat Republican George Allen.[37]

The example groups discussed so far, such as the NRA and the AFL-CIO, all have well-known issue positions and have been long-time players in electoral politics, consistently aligned with one of the two major parties. Their names alone are public indicators of the interests they represent, and their issue advocacy efforts typically parallel those of the parties and reinforce candidate themes during the campaign, but not all issue advocacy campaigning is done by such easily identifiable groups.

527 Committees: The "Stealth PACs"

In 2000 the largest practitioner of issue advocacy advertising was not well known to the public or even to politicians and close political observers among the press. The biggest spender was an organization named Citizens for Better Medicare (CBM), whose outlays during the election have been estimated as between $40 and $65 million.[38] As an outlay of funds, this would represent a figure equivalent to more than 20 percent of all the soft money funds contributed to either the Democratic or the Republican parties at the national level during the 1999–2000 electoral cycle! During the period from January 1, 1999, and August 31, 2000, the organization spent an estimated $34 million on issue ads alone, topped only by the Democratic National Committee ($35 million) and the Republican National Committee ($51 million) among issue advertisers.[39] The organization's activities helped make the health care arena the single most dominant focus of issue ads in 2000, representing nearly a quarter of all issue ads aired during this period.[40]

Despite the name, which most voters would probably associate with a senior citizens' advocacy group pushing for prescription drug coverage under Medicare, CBM produced issue ads that were unalterably opposed to the highly publicized Democratic plan to expand Medicare coverage. The organization preferred the Republican alternative, which called for government reimbursement to private insurance firms to increase drug coverage.

The organization ran negative issue ads nationally, typically against Democratic incumbents in close races who had embraced Clinton's plan to expand Medicare coverage, or sponsored positive issue ads in support of Republicans who had taken the lead against the plan. But some Democratic challengers drew extra attention, including Brian Schweitzer, a Senate candidate from Montana. Schweitzer, a political newcomer on a virtual crusade against big drug companies, had gotten national media attention early in 2000 for organizing senior citizen bus trips to Canada to purchase drugs manufactured in the United States. Such drugs are less expensive across the border. Citizens for Better Medicare ran attack ads throughout the state accusing Schweitzer of wanting "Canadian-style government controls on medications here in America." Schweitzer was forced to start his television advertising much earlier than planned to answer the charges.[41] Interestingly, Republican incumbent Conrad Burns opposed CBM's activity in the state, feeling that the ads altered his preferred campaign agenda by focusing too much attention on the prescription drug issue.[42]

Who exactly were the individuals or institutions behind CBM and what interests did they represent? Early in the election cycle, it was hard to tell. It was later revealed that CBM claimed to represent a coalition created in 1999 by the Pharmaceutical Research and Manufacturing Association of America (PhRMA), a drug industry trade group, and the Healthcare Leadership Council, which speaks for fifty drug companies, hospitals, and healthcare providers. But no information was ever revealed during the election concerning the group's financial support.[43]

Citizens for Better Medicare considered itself a 527 committee under the Federal Tax Code, thanks to provisions incorporated in 1974 that enabled political groups to benefit from certain tax advantages without any public disclosure. Section 527 organizations need not report to the FEC, nor is there any approval process necessary for IRS certification. Essentially, such groups merely claim they meet the provision of section 527.[44] As long as any such group refrained from express advocacy or any hard money activity, while still claiming to be a political organization that exists to influence federal elections, it is exempt from federal taxation. One further stipulation is that the funds they collect from donors must be in noninterest-bearing accounts.

In a real sense, 527 committees even receive a public subsidy for their activities to influence elections, a big advantage over other forms of political organization. Donors to other forms of nonprofit organizations that may engage in certain political activity such as social welfare groups, which typically register with the IRS as 501 (C)(4) organizations, face a steep federal gift tax if their donations exceed $10,000. In contrast, 527 donors may contribute unlimited amounts to the committee without triggering the tax.

In short, 527 committees were unregulated political organizations whose donors were undisclosed and unlimited in the amounts they could contribute. As long as they refrain from express advocacy, such committees can also spend unlimited amounts to influence elections, earning them the title "Stealth PACs."[45]

The advantages of 527 committees were not widely known before the mid-1990s. Before then, only a few groups tested the waters to take advantage of section 527 to form election issue advocacy groups.[46] But by the 1999–2000 election cycle the advantages of a 527 committee had become attractive to interests across the political spectrum. The Sierra Club organized a 527 committee in anticipation of the 2000 elections, as did the NAACP, which created Americans for Equality as an organization separate from the National Voter Fund.[47]

Although it had materially little effect on 527 committee issue advocacy efforts in the 2000 elections, a law was signed in July 2000 that requires any group that organizes as a 527 committee to register with the IRS within one day. Any donations over $200 received after July 1, 2000, had to be disclosed as well as expenditures over $500, providing the group had intentions of spending more than $25,000. Election advocacy efforts by CBM were not affected. The organization simply stopped receiving contributions after the law was passed and later formally registered with the IRS as a 501 (C)(4) social welfare organization, a classification where donors are still not identified publicly.[48]

Until the next election cycle, we will not know whether or not 527 committees will cease to be major vehicles for groups engaging in issue advocacy campaigning. Groups will have to decide whether or not disclosure is offset by such favorable tax rules. Wealthy individuals seeking to influence elections may simply choose to engage in issue advocacy campaigning as individuals instead of through groups.

Conclusion

To the observer of American elections, there was little genuinely new or innovative in the behavior of groups active in the 2000 campaign. Many of the patterns that emerged during the 1996 election continued unabated, most notably the increasing tendency for groups of all kinds to engage in electoral activity outside the confines of federal election law. Although regulated group hard money activity did increase, it was clearly overshadowed by the huge escalation of group fund-raising and campaign spending not regulated by the FEC and shielded from public scrutiny. More and more groups learned that contemporary electoral politics is more about soft money contributions to the parties and the strategic use of issue advocacy campaigning in support of or against a candidate, than about merely contributing to the candidate of their choice. With its focus only on hard money activity, "The FEC, as currently interpreted and enforced, could no longer restrain most of the financial activity that takes place in modern elections."[49]

Not surprisingly, such an environment calls for reform. Talk about campaign finance reform abounded during and after the election. Senator John McCain made campaign finance the centerpiece of his quest for the Republican presidential nomination during the spring of 2000, and eventual party nominees Democrat Al Gore and Republican George Bush each articulated positions on how to reform the current system, though their proposals had little in common. At this writing, the new congress is considering several campaign finance bills that would affect group activity during elections. The most extreme legislation would totally ban national party soft money fund-raising and spending and would greatly curtail broadcast issue advocacy close to Election Day. These provisions would also include timely disclosure of the groups engaged in electioneering communication and their donors.

Still, one must be pessimistic about the possibility of sweeping campaign finance reform. Despite public cynicism about money and politics, there seems to be no groundswell among the public to pressure legislators into taking action. The legislators themselves, while irritated at the need for continual fund-raising and fearful of the loss of control over campaign agendas when confronted with opposition by group issue advocacy during the race, understand that overall they are benefactors of the current system and are risk averse as a consequence. Their public pronouncements and their behavior in Congress on the campaign finance issue may be at odds. Groups at both ends of the political spectrum, from the National Rifle Association to the AFL-CIO, are leery of changing the current system of largely unrestricted issue advocacy, which they see as essential to their ability to influence the course of public policy. And both national parties and their relevant committees have learned to adapt nicely to the new campaign finance environment; they have relished their recent importance in campaigns. The organized interests, such as Common Cause, arguing on behalf of genuine campaign finance reform, are greatly outnumbered.

The federal courts perhaps loom as the biggest barrier to sweeping change. The courts have proved vigilant in protecting political expression in the context of elections. Legislative efforts to single out and restrict broadcast issue advertising within a month or two of an election, for example, are unlikely to be viewed favorably by the judiciary. Vague guidelines defining "electioneering communication" and what constitutes a "targeted electioneering issue ad," with determination left to an FEC that has proved unwilling to aggressively enforce existing law, is sure to draw the ire of the courts.

The prospects for improvements in disclosure are somewhat better. For example, nonprofit organizations, such as 501 (C) (4)s, currently enjoy special protection under the law, with their donors not being identified as long as they refrain from "express" advocacy. Treating nonprofits in the same manner as 527 committees, which now must identify donors and amounts of group expenses involved in electioneering activity, does not seem unreasonable.

But none of the reforms likely to be adopted and able to pass court scrutiny will address the fundamental problem of the disproportional impact of organized interests with resources upon the electoral system, a problem that in some form has been part of American electoral politics since the nation's founding. Particularly bothersome in the current era is the relationship between political parties and organized interests as parties have evolved to be largely fund-raising conduits and service vendors to candidates. An electoral system based largely on the ability of parties and their candidates to raise financial resources from special interests inevitably clashes with the notion that parties are aggregators of broad interests, potential counterweights to the excessive demands of special interests. The blurring of lines among candidate, party, and organized interest activity in elections is not just confusing to the electorate but raises real questions about political accountability and the nature of representation.

It seems unlikely that the role of groups in upcoming elections will be all that different than was the case in the 2000 elections. Even if modest reforms take place, we should recognize that organized interests have proved creative in adapting to periodic efforts to change the campaign finance laws. Restrictions in broadcast issue advocacy, if adopted and able to pass court scrutiny, are likely to only encourage stepped-up activity in other forms of electioneering communication, for example. Banning organized interest soft money contributions to parties probably would have the effect of merely channeling such funds into more group and issue advocacy activity. Owing to innovations, the impact of unregulated interest group fund-raising and expenditures in elections is likely to grow.

Notes

1. Allan J. Cigler and Burdett A. Loomis, "From Big Bird to Bill Gates: Organized Interests and the Emergence of Hyperpolitics," in Allan J. Cigler and Burdett A. Loomis, eds., *Interest Group Politics*, 5th ed. (Washington: Congressional Quarterly, 1998), pp. 389–403.

2. See Mark J. Rozell and Clyde Wilcox, *Interest Groups in American Campaigns: The New Face of Electioneering* (Washington: Congressional Quarterly, 1999).

3. The term "permanent campaign" was first used by Sidney Blumenthal in *The Permanent Campaign* (Simon and Schuster, 1982).

4. Norman Ornstein and Thomas Mann, eds., *The Permanent Campaign and Its Future* (American Enterpise Institute for Public Policy Research and Brookings, 2000).

5. Allan J. Cigler, "Political Parties and Interest Groups: Competitors, Collaborators, and Uneasy Allies," in Eric Uslaner, ed., *American Political Parties: A Reader* (Itasca, Ill.: F. E. Peacock, 1995), pp. 407–33.

6. The Christian Right is often cited as an example. See James L. Guth and others, "Thunder on the Right? Religious Interest Group Mobilization in the 1996 Election," in Cigler and Loomis, *Interest Group Politics,* pp. 169–92.

7. The growth of soft money was especially prominent in the 1999–2000 election cycle, as both parties raised record amounts, primarily from corporations, individuals, and unions. The Democratic national party committees raised $245.2 million, an increase of 98 percent from the 1995–96 cycle; Republicans raised $249.9 million, up 81 percent from the last presidential election. See www.fec.gov/press/051501partyfund.htm1 (June 1, 2001).

8. David B. Magleby, ed., *Getting Inside the Outside Campaign* (Brigham Young University, Center for the Study of Elections and Democracy, 2000).

9. Anthony Corrado, "Financing the 2000 Elections," in Gerald M. Pomper, ed., *The Election of 2000* (Chatham House Publishers, 2001), p. 95.

10. 424 U.S. 1[1976], 44.

11. 424 U.S. 1 [1976], note 52.

12. Paul Herrnson, *Congressional Elections: Campaigning at Home and in Washington* (Washington: Congressional Quarterly, 1997), pp. 123–24.

13. Anthony Corrado, "Financing the 1996 Election," in Gerald Pomper, ed., *The Election of 1996* (Chatham House Publishers, 1997), pp. 162–63

14. David B. Magleby, *Outside Money: Soft Money and Issue Advocacy in the 1998 Congressional Elections* (Rowman and Littlefield, 2000).

15. M. Margaret Conway and Joanne Connor Green, "Political Action Committees and Campaign Finance," in Cigler and Loomis, *Interest Group Politics,* p. 194.

16. www.fec.gov/press/053101pacfund/tables/pacsum00.htm (June 2, 2001). All the 2000 data on PACs to be presented come from various FEC reports made available during May and early June 2001, representing final information for the 1999–2000 cycle. For detailed reports see the summary FEC website at www.fec.gov/press.

17. Corporate soft money contributions are especially important to the Republican Party, with eight of the top ten donors to the party being individual corporations, led by AT & T, which contributed more than $2.4 million. In contrast, seven of the top ten soft money donors to the Democratic Party were unions. See Center for Responsive Politics, "Top Soft Money Donors: 2000 Election Cycle" (www.opensecrets.org/parties/asp/softtop.asp?txtCycle=2000&txtSort=amnt [June 10, 2001]).

18. In 1982 NCPAC apparently even considered becoming a political party. It not only contributed to candidates who agreed with its political agenda but also ran negative campaigns against candidates from both political parties. See Larry Sabato, *PAC Power* (Norton, 1985), pp. 97, 101–04.

19. Data from Bob Biersack compiled from FEC data. David B. Magleby, "Election Advocacy: Soft Money and Issue Advocacy in the 2000 Elections," in David B. Magleby, ed., *Election Advocacy: Soft Money and Issue Advocacy in the 2000 Congressional Elections* (Brigham Young University, Center for the Study of Elections and Democracy, 2000), p. 39.

20. Ibid., pp. 40, 41.

21. From the University of Pennsylvania, Annenberg Public Policy Center ad collection (www.appcpenn.org/issueads/NAR.htm [March 21, 2001]).

22. www.appcpenn.org/issueads/estimate.htm (June 3, 2001). Estimates probably understate expenditures since not all ads are picked up by the researchers, and many groups simply do not reveal spending totals.

23. "2000 Presidential Races First in Modern History Where Political Parties Spent More on TV Ads Than Candidates " (www.brennencenter.org/presscenter/pressrelease_2000_1211cmag.htm1 [March 23, 2001]).

24. Magleby, *Election Advocacy,* p. 2.

25. Frank Swoboda, "AFL-CIO Plots a Push for Democratic House," *Washington Post,* February 18, 1999, p. A1.

26. www.aflcio.org/labor/2000/election.htm (May 21, 2001).

27. Joseph Serwack, "Day Off Helps UAW Flex Muscle; Union Turnout Boost Democrats," *Crains's Detroit Business,* November 13, 2000, p. 1.

28. Robert Dreyfuss, "Rousing the Democratic Base," *American Prospect,* vol. 11 (November 6, 2000), pp. 20–23.

29. Ibid., p. 22.

30. Magleby, *Election Advocacy,* p. 46

31. Ibid., p. 27–28.

32. Targeted direct mail efforts by a range of interest groups were especially prominent in many competitive electoral contests in 2000. See, for example, the case studies in Magleby, *Election Advocacy,* especially Craig Wilson, "The 2000 Montana at Large Congressional District Race," pp. 206–16; Craig Wilson, "The 2000 Montana Senate Race," pp. 92–105; and Todd Donovan and Charles Morrow, "The 2000 Washington Second Congressional District Race," pp. 261–76.

33. See Michael W. Traugott, "The 2000 Michigan Senate Race," in Magleby, *Election Advocacy,* pp. 62–74; and Bob Dudley and others, "The 2000 Virginia Senate Race," *Election Advocacy,* pp. 106–20.

34. www.appcpenn.org/issueads/national%20rifle%association.htm (March 20, 2001).

35. www.appcpenn.org/issueads/handgun%20control.htm (March 20, 2001).

36. Ibid.

37. Dudley, "The 2000 Virginia Senate Race," in Magleby, *Election Advocacy,* p. 117.

38. Estimates vary because CBM did not release expenditure data. The conservative estimate comes from John Mintz and Susan Schmidt, "Stealth PACs

Report Campaign Financing; First Data Available under New Reform Law." *Washington Post,* November 1, 2000, p. A17. The high estimate comes from Magleby, *Election Advocacy,* p. 28.

39. Erika Falk, "Issue Advocacy Advertising through the Presidential Primary 1999–2000 Election Cycle," September 20, 2000, press release www.appcpenn.org/issuead/forjs/2000issuead.htm (March 20, 2001), pp. 11–12.

40. Together nine health care groups, including CBM, spent more than $86 million on the issue of health care during the primary season, 24 percent of the total spent on issue advocacy advertising. Spending on environment issues was next with 15 percent of the total. Ibid., p. 9.

41. Wilson, "The 2000 Missouri Senate Race," in Magleby, *Election Advocacy,* p. 66.

42. Ibid. The Burns campaign attempted to get CBM's negative advertising attacks against his opponent stopped but was unsuccessful.

43. While the group had a website (www.bettermedicare.org) that did list all the members of the association, which ranged from the Pharmaceutical Research and Manufacturers Association to the Chamber of Commerce to the AIDS Policy Institute and the Log Cabin Republicans, the sources of funds for the 1999–2000 issue advocacy campaign were nowhere listed. It is widely believed that major funding for the effort came from individual drug companies. The connection with the Republican Party was close. CBM's media consultant, Alex Castellanos, also worked for the Republican National Committee and the Bush presidential campaign. See Campaign Finance Institute, "Issue Ad Disclosure: Recommendations for a New Approach," p. A8 (www.cfinst.org/disclosure/report.htm [May 28, 2001]).

44. Marie B. Morris, "527 Organizations: How the Differences in Tax and Election Laws Permit Certain Organizations to Engage in Issue Advocacy without Public Disclosure and Proposals for Change," Congressional Research Service Issue Brief, June 26, 2000, made available by the National Council for Science and the Environment (www.cnie.org/nle/rsk-41.html [March 27, 2001]).

45. Michael Trister, "The Rise and Reform of Stealth PACs," *American Prospect,* vol. 11 (September 24, 2000), pp. 32–35.

46. Ibid. Perhaps the most prominent of the 527 committees were the Citizens for Reform and Citizens for the Republic Education Fund, created by Triad Management, a consulting organization to conservative interests, which spent between $3 and $4 million in the 1996 election supporting Republican and Senate candidates in twenty-nine races. Originally registered as 501(C)(4) organizations, the organizations later registered as 527 organizations in anticipation of the 1998 elections.

47. The NVF apparently was funded primarily by one unknown donor. See Campaign Finance Institute, "Issue Ad Disclosure," p. A10.

48. Ibid., p. A9.

49. Corrado, "Financing the 2000 Elections," p. 120.

EIGHT   *Financing Gubernatorial*
and State Legislative
Elections

ANTHONY GIERZYNSKI

S TATE ELECTIONS AND their financing have be-
come increasingly important during the past few decades. Twenty years
of devolution and increases in the professionalism of state governments
have made state capitols centers of power where important decisions are
being made, decisions that affect a variety of interests. Add to these newly
conferred and adopted powers the states' historic role in drawing congressional district maps (the state legislatures and governors draw the congressional district maps in most states, a power that can affect the balance
of power in Congress), and it becomes clear why.[1] Political money flows
to the places of power within a political system, and as states become
more powerful, more political money flows into state elections. This flow
has been documented in the growing amount of money involved in state
campaigns, as well as in the increase in lobbying activity in state capitals
around the nation.[2] In recent election cycles, states have also been a part
of the dramatic expansion in soft money. A recurrent lesson in campaign
finance is that political money flows to the places of least resistance, and
one of those channels has increasingly been nonfederal, or soft, money.
The door to soft money was opened by a 1979 amendment to the Federal
Election Campaign Act (FECA) and greatly expanded by Federal Election

Leslie-Anne Hinton helped amass data on gubernatorial elections and Stefanie
Lynch assisted with the data on legislative races. I would also like to thank the
staff of state offices that handle campaign finance records for their speedy responses to my data requests.

Commission (FEC) rulings. The purpose of the congressional amendment was to allow state and local party organizations to carry out traditional party campaign activity—such as grassroots campaigning on behalf of the parties' candidates, voter registration, and get-out-the-vote drives—that indirectly benefited federal candidates without that spending being considered an in-kind contribution to federal candidates.[3] The FEC has also ruled that national parties can raise soft money and transfer it to state and local parties who can spend it in ways that indirectly benefit federal candidates. Although soft money is unlimited at the federal level, it may be regulated by state governments. States regulate the financing of state and local campaigns, and because soft money is used in part for those campaigns, it falls under the jurisdiction of state law. States may limit or prohibit contributions to state parties for state election purposes. In fact, thirty-five states impose some limits on contributions to parties or on party contributions to candidates.[4] And two states, Alaska and Connecticut, ban the use of soft money in their states.

More broadly, states have been active in campaign finance reform. Michael Malbin and Thomas Gais report that "about two-thirds of the fifty states have enacted major new campaign finance laws since . . . 1979," a sharp contrast to the absence of new federal legislation in this area.[5] In the two decades since 1980, twenty-two states either adopted limits on individual contributions or reduced the limits they had in place, and twenty-three states publicly finance political parties or candidates in some races.[6] Included among those are four states—Maine, Vermont, Arizona, and Massachusetts—which have recently adopted so-called Clean Elections public financing programs that attempt to eliminate most private money from elections. Under these laws, candidates qualify for public funding if they are able to raise a specified number of small contributions ($5 in Maine and Arizona, $50 in Vermont). As part of accepting the public funds, candidates agree to spending limits and raising no additional private money. To encourage participation in the public financing system these states (except Vermont) also lower contribution limits for those who choose not to participate. Fourteen states have some form of public funding for gubernatorial elections. Minnesota and Wisconsin have long had partial public financing with corresponding expenditure limits for state legislative candidates who agree to campaign spending limits and meet eligibility requirements. These candidates can receive public funds to cover campaign expenses.

States have also attempted to deal with several other campaign finance issues. Oregon, for example, enacted a law that restricted the percentage of money candidates could raise outside of their district. Minnesota tried to mitigate the impact of independent expenditures by adjusting public funds and spending limits for candidates, and Missouri prohibited incumbents from carrying over excess campaign funds from the previous election. Arkansas, Virginia, Minnesota, Ohio, and Oregon give tax credits to citizens who make small contributions of $25 to $50 to candidates who abide by expenditure limits.[7]

Local governments have also been active, testing different approaches to regulating campaign finance. The two largest cities in the United States, New York and Los Angeles, have adopted systems of public funding with corresponding spending limits for city candidates. Qualified city council candidates in both cities who are willing to abide by spending limits receive public funds to match contributions of a certain size.[8] Seattle had a partial public funding system with expenditure limits in place until Washington voters passed an initiative that prohibited public funding of campaigns in the state.[9] And, finally, in what is the Galapagos of campaign finance, Albuquerque, New Mexico, has had mandatory spending limits in place since the 1970s because the statute has never been successfully challenged in court. Mayoral and city council candidates in Albuquerque cannot spend more than twice the annual salary for the office they seek (the current salary for mayor is $87,360, and the salary for council members is $8,528).

Many of these state and local innovations in campaign finance regulation have been tested in court before they took effect. For example, Oregon's out-of-state provision, Minnesota's attempt to regulate independent expenditures, and Missouri's ban on carryover funds were ruled unconstitutional. Still, elections have been conducted under many of these innovations—Maine and Arizona's "clean election" laws still stand, and the U.S. Supreme Court recently upheld Missouri's contribution limits.[10] And state and local laws continue to provide a steady diet of cases for the courts to reconsider or elaborate on the seminal *Buckley* v. *Valeo* case (424 U.S. 1 [1976]). In *Nixon* v. *Shrink Missouri Government PAC* (2000) the Supreme Court allowed Missouri's relatively low contribution limits to stand, but in *Landell* v. *Sorrell* the federal district court ruled Vermont's mandatory expenditure limits unconstitutional.[11] The expenditure limits were enacted by the state's legislature with the intent of challenging the *Buckley* ruling on such limits. The case is currently on appeal. In August 2001, federal district Judge Martha Vazquez upheld the city of Albuquerque's mandatory spending limits in the first federal court ruling to uphold such limits since *Buckley* (*Homans* v. *City of Albuquerque*, No. CIV 01-917 MV/RLP). Judge Vazquez wrote in her opinion that the Albuquerque election "record clearly establishes 25 years of expenditure limits that have preserved the integrity of Albuquerque's electoral process and the public's faith in its elections."[12] Her ruling was, however, overturned by the Tenth Circuit Court of Appeals, which suspended the limits for the 2001 city election. This case has become another vehicle to challenge the *Buckley* ruling: it will have a full hearing in federal district court.

The wide range of state and local government campaign finance reforms occur in states that vary significantly in population and geographic size, timing of elections, length of the general election campaign, media market size and coverage, and political culture. This range of experience and variety of settings provide campaign finance students with ample opportunities to assess the impact of different practices and reforms.

Gubernatorial Elections: 1997–2000

Following the 2000 election, Republicans controlled twenty-nine of the governorships, Democrats nineteen, and independents two. The Democrats had gained one governorship. But most states hold their gubernatorial elections in nonpresidential election years (thirty-nine states), which has had the effect of insulating gubernatorial elections from national party trends associated with presidential elections. States like Kentucky, Louisiana, Mississippi, New Jersey, and Virginia hold their contests in odd-numbered years, insulating them even more from the influence of national party trends. New Hampshire and Vermont still elect their governors every two years during both presidential elections and midterm elections. To get as complete a picture of gubernatorial election financing as possible, gubernatorial races between 1997 and 2000 were examined.

In recent years, gubernatorial election financing has been capturing its share of headlines with candidates breaking spending records in many states, large and small alike. Spending toppled records in nine of the eleven states that held gubernatorial races in 2000. In Indiana, "Democrat Frank O'Bannon and Republican David McIntosh raised just under $20 million for governor, making it the most expensive campaign in state history."[13] Similarly in New Hampshire, "Combined spending by the two lead candidates . . . totaled $4.3 million this year. . . . The previous record for a governor's contest, including primary spending by all candidates, was

$3.1 million."[14] And the tightly contested Missouri gubernatorial race "was one of the most expensive contests in state history."[15] In Washington the spending record "was broken in the gubernatorial race. Democratic incumbent Gary Locke put $3.7 million into his campaign, while Republican John Carlson raised $2.5 million. The previous record of $2.9 million was set in 1984."[16] In North Carolina, "the $19.6 million spent by [gubernatorial candidates] Easley and Vinroot surpassed the $15.9 million spent in 1996," which had held the record for the costliest governor's race.[17] "Election 2000 in Vermont was marked by unprecedented spending for and by candidates," including record spending in the governor's race.[18] And in 2000, North Dakota had "the most expensive campaign for governor" in its history.[19]

This tendency to set new records for spending in the 2000 gubernatorial races followed the record spending in the 1998 California gubernatorial primary election. In this contest two millionaires each spent part of their fortunes ($64.3 million) in unsuccessful attempts to secure the Democratic nomination.[20] In contrast Al Gore and Bill Bradley spent $83.5 million vying for the 2000 Democratic nomination for president.[21] In combined primary and general election spending, the gubernatorial candidates in California spent a grand total of $124.5 million. That is more than was spent on all of the eleven gubernatorial races in 2000 combined.

So, how do the rest of the states compare in spending and fund-raising in gubernatorial contests? Figure 8-1 presents the total receipts and expenditures in primary and general elections by gubernatorial candidates in the most recent general elections for each of the states.[22] Not surprisingly financing in California's gubernatorial races far outstrips the financing in any of the other states, and was more than twice the amount spent in New York and Texas—its closest competitors. This may not, however, be an entirely valid comparison, considering the weak competition in New York and Texas races in 1998. Nonetheless, even if adjusted for inflation, the spending in the very competitive 1994 elections in these states, $22.8 million in New York and $26.4 million in Texas, is dwarfed by the $69.2 million spent by the two general election candidates for governor in California in 1998.[23] In the 2000 election, the most expensive races took place in Indiana, Missouri, and North Carolina and in 1998 Georgia, Ohio, and Illinois came behind California, New York, and Texas in levels of financing. And New Jersey and Virginia (1997 election) are clearly in the same league.

The amount of money spent in gubernatorial races is partly a function of the state's population. When spending is divided by the number of eli-

Figure 8-1. *Total Raised and Spent by Major Candidates in Gubernatorial General Elections, 1997–2000*

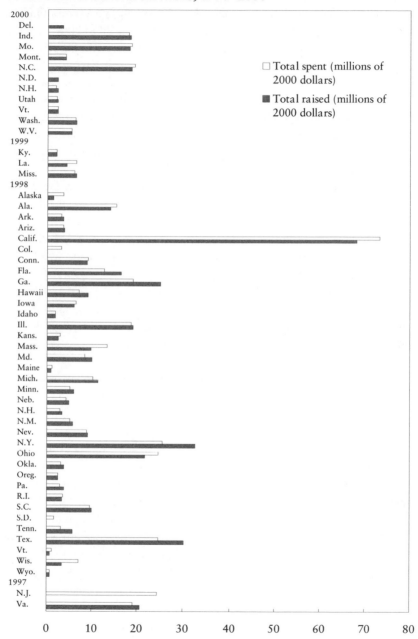

Source: Gubernatorial Campaign Expenditures database, compiled by Thad Beyle and Jennifer Jensen, secretaries of state and state ethics committees, and the National Institute on Money in State Politics, Helena, Montana.

gible voters in the state, the rankings of spending in states changes.[24] The states with the highest spending per eligible voter in the 1997 to 2000 gubernatorial elections were Alaska ($8.64 per eligible voter), Hawaii ($8.27), Nevada ($6.75), Montana ($6.30), and Vermont in 2000 ($4.91), while in California spending per eligible voter in the gubernatorial general election was $3.08.[25] These high-spending-per-voter states are all states with small populations, suggesting that there are probably some economies of scale that accompany campaign spending in larger states, most likely in mass media expenditures. And as Thad Beyle points out, the population in states like Alaska, Hawaii, and Montana is spread out in unique ways that make reaching voters more costly.[26] Although states with small and widely dispersed populations are usually at the top in spending per voter, Vermont's appearance in the top five is because of an unusually competitive campaign in 2000, following the state's passage of the Civil Unions law that granted marriage benefits to same sex partners and a public funding law that provided a third party candidate with $300,000 in public campaign money; spending per eligible voter in the 1998 Vermont gubernatorial contest was $2.16.

Figure 8-2 shows the median spending levels for gubernatorial candidates according to the outcome of the election and the party and incumbency status of the candidate. Winning candidates outspent losing candidates by a ratio of 1.4 to 1. Incumbents had a 2.6 to 1 edge over challengers in median spending. Open-seat candidates, reflecting the competitive nature of their races, spent more than both incumbents and challengers. It should be noted that incumbents tend to raise more money than they spend (data not shown), whereas challengers and open-seat candidates are likely to spend more money than they raise.

A factor that affects a candidate's ability to raise campaign money besides incumbency is party. During this election cycle, there was a party difference evident in election financing among incumbent and open-seat gubernatorial candidates. The differences in the average spending of Democratic and Republican challengers were marginal. Republican incumbents, though, spent more than twice as much as Democratic incumbents, and Republican open-seat candidates spent almost twice as much as Democratic open-seat candidates. The party difference among incumbents supports the notion that when Republicans hold power, they have a significant advantage in fund-raising. Contributors want access to power and to support those they most agree with. The interests that contribute the most money in politics tend to prefer Republicans, but the fact that Democrats

Figure 8-2. *Median Spending in Gubernatorial Elections, 1997–2000*

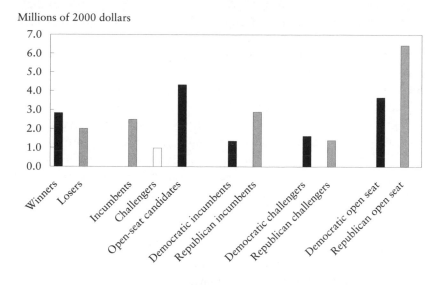

Millions of 2000 dollars

often hold power means that some of their money must go to Democratic candidates as well. When Republicans are in power, however, the interests' desire for access and preference for Republican ideology converge, so money flows more freely to Republicans. This dynamic can also be seen in the shift of business sector contributions before and after the 1994 Republican takeover of Congress.[27]

At first glance, there seems to be a gender gap in campaign spending in gubernatorial races, though when one examines the cases a bit more closely, the picture becomes more complicated. If one looks at the median spending of male and female candidates, holding constant the incumbency status, one sees that women were unable to spend as much as their male counterparts. The spending gap was evident among incumbents and challengers but was especially large among open-seat candidates, when the median spending by male candidates was $5.4 million compared with $1.2 million for the women.[28] In three of the five open-seat races in which a woman was one of the major party candidates the female candidates were outspent on average by more than $2 million. One of these candidates, Republican Judy Martz, however, won her race for the Montana governorship, despite being outspent three to one. That Montana is one of the most Republican states in the nation may have mitigated her being so heavily outspent. In Delaware and North Dakota (where spending data are not available), female candidates raised slightly more money than male candidates. One, Democrat Ruth Ann Minner, won her bid for the Delaware governorship; the other, Democrat Heidi Heitkamp, lost the North Dakota race.

Among gubernatorial challengers, the median male challenger spent more than the median female challenger, $1,249,000 to $633,000, but the median spending gap between female challengers and their incumbent opponent was $527,000, while for males the gap was $827,000.[29] In percentages, however, the median female challenger spent 55 percent of the amount spent by her incumbent opponent, while the median male challenger spent 72 percent of the incumbent's spending, suggesting that female challengers did not fare as well in obtaining money as their male counterparts. One female incumbent, Democrat Jean Shaheen, was outspent in two consecutive winning elections by her male challengers. In the 2000 New Hampshire election, her opponent outspent her by $635,695, or 34 percent, and in the 1998 election, she was outspent by a smaller margin. Only two of the other thirty-four incumbents who ran for reelection between 1997 and 2000 were women.

Besides the size of the state's population, incumbency status, party, and gender, it is reasonable to suspect that the wealth of a state, the strictness of campaign finance laws, the competitiveness of the election, and the cost of mass media campaigns would all affect the amount of money spent in gubernatorial elections. The wealth of the state limits the pool of money from which contributions may be raised; candidates in poor states will have a harder time raising as much money as their counterparts in wealthier states even with contributions that come from outside the state. Campaign finance laws are designed to restrict the amount of money candidates can raise, so it is reasonable to assume that candidates in largely unregulated states will be able to raise more money.[30] Also, the more competitive the election, the more likely contributors will be to give and the more likely candidates will be to spend more money. The use of mass media is a given in modern gubernatorial campaigns. Thus higher costs of mass media campaigning are another factor driving up overall campaign costs.

A simple examination of spending data in gubernatorial elections finds that these assumptions are correct. Greater levels of competition are associated with higher levels of campaign fund-raising (Pearson's R of .24).[31] There is a negative association between the strictness of campaign finance regulations and amounts raised (R of −.24) and a very strong positive correlation between the gross state product of the state and fund-raising (R of .83). And more expensive media markets, as well as the number of media markets in a state, are associated with higher spending (R of –.38 with ranking of media market high to low and an R of .64 with number of media markets).[32]

A more rigorous examination using multiple regression analysis (which assesses the relative impact of each of the above factors on fund-raising while holding all other factors constant) bears some of these relationships out. The wealth of the state, level of competitiveness, strictness of campaign finance laws, and the party and incumbency status of the candidates are related to how much a candidate can raise (regression results in the appendix to this chapter, table 8A-1).Candidates in wealthier states raise significantly more money than candidates in poorer states. Candidates in competitive elections (as measured by the margin of victory) raise far more than candidates in noncompetitive races. Incumbents and open-seat candidates raise significantly more money than challengers. Democratic gubernatorial candidates collect much less money than Republican candidates. And candidates in states with stricter campaign finance laws raise less than candidates in more loosely regulated states. The last finding suggests that, at least in terms of describing the 1997–2000 gubernatorial elections, campaign finance regulations do make a difference when it comes to how much candidates raise. Once all other factors are controlled for, neither gender differences among candidates nor media costs are related to revenues raised.

These findings beg the question, does candidate spending matter when it comes to who wins elections? The answer is yes. Despite instances when the candidate who spends the most does not win, such as the 2000 Montana race in which the loser outspent the winner three to one (in all, twelve of the forty-nine winning candidates were outspent by their opponents), the general pattern is that spending by gubernatorial candidates is associated with how well they do on election day. Figure 8-3 demonstrates this pattern by plotting candidate spending (as a percent of the total spent in their race) with the percent of the vote won in the election. The figure shows that the greater the share of spending, the greater the share of the vote. This relationship between spending and the vote holds when other factors—such as the partisan nature of the state, incumbency, the quality of nonincumbent candidates, party, and gender—are also considered and when one looks at the percent of spending or the actual amount spent.[33] This finding fits well with the political science literature on the role of money and electoral out-

Figure 8-3.   *Plot of Candidates' Percent of Spending in Race with Percent of Their Vote*

Percent of the vote

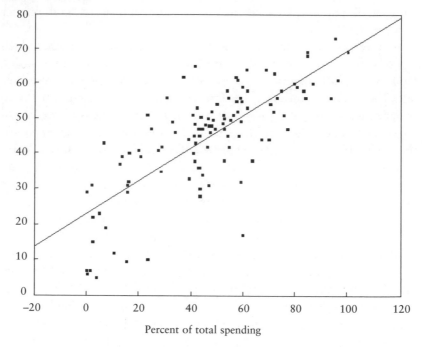

Percent of total spending

comes for many U.S. offices.[34] It also fits in with the recent work of Sarah Morehouse and Thomas Carsey on gubernatorial elections.[35]

Legislative Races 1999–2000

Most legislatures elected in 2000, just as at the beginning of each decade since 1960, have an additional power that makes the outcome, and thus the financing, of these races even more important than usual. The power is the power to create new district maps that determine voting districts within the state. The manner in which the districts are drawn following the decennial census can determine which party controls both the U.S. House of Representatives and the state legislatures. This results in intense competition for control of the legislature. A major component of this competition is, presumably, increased party and interest group spending in state legislative elections. In an analysis of the fund-raising for state legislative races conducted by the National Institute on Money in State Politics, the political parties were the top contributors in most of the states examined in 2000. This was true of Iowa, where the top three contributors were political parties; it was also true in Illinois, where the contributions from the parties plus the legislative party leaders constituted 30 percent of all contributions to state legislative candidates; it was also true of Washington, Tennessee, Florida, Texas, and Missouri.[36]

There were 5,918 legislative seats up for election in the forty-five states holding state legislation elections in 2000. Four states hold their elections in odd-numbered years—New Jersey, Mississippi, Louisiana, and Virginia—and one, Maryland, picks its house and senate every four years during midterm elections. Following the 2000 election, Republicans control both houses of seventeen state legislatures, Democrats control sixteen, and sixteen legislatures are split with each house controlled by a different party. Before the election, Republicans controlled seventeen, Democrats nineteen, and thirteen were split. One state, Nebraska, has a unicameral, nonpartisan legislature.[37]

How much money was involved in these state legislative races? Figure 8-4 presents the total raised or total spent in state senate and house districts in 2000 (Mississippi, New Jersey, and Virginia data are from the 1999 election) for the twenty-eight states with available data.[38] Just as with the gubernatorial races, there is a great deal of variation in campaign finance activity in state legislative races. Florida, Illinois, New York, and Texas top the list in the amounts raised or spent in state house and senate campaigns, though California (whose results are not available at this time) likely hosted the most expensive state legislative races since California legislative candidates spent $90.7 million in 1998.[39] The amounts involved in legislative contests are similar to the amounts in gubernatorial contests for most states (compare figure 8-1 with figure 8-4), which suggests that, in financial terms, who controls the state legislature is deemed as important as who controls the governorship. The amount of money involved in legislative races in most of the larger states—Florida, Illinois, New York, and Texas—is far higher than the amount involved in gubernatorial contests in those states. Besides the size of the state, the relative amount of money involved in legislative and gubernatorial races probably depends on party competition and the size of the legislative districts.[40]

The amount raised and spent in legislative races is dependent, in part, on the number of races held each year (some states follow the U.S. model and stagger the election of their senators so that only a portion of sena-

Figure 8-4. *Total Raised and Spent in State Legislative Races, Selected States, 1999–2000*

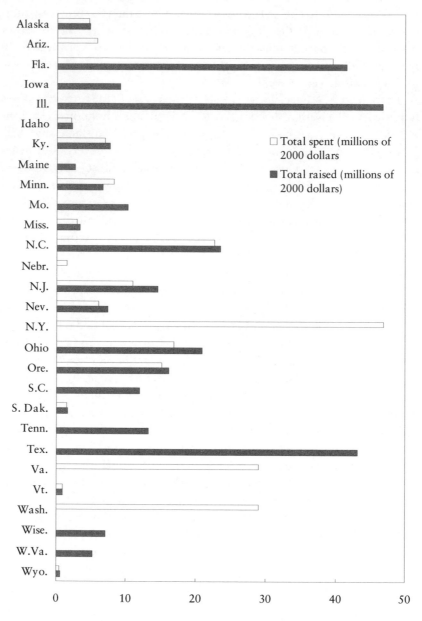

Source: Secretaries of state, state ethics commissions, and the National Institute on Money in State Politics.

tors are up for re-election in any particular year) and the population of the legislative districts in the state. Legislative districts vary in population, from state senate districts in California, which contain more than 750,000 people—larger than some states—to state house districts in New Hampshire, which contain about 3,000 people. To standardize across districts figure 8-5 represents the average district spending per eligible voter for senate and house districts (Nebraska has only one legislative chamber, and New Jersey had no senate elections in 1999).[41] There is greater similarity among the states when the spending is examined from this perspective, though one state, Alaska, stands out, much as it did in gubernatorial candidate spending per eligible voter, again because of its small and widely dispersed population.

Are the amounts of money involved in the 1999 and 2000 elections typical for legislative elections in all years? Or do these levels of activity represent a trend toward higher spending or an influx of money because the 1999 and 2000 legislatures will have power over redistricting? Several media accounts provide some anecdotal evidence that this is true either in overall spending or in individual spending records in battleground districts. An analysis by the Wisconsin Democracy Campaign found that legislative candidate spending in Wisconsin was 26 percent higher in 2000 than in 1998.[42] A spending analysis in New York found that "candidates for state legislature spent $47 million on the last election, a dramatic rise over previous contests."[43] The $47 million raised by legislative candidates in Illinois topped the 1998 total of $45.8 million. An analysis of Texas legislative races found a 24 percent increase in 2000 fund-raising over 1998 even though there were fewer candidates in 2000.[44] And in Iowa, legislative candidates' $9 million in fund-raising surpassed the $7.5 million raised in 1998.[45] And campaign finance reports show records set in individual races in Kansas, New Hampshire, and Vermont.[46]

Robert Hogan and Keith Hamm's analysis of state house races in 1992 allows a comparison of the spending per eligible voter in ten states in the first postredistricting election for this decade with the preredistricting election in 2000.[47] During the decade, the average district level spending per voter (in 2000 dollars) increased in half of the twelve states for which we have data, and some of the increases were substantial. Four of the states that did not see an increase were Maine, Minnesota, Missouri, and Wisconsin; each one had public funding or tight contribution limits for legislative candidates in 2000. The $2.40 average spending per voter by state house candidates in North Carolina was more than double the $0.98 spent

Figure 8-5.   *Average District Spending or Revenues per Eligible Vote,*
House and Senate Races

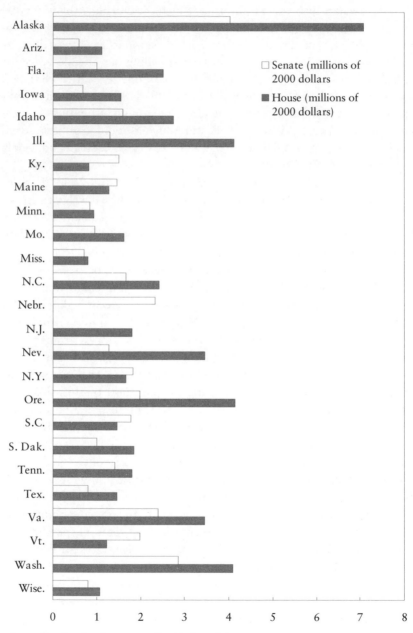

Source: Based on data from sources listed in figure 8-4.

in 1992, possibly reflecting the increasing party competition in that state.[48] Spending in house districts in Washington was $4.09 per voter in 2000 compared with $1.47 in 1992. And even small states, such as Idaho, saw a jump in district-level spending, which went from $0.98 per eligible voter in 1992 to $2.74 in 2000. The data suggest an increase in funding of state legislative races in several states, reflecting, perhaps, the importance of these positions to the fortunes of the political parties and the interests that are aligned with them. However, more data are needed to confirm this pattern. There is reason to assume that spending in 1992 would be high compared with other years because in the first election following a redistricting there are often more open seats, and incumbents often spend more to campaign in their realigned districts.

Political Party Money

Political party money has been greatly affected by the rise of soft money, and the growth of soft money seems to have accompanied a renaissance in the role of political parties in funding elections at the state as well as the national level.[49] Party organizations in the states and at the national level have adapted to the cash economy of candidate-centered campaigns, developing organizations that raise money and provide services for the candidates. Party organizations are often among the top contributors to state legislative and gubernatorial races, focusing their resources on key competitive races, and thus becoming important forces in competitive electoral contests.[50] And, according to an analysis by Malcolm Jewell and Sarah Morehouse, state parties "contribute on average half of all party money spent within their borders in a presidential election year."[51] The development of soft money has, by most accounts, helped strengthen state party organizations, assisting in the development of the electoral infrastructure—such as voter files, contributor lists, full-time staff, and get-out-the-vote machinery—making state parties more important players in elections.[52]

Soft money, by its nature, involves state party organizations, whether by assisting in the raising of money, acting as a conduit for the national parties, or carrying out the grassroots voter identification and mobilization and party campaigning that the FEC rulings were originally designed to encourage. Soft money represents a tremendous influx of campaign dollars to the state party organizations and campaigns, especially for the states that are presidential battleground states or ones in which a key

Table 8-1. *Party Activity, 1999–2000*

Item	Total raised	Transferred to state parties (dollars)	Transferred to state parties (percent)	Contributed to state candidates (dollars)
Democratic				
committees, totals	619,205,332	227,632,170		6,101,449
National hard	212,880,651	77,791,446	36.5	
Soft	256,983,424	149,840,724	58.3	
State hard	149,341,257			
Republican				
committees, totals	796,300,920	187,360,417		12,772,670
National hard	361,588,430	57,503,378	15.9	
Soft	258,156,288	129,857,039	50.3	
State hard	176,556,202			

Source: Compiled from Federal Election Commission data, Washington.

congressional race is being fought. In the 2000 election cycle, the Democratic and Republican national committees (both national and congressional campaign committees) of the Democratic and Republican parties transferred $415 million in both "hard" and soft money to state and local party committees.[53] The amounts broken down by party and type of money can be found in table 8-1. A look at the total funds raised by party committees shows clearly that the Republicans have a significant advantage, raising $177 million more than Democratic committees. This advantage comes from the Republicans' superior ability to raise hard money because the difference in the parties' soft money totals is minimal. Democratic committees transferred 36.5 percent of their hard money and 58.3 percent of soft money to state and local parties. Republicans transferred 15.9 percent of hard money and 50.3 percent of soft money. Though this influx of money from the national parties may be intended mainly to benefit federal candidates (and is often "run" through state parties to pay for issue ads), it also indirectly helps state campaigns that benefit from better-financed and better-staffed state parties and from the state parties' mobilization and campaign efforts carried out on behalf of all candidates.[54] Some state parties actually receive a "cut" or commission on soft money raised or used in their state.[55]

Although states receive funding from national parties, states also raise funds for federal campaigns. Table 8-1 also shows the money raised by state parties for federal campaigns. Because this money is for federal campaigns, it is regulated by federal election law and thus considered hard money. Democratic state party hard money constituted 24.1 percent of the total raised by Democratic committees, and Republican state party hard money constituted 48.4 percent. Unfortunately, this picture of party funding is incomplete because it is nearly impossible to find out the amount of money that stays in the state parties' coffers. However, as I have demonstrated elsewhere, the Democrats fail to make up any financial ground on the Republicans with these funds.[56]

The amounts received by state party organizations vary depending on whether the state was considered a battleground state for the presidential election or held an important congressional race. The top ten states receiving transfers from the Republican national committees (all of them receiving in excess of $10 million) were Florida, Michigan, Missouri, Pennsylvania, California, Washington, Ohio, Virginia, Illinois, and Wisconsin. The top ten states receiving transfers from the Democratic national committee were Michigan, Florida, Pennsylvania, New York, Missouri, California, Ohio, Washington, Virginia, and Illinois. As you can see, there is a great deal of overlap between the two parties' top ten lists. If the amount transferred per eligible voter is considered, Missouri, Michigan, and Washington (and Pennsylvania for the Democrats) are still among the top ten states receiving money from the national parties. Although the pattern of party transfers suggests that the money is being funneled to the states for federal campaigns, state parties and candidates benefit indirectly from increased voter mobilization and stronger electoral infrastructure, or directly when party organizations take a cut of the transferred money. It is also important to note that the committees of both national parties transferred at least some money to their state affiliates in every state.

Finally, a relatively small amount of national party money is contributed directly to state candidates—in 2000 Democrats gave $6.1 million and Republicans $12.8 million to state candidates. In 1998, amid a greater number of gubernatorial elections, Democratic national committees contributed $3.8 million and Republican national committees $11.1 million ($4.0 and $11.7 million in 2000 dollars). Note the Republicans' large financial advantage in this area too. These amounts seem low relative to the soft money transfers, but a couple of cases illustrate that the parties were not unwilling to pour money into state contests and that such contributions can be of great importance. In 2000 Vermont's Democratic candidate for governor, Howard Dean, received $572,500 from the Democratic National Committee, which was more than half of the $945,444 he spent in his re-election bid. His opponent, Ruth Dwyer, received $255,000 from the Republican National Committee plus $100,000 from the Republican Governors' Association, more than one-third of her total spending of $899,582.[57] That is a tremendous amount of money contributed by the parties to the second smallest state in the union. In Indiana, the RNC contributed more than $1.5 million to David McIntosh for his bid for the governorship, well over one-third of his receipts.[58] In North Dakota, Republican John Hoeven received $300,000, or almost one-third of his revenues, from the National Republican Party.[59] And, the Republican Governors' Association contributed $1.3 million to North Carolina gubernatorial candidate Richard Vinroot, an amount that constituted one-third of Vinroot's revenues.[60] In 1998 Dan Lungren, a California gubernatorial candidate, received $1.3 million from the RNC, $1.4 million from the National Republican Senatorial Committee, and $250,000 from the National Republican Congressional Committee (NRCC).[61] The governors' role in redistricting is undoubtedly one of the key reasons the national party committees are so generous to gubernatorial candidates. Governors in most states play a role in redistricting through their veto power or their power to appoint members of redistricting commissions. In 1998 and 2000, national committees also contributed to select state legislative leaders who can redistribute the money to candidates in competitive races. Lee Daniels, the Republican leader in the Illinois House, for example, received $125,000 from the NRCC in 1998.[62] And the Democrats have even created an arm of the national party, the Democratic Legislative Campaign Committee, whose purpose is to support Democratic state legislative candidates.

Soft money, especially in the form of transfers from national parties to state parties, has been instrumental in increasing the power and importance of state parties. This raises the question as to what impact the McCain-Feingold ban on soft money would have on the state parties. Clearly, given the amounts of money just discussed, state party committees would suffer an initial setback, losing a sizable source of revenue that has allowed them to enhance their electoral capabilities. It is also clear that the effect on the parties would be uneven. The Democrats, who have achieved a rough parity with the Republicans in soft money funds while lagging far behind in hard money, would be hurt the most. However, much of the state and local party infrastructure for these electoral capabilities is probably in place by now. That the state parties seem capable of raising significant amounts of hard money for federal campaigns suggests that the state parties would not suffer too greatly if soft money were banned (table 8-1). Still, given the beneficial uses of soft money—registering voters, getting them to the polls, and campaigning for all of the parties' candidates—a better solution would be to more tightly limit soft money rather than ban it. Such regulations might include limiting the amounts that can be contributed and more clearly delineating the purposes for which soft money can be used.

Conclusion

A tremendous amount of campaign finance activity takes place at the state level, and this chapter did not even cover campaign financing for statewide offices other than governor, that is, lieutenant governor, secretary of state, and so on; financing for ballot measure campaigns; or financing for city and county elections. In a sense, financing congressional and presidential elections is only the tip of the iceberg when it comes to campaign finance, and while we have begun to learn more about some state-level practices, vast areas of election financing remain well below the surface of our knowledge. One study estimated that "one-fifth of all money spent in American campaigns is spent at the local level" alone.[63]

The amount of money involved in state elections is not surprising given the growing power of state government and the role that state party organizations play in the soft money equation. The campaign finance activity of gubernatorial candidates, state legislative candidates, and political parties during the 2000 election cycle is likely to spur additional attempts on the part of the states to regulate campaign finance activity; and, the findings of the analysis of gubernatorial elections above suggest that limits on fund-raising do indeed work to limit the amounts raised and ultimately spent in elections. In the 2000 election California voters approved Proposition 34, which places limits on campaign contributions. Previously, California did not limit contributions or prohibit contributions from corporations and unions. Following the most expensive gubernatorial campaign in history, North Dakota legislators are considering changes in their state's campaign finance law. In fact, in the eight months following the election, well over a hundred pieces of campaign finance legislation have been introduced in state legislatures. And if the McCain-Feingold bill fails to pass, many states may take up the cause and ban or further regulate state soft money. How far the states can go depends in part on what the courts will allow them to do. While tough contribution limits were recently upheld in Missouri, and the so-called clean election reform has withstood a challenge in Maine, states seem to have little room to maneuver. The challenges to the 1997 Vermont campaign finance law and Albuquerque's that put mandatory limits on campaign expenditures are the only case in the legal pipeline right now that challenge the *Buckley* distinction between limited contributions and unlimited expenditures, and given the current makeup of the Supreme Court and the current resident of the White House, it is unlikely that these cases will reverse the *Buckley* decision. Still, state legislatures, local governments, and voters have shown a greater willingness to tackle issues surrounding election financing than Congress, and they will probably continue to do so in the years to come, acting as laboratories testing new approaches to regulate election financing.

Table 8A-1.   *Regression Analysis of Gubernatorial Fund-Raising*

Item	B	Standard error	Significance level (1-tailed test)
Gross state product	30.29	12.59	.01
Candidate quality	193,034	314,867	.27
Margin	67,377	41,787	.06
Campaign finance law	−653,268	280,302	.01
Rank of highest media market	−1,983	8,560	.40
Number of media markets	89,158	145,444	.27
Democrat	−1,127,323	630,327	.04
Other party	460,077	1,502,304	.38
Incumbent	1,665,387	900,049	.03
Open-seat candidate	1,753,402	905,017	.03
Woman	39,426	849,318	.48
Voting age population	−.40	.63	.25
Year 2000	−690,788	2,286,092	.38
Year 1999	−2,139,617	2,520,594	.18
Year 1998	−1,585,679	2,249,677	.24
Adjusted R^2	.745		
N	103		

Note: The dependent variable is the total amount of revenues raised by each major gubernatorial candidate in gubernatorial general elections between 1997 and 2000.

Notes

1. Thad Beyle, "The Governors," in Virginia Gray and others, eds., *Politics in the American States: A Comparative Analysis* (Washington: Congressional Quarterly, 1999), pp. 191–231; Anthony Gierzynski and David Breaux, "Money and Votes in State Legislative Elections," *Legislative Studies Quarterly* vol. 16 (May 1991), pp. 203–17; Michael J. Malbin and Thomas L. Gais, *The Day after Reform: Sobering Campaign Lessons from the American States* (Albany: Rockefeller Institute Press); and Gary F. Moncrief, "Candidate Spending in State Legislative Races," in Joel A. Thompson and Gary F. Moncrief, eds., *Campaign Finance in State Legislative Elections* (Washington: Congressional Quarterly, 1998), pp. 37–58.

2. See Clive S. Thomas and Ronald J. Hrebenar, "Interest Groups in the States," in Virginia Gray and others, eds., *Politics in the American States* (Washington: Congressional Quarterly, 1999), pp. 113–43.

3. See Anthony Corrado, "Party Soft Money," in Anthony Corrado and others, eds., *Campaign Finance Reform: A Sourcebook* (Brookings, 1997); and Malcolm E. Jewell and Sarah M. Morehouse, *Political Parties and Elections in the American States*, 4th ed. (Washington: Congressional Quarterly, 2001).

4. Jewell and Morehouse, *Political Parties and Elections.*

5. Malbin and Gais, *The Day after Reform*, p. 13.

6. Ibid. Vermont, which lowered its contribution limits in 1997, can be added to the twenty-one states reported by Malbin and Gais. Examples of low limits include Colorado's now defunct Amendment 15 which set $100-per-election limits on contributions to state legislative candidates and $500-per-election limits on contributions to statewide candidates; Minnesota limits contributions to legislative candidates at $100 per election from individuals and PACs; Missouri limits contributions to state house elections to $275 per election and to statewide candidates to $1,075; and Vermont limits contributions to state house candidates to $200 per election cycle, $300 for contributions to state senate candidates, and $400 for contributions to statewide candidates.

7. See Council of State Governments, *The Book of the States, 2000–2001*, vol. 31 (Lexington, Ky.: Council of State Governments, 2000).

8. Anthony Gierzynski and others, *The Price of Democracy: Financing Chicago's 1995 Election* (Chicago Urban League, 1996).

9. Carolyn M. Van Noy, "The City of Seattle and Campaign Finance Reform: A Case Study," *Public Integrity*, vol. 2 (Fall 2000), pp. 303–16.

10. *Nixon v. Shrink Missouri Government PAC* (528 U.S. 377[2000]).

11. Docket 2:99-cv-146, 2000.

12. The record, which was documented in part by the research of this author as an expert witness in the case, is truly an impressive one in favor of mandatory spending limits. Elections in Albuquerque have higher turnout than most cities, a lower incumbency success rate, almost no incumbency advantage in campaign spending, and the citizens of Albuquerque have a high level of trust in their elections, expressing the belief that they have information sufficient to make informed choices in city elections.

13. The Associated Press State and Local Wire, "2000 Governor's Race Most Expensive Campaign in State History," January 17, 2001.

14. Tom Fahey, "In the Race for the Corner Office, Shaheen, Humphrey Spent $4.3 Million," *Manchester Union Leader*, November 16, 2000, p. A13.

15. Kit Wagar, "Political Contest among Costliest: Holden's Bid Took in $9.7 Million," *Kansas City Star*, December 9, 2000, p. B1.

16. Beth Silver, "It's in Voters' Hands Now: Battleground 2000 Has Proven to Be an Exciting and Highly Competitive Election Year for Washington," *News Tribune*, November 5, 2000, p. A1.

17. Associated Press, "Democrats Tops in Campaign Spending," *Herald Sun*, January 19, 2001, p. C6; and Eric Dyer, "Easley Outraises, Outspends Vinroot in Bid for Governor; the Race Could Set a New North Carolina Spending Record," *Greensboro News and Record*, November 1, 2000, p. B1.

18. Ross Sneyd, "Campaign 2000 Involved Lots of Spending," *Associated Press State and Local Wire*, December 18, 2000.

19. Dale Wetzel, "Costly Campaign Spurs New Campaign Finance Proposals,"*Bismarck Tribune*, January 28, 2001, p. 6C.

20. California Secretary of State (www.ss.ca.gov/prd/finance_98/constitutional_officers.htm, [June 7, 2001]).

21. Federal Election Commission (www.fec.gov/finance/pdism8.htm [June 7, 2000]).

22. All candidates who received 5 percent of the vote or more in the general election are included in the figures and in the rest of the analysis in this section unless specified otherwise.

23. The amounts in 1998 dollars are $25.1 million for New York and $29 million for Texas.

24. Eligible voters were used in the denominator rather than actual voters to avoid the problem posed by the fact that voter turnout is higher in presidential election years than other election years.

25. All dollar amounts in this paragraph are in 2000 dollars.

26. Beyle, "The Governors," pp. 191–231.

27. For a lengthier discussion of this argument see Anthony Gierzynski, *Money Rules: Financing Elections in America* (Westview Press, 2000).

28. The median spending by women open-seat candidates includes only three of the five races for which spending data were available.

29. These calculations include major party challengers only.

30. See Janet Box-Steffen Steffensmeier and others, "Campaign Contributions in an Unregulated Setting: An Analysis of the 1984 and 1986 California Assembly Elections," *Western Political Quarterly*, vol. 45 (September 1992), pp. 609–28; and Malbin and Gais, *The Day after Reform*, for different takes on this point. See also Robert Hogan, "The Costs of Representation in State Legislatures: Explaining Variations in Campaign Spending," *Social Science Quarterly*, vol. 81(December 2000).

31. Correlation coefficients measure the strength of association between variables and range from 1 (a perfect positive association, that is, as one variable increases the other increases at an equivalent rate) to –1 (a perfect negative asso-

ciation). All correlation coefficients reported in this paragraph are significant at the .05 level or better, one-tailed test.

32. The correlations with the amount of money raised are as follows (all statistically significant at the .05 level or better, one-tailed test): Ranney competition index, .321; the margin of victory in the race, .231; campaign finance regulations (scored on a scale between one and five where states with no limits on contributions or prohibitions on corporations or labor unions were scored a '1,' states with some limits on contributions but no prohibition on corporate or labor contributions were scored a '2,' states with relatively tight limits on contributions and prohibitions or strict limits on corporate and labor contributions were scored a '3,' partial public funding with corresponding limits on expenditures as well as contributions were scored a '4,' and full public funding or partial public funding that applied to a wide number of state offices was scored a '5'), –.237; gross state product, .832; and, for media costs, the rank of the highest media market in the state, –.376, and the number of media markets in the state, .637.

33. This information is taken from a regression analysis calculated by the author but not shown here.

34. Sarah McCally Morehouse, *The Governor as Party Leader: Campaigning and Governing* (University of Michigan Press, 1998).

35. Thomas M. Carsey, *Campaign Dynamics: The Race for Governor* (University of Michigan Press, 2000).

36. The National Institute on Money in State Politics (www.followthemoney.org/ [June 5, 2001]).

37. National Conference of State Legislatures (www.ncsl.org, [June 5, 2001]).

38. Collecting campaign finance data on state races is rather challenging. It requires that the state make the data available (and many states have not processed their data at the time of writing this chapter) and that the data are made available in a usable format. Nonetheless, I received some much appreciated help from people who are responsible for handling the campaign finance and election information in a number of states.

39. California Secretary of State, "Total Campaign Expenditures by Candidates for the California State Legislature: 1976–1998" (www.ss.ca.gov/prd/finance98_general_final/figure_2.htm [June 7, 2001]).

40. Robert Hogan and Keith Hamm, "Variations in District-Level Campaign Spending in State Legislatures," in Thompson and Moncrief, eds., *Campaign Finance in State Legislative Elections*, pp. 59–79, found a positive relationship between district level spending and the competition over control of state house chambers. The analysis of gubernatorial elections in this chapter found a link between competitiveness and fund-raising.

41. Owing to limitations of available data (state totals for candidates were only available in a number of states) the spending per eligible voter per district was calculated by dividing the total spending or revenues by the number of districts and then dividing that by the number of eligible voters per district.

42. Wisconsin Democracy Campaign, "Candidate, Special Interest Spending Soars in 2000: Independent Spending Balloons 134 Percent to $2.5 Million" (www.wisdc.org/PRWeb.htm [February 8, 2001]).

43. James M. Odato, "Campaign Spending Soared, Study Says," *Times Union,* April 20, 2001, p. B2

44. The National Institute of Money in State Politics, Helena, Montana.

45. The National Institute of Money in State Politics.

46. Scott Rothschild, "Helgerson, Wagle Top Campaign Spending List," *Wichita Eagle,* October 31, 2000, p.A1; and Tom Fahey, "In the Race for Governor," p. A13.

47. Hogan and Hamm, "Variations in District-Level Campaign Spending," pp. 59–79.

48. All of the dollar amounts cited in this paragraph have been adjusted for inflation in 2000 dollars.

49. See Jewell and Morehouse, *Political Parties and Elections.*

50. See Anthony Gierzynski, *Legislative Party Campaign Committees in the American States* (University Press of Kentucky, 1992); and Anthony Gierzynski and David Breaux, "The Financing Role of Parties," in Thompson and Moncrief, eds., *Campaign Finance in State Legislative Elections,* pp. 185–205.

51. Jewell and Morehouse, *Political Parties and Elections,* p. 271.

52. Jewell and Morehouse, *Political Parties and Elections;* and John Kenneth White and Daniel M. Shea, *New Party Politics: From Jefferson and Hamilton to the Information Age* (Bedford/St. Martin's, 2000).

53. Calculated by the author from Federal Election Committee data.

54. See Marianne Holt, "The Surge in Party Money in Competitive 1998 Congressional Elections," in David B. Magleby, ed., *Outside Money: Soft Money and Issue Advocacy in the 1998 Congressional Elections* (Rowman and Littlefield, 2000), pp. 17–40; and Jewell and Morehouse, *Political Parties and Elections.*

55. Jewell and Morehouse, *Political Parties and Elections.*

56. Gierzynski, "Money Rules."

57. Ross Sneyd, "Campaign 2000 Involved Lots of Spending."

58. Linda Casey, "Race to Governor's Mansion 2000: The Major Parties Are Paying Attention," National Institute of Money in State Politics, Helena, Montana, November 1, 2000 (www.followthemoney.org/issues/governor/governor.html [June 28, 2001]).

59. Casey, "Race to Governor's Mansion 2000."

60. Dyer, "Easley Outraises, Outspends Vinroot," p. B1.

61. Edwin Bender, "States, Redistricting and Election 2000," National Institute of Money in State Politics, Helena, Montana, March 14, 2000 (www.followthemoney.org/issues/redistricting.html [June 28, 2001]).

62. Bender, "States, Redistricting and Election 2000."

63. California Commission on Campaign Financing, *Money and Politics in the Golden State: Financing California's Local Elections* (Los Angeles: Center for Responsive Government, 1989), p. 3.

NINE   *Financing Judicial*
        Elections

ROY A. SCHOTLAND

For years, the public, press, and political pundits have largely ignored judicial elections, because "political campaigns for judicial posts are generally about as exciting as a game of checkers played by mail."[1] They have been "low-key affairs, conducted with civility and dignity."[2] However, during the past twenty years, judicial elections have changed a great deal, starting in 1978 in Los Angeles County and erupting in the 1980s in Texas.[3] As the changes spread in more and more states, judicial elections have become "nastier, noisier and costlier."[4]

The 2000 cycle was unprecedented, with $45,495,420 raised by supreme court candidates, a 61 percent increase over the previous peak in 1998, setting records in ten of the twenty states that held such elections.[5] Noncandidate spending in just the five states with the most heated supreme court elections totaled at least another $16,000,000.

A primary catalyst of change in judicial elections has been the courts' increasingly prominent role in high-visibility policy matters such as abortion, gun control, death penalty, and vouchers. Judicial elections have heated up also because of "the changing nature of campaigning and growth of the mass media as a campaign tool," the growth of two-party competition in many States, and more growth in lawsuits than in population. More litigation means more lawyers, more specialization with arrays of "plaintiffs' personal injury lawyers" opposing the "defense bar," and more judges.[6]

The magnitude of the spending and the ferocity of many of the campaigns in 2000, transform a fundamental tension inherent in judicial elections into an acute, pressing challenge to the integrity and public perception of state courts: can a judge remain impartial when pressed to campaign, raise funds and take positions on issues? This chapter examines the unique aspects of judicial elections in the context of the 2000 elections, the changes in judicial elections, and the challenges these changes pose for our government and for campaign finance reform.

The Context and Unique Aspects of Judicial Elections

Of 1,313 state appellate judges and 11,118 state trial judges (general jurisdiction), 87 percent face elections of some type.[7] If we exclude "retention-only" elections, we find 53 percent of appellate judges facing contestable elections, and 77 percent of trial judges. Only seven states have no judicial elections; in another six, all judges run in partisan elections; and the remaining states have a variety of appointed judges, contestable elections, and "retention" elections in which judges have no opponent but must win a majority of "yes" votes for another term.[8] In some states, the ballot has far more judicial than legislative candidates: for example, Florida has 160 legislators and 536 judges, Illinois has 177 legislators and 556 judges, and Ohio has 132 legislators and 445 judges.

Whatever the selection system, a great many judges start on the bench by appointment to fill vacancies; nationally, that is the route for at least one-third of state judges.[9] Initial terms, even full ones, are often short. For subsequent terms: 45 percent of elected appellate judges have six-year terms, 16 percent have eight years, the remaining 38 percent have ten years or longer. Of elected trial judges (general jurisdiction), 19 percent have four years, 62 percent have six years, and 13 percent have ten years or longer.[10] Further, while there cannot be an opponent in a "retention" election, even in most contestable judicial elections candidates run uncontested.[11] While contests are more frequent for supreme courts than for lower courts, a study of high court elections, 1980–95, found that 48 percent of the incumbents were not challenged.[12] For example, of Texas's 481 judges sitting in 1993, "over 80 percent were unopposed in both the primary and general election when they first sought reelection. And in bids for subsequent terms, that trend accelerates. . . . [Of those] who initially reached the bench by appointment . . . *55 percent have never had an opponent . . . either in a primary or a general election.*"[13]

"Retention" elections are unique to judges, although nonpartisan elections are not.[14] Both retention and nonpartisan elections are presumed to provide a better balance of accountability and protection for judicial independence, than partisan contestable elections (table 9-1).

Having judges face elections raises a fundamental tension between, on one hand, the judges' basic obligations of independence and impartiality and, on the other hand, the necessities of campaigning, including the necessity of funding the campaigns and appealing to voters on issues related to the office.[15] Edward Ryan, a delegate to the 1846 Wisconsin constitutional convention who later became a chief justice of the Wisconsin supreme court, captured the tension between neutral judges and judicial elections well when he said the judiciary "represents no man, no majority, no people. It represents the written law of the land . . . it holds the balance, and weighs the right between man and man, between rich and poor, between the weak and the powerful."[16] Judges' actions directly affect the plaintiffs and defendants who basically stand alone before the judge. Our commitment to the "due process of law" means that litigants depend mainly on the judges' impartiality and independence. In contrast, contestants in the political process usually depend on being parts of organized groups of like-minded people, which produces electoral accountability. Judicial elections reflect the differences between judges and other elected officials.

Several key features differentiate judicial elections from other elections, rendering them "quasi-elections":

Timing

At least five states hold judicial elections in "off" times, as is true of many local elections. For example, all Pennsylvania judicial elections are held with municipal elections in odd-numbered years, and Tennessee's on the first Thursday in August of even-numbered years. In Tennessee in 2000, the highest vote cast in a judicial race was 293,127, compared with 1,996,573 cast in the November presidential election (no other statewide offices were on the ballot in 2000).[17]

Low Voter Awareness

Polls show a startling lack of voter awareness of even the names of the judicial candidates.[18] Judicial races almost never draw press coverage, thereby increasing the candidates' need to raise funds to communicate their existence, let alone any message.[19]

Ballot Length

Ballot length and a candidate's placement on the ballot are well-known shapers of voter participation. Long ballots result in more spoiled ballots and more voter drop-off (people who skip voting for some offices). Notoriously long ballots, with a legion of judicial candidates at the end, are the norm in Cook County (Illinois), Harris County (Houston), and Cuyahoga County (Cleveland). Last year's ballot in Cook County included so many justices and judges that the county's proportion of spoiled ballots exceeded Florida's.[20] In the general election, in addition to Cook County's candidates for a supreme court seat, there were seventy-seven lower-court candidates for retention and eighty-three candidates for twenty-two lower-court seats.

One consequence of having so many candidates is that names matter more. For example, in 1990 Washington State's able chief justice lost to an unknown Tacoma lawyer who did not campaign and spent only $500 but had the same name as Tacoma's well-known statewide TV anchor, Charley Johnson.[21] In San Antonio that year, an intermediate appellate judge who miraculously had the support of both the plaintiffs' and the defense bar, lost the primary to a recent retiree from Army JAG whose name was Gene Kelly. In the general election Kelly spent $7,595; his opponent spent $1,000,000 (mainly on TV ads saying "He's Not That Gene Kelly"), but Kelly, though losing, received 44 percent of the vote.[22]

The Special Role of Attorneys

It is widely assumed that most judicial candidates rely mainly on lawyers for campaign funds. In fact, while many judicial campaigns are funded significantly by lawyers' contributions, that is not a prevailing pattern.[23] Attorneys play another role in judicial elections through "ratings" of judicial candidates conducted by local bar associations.

Characteristics of Judges That Affect Their Behavior as Candidates

Reflecting the judges' special position, fund-raising in judicial campaigns is uniquely constrained. "There is no aspect of the electoral system of choosing judges that has drawn more vehement and justifiable criticism than the raising of campaign funds."[24] Numerous recent polls report findings such as "nine out of ten Ohioans believe judicial decisions are influenced by contributions to political campaigns."[25] In all but four of the thirty-nine states with judicial elections, a legally binding Canon of Judicial Conduct bars personal fund-raising and requires that all fund-raising be done by the candidate's campaign committees, in order to at least reduce the candidate's involvement in fund-raising. And in at least twenty–

Table 9-1. *States and the Types of Judicial Elections for Some or All of Their Judges*

Italicized states have different judges facing different types of elections

Partisan[a]	Retention[b]	Nonpartisan	No judicial elections[c]
Alabama	Alaska	Arkansas	*Connecticut*
Idaho	*Arizona*	*Arizona*	Delaware
Illinois	*California*	*California*	Hawaii
Indiana	Colorado	*Florida*	Massachusetts
Kansas	*Florida*	Georgia	*Maine*
Louisiana	*Illinois*	*Idaho*	New Hampshire
Michigan	*Indiana*	*Indiana*	New Jersey
Missouri	Iowa	Kentucky	Rhode Island
New Mexico	*Kansas*	Minnesota	*South Carolina*
New York	Maryland	Mississippi	*Vermont*
North Carolina	*Missouri*	Montana	Virginia
Ohio	Nebraska	Nevada	
Pennsylvania	*New Mexico*	*North Carolina*	
Tennessee	Oklahoma	North Dakota	
Texas	*Pennsylvania*	*Oklahoma*	
West Virginia	South Dakota	Oregon	
	Tennessee	South Dakota	
	Utah	Washington	
	Wyoming	Wisconsin	

a. In Michigan and Ohio, and recently in Idaho, judicial candidates appear on the general election ballot without party labels, but their selection and campaigns are otherwise partisan.

b. In Illinois, New Mexico, and Pennsylvania judges are initially elected in partisan elections, but their continuance is determined in retention elections; New Mexico has a uniquely hybrid process.

c. Included are Connecticut, Maine, South Carolina, and Vermont, with probate judges elected. Except for this note, this table includes only appellate and general-jurisdiction trial judges.

four states, the law limits the time period during which fund-raising is permitted, both before and after the election.[26]

Nonjudicial candidates seek support by making promises about how they will perform. Judges cannot make such promises because of their obligation to decide on the basis of proven facts and applicable law, and so their campaign statements are circumscribed by Canons of Judicial Conduct.[27] It is inconceivable that we would try to have legal limits on what legislative or executive candidates say in campaigns.

Other elected officials are free to meet—at any time, openly or privately—their constituents or anyone who may be affected by their action in pending or future matters. In contrast, judges are insulated from contact with the parties to a matter before them, by both norms and legal limits on *ex parte* contacts.[28]

To note these limits on judicial candidates' campaign conduct is not to deny that some express campaigning exists. "Tough on crime" is surely the major "platform" of more than a few judicial candidates, whether explicit or only "signaled."[29] However, the overwhelming proportion of judicial campaigners refrain from taking or signaling any such positions.[30] Consider a dispute over "signaling" in New York, where candidates may be endorsed by more than one party. The relevant official committee split on whether it is ethical for a judge to accept the endorsement of the Right to Life Party.[31] Indeed, the limits on judicial campaigns account for their dullness and are the precise ground the media cites to explain their nearly complete neglect (until 2000) of judicial campaigns.

Unlike other incumbents, judges cannot build up support through "constituent casework," patronage, securing benefits for their communities, and so on. Doubtless there are some judges who have won votes because of their decisions in particular cases, but more likely judges are losing votes, and sometimes even their seats, because of decisions in particular cases.[32] Typically, judges draw little, if any, support for "services rendered."[33]

Almost all other elected officials anticipate electoral competition and have a talent for campaigning. Otherwise, they would not survive in elective office. In contrast, few judges face challengers; most hope they will avoid real competition and not have to campaign. Although there is now more electoral competition in judicial elections than before about 1980, we do not yet know how much the rise of competition in judicial elections will change the kinds of people who seek to serve—and to stay—on the bench.

The 2000 Judicial Elections

In 2000, the United States saw an unprecedented number of intensely fought campaigns, some described as "sleazy," "a national disgrace," and "rotten to the core," and many that were dramatically more costly than ever before.[34] In these campaigns interest group activity was unprecedented, not merely an increase but a change in kind.[35]

The 2000 elections broke spending records both for the national total and in ten states, soaring past all but two previous records.[36] The record spending in one race is still Texas's 1994 Democratic primary, $4,490,000.[37] In 2000, supreme court candidates in just five states, Alabama, Illinois, Michigan, Mississippi, and Ohio raised $34,883,523 (table 9-2).[38]

Table 9-2. *The Five States with 2000's Hottest Elections*

	2000				Prior peak year	
State and election	Total raised by candidates—all races, general and primary (dollars)	Average per candidate[a] (dollars)	Per vote in most expensive race (dollars)[b]	Number of seats	Total raised by candidates—all races, general and primary (dollars)	Average per candidate[a] (dollars)
Alabama				5		
Republican primary (Monroe)[d]	13,104,909[c]	1,092,076	7.14		7,610,718 (1998)	2,244,252 (1996)
Illinois[e]	8,058,000	740,451		3	2,001,885 (1992)	117,756 (1992)
Democratic primary (Fitzgerald)			5.36			
Republican primary (Thomas)			11.36			
Michigan	7,058,914	1,008,416		3	2,726,833 (1998)	405,981 (1996)
General election (Taylor)[f]			0.82			
Mississippi[d]	3,383,000	375,888		4	747,105 (1996)	106,729 (1996)
General election (Diaz)[f]			4.66			
Ohio	3,278,700	730,525		2	4,645,512 (1992)	516,168 (1992)
General election (Resnick)[f]			0.48			
Total	34,883,523			17	17,732,053	

a. Counting no candidate who raised no funds.
b. Total contributions to candidates in that race/total votes cast in that race.
c. Bold indicates a record for that state.
d. Winner of the race is named in parentheses.
e. In Illinois and Mississippi, Supreme Court candidates run not statewide but in geographic districts.
f. Includes sums spent in their uncontested primaries.

Last year's noncandidate spending in judicial elections is also noteworthy. In the same five states mentioned above, at least $16,000,000 was spent on campaigns by noncandidate groups (and four of those states accounted for all but $25,000 of that sum). This, combined with candidate expenditures, brings the total for judicial elections in these states to at least $62,000,000.[39] In the five states with the highest level of judicial candidates' funds, the seventeen contests averaged $2,053,000. The average per seat sum in 2000 nearly doubles the average for 1990–99, $540,067 (189 seats).

As for lower courts, little information is available about 2000.[40] In Florida—surprising even people familiar with judicial elections— candidates raised $8,638,000 for 182 general-jurisdiction trial court seats, although only 17 seats were contested (four of those involved runoffs).[41] New Mexico adds to the sense that unexpectedly large sums are involved in many places: candidates for six trial-court seats raised $407,000, and for three intermediate appellate seats, $754,000.[42]

2000's Hottest Judicial Elections

Texas has drawn more attention for its judicial elections than any other state, but in 2000 it (like California, New York, and Pennsylvania) was quiet. However, judicial elections in a number of other states typified many of the problems associated with such elections, as well as some of the challenges confronting reform.

Alabama

Five states had fiery supreme court contests in 2000. Alabama, with sharply partisan judicial races for five seats, was the state with the most in candidates' funds and perhaps also with the most at stake. Four of their nine justices were up for reelection, and another one sought to succeed the retiring chief justice. At the election's end, two incumbents lost their seats, and the chief justiceship went to trial judge Roy Moore, who had gained national note for posting the Ten Commandments in his courtroom and keeping them there despite court orders. Thirteen candidates, including three primary election losers and one Libertarian who spent nothing, spent $13,104,909 and averaged $1,092,076 (excluding the Libertarian nonspender).

Big spending in Alabama is not new. Since at least the early 1990s, Alabama, which has led the nation in punitive damages awards, has regularly seen well-funded contests between Democratic candidates supported largely by plaintiffs' trial lawyers and Republican candidates supported largely by business interests.[43] In 1998, seven candidates vying for three seats raised $7,610,718; the average that year was $1,087,245.[44]

The Alabama contest in 2000 had, besides candidates' spending, high expenditures by outside interest groups. One Christian conservative grassroots group raised $177,000 supporting Judge Moore in the Republicans' four-way primary. Several other groups made considerable expenditures—most likely more than $800,000—on statewide TV issue ads.

However, because Alabama does not limit direct contributions to candidates, except contributions by corporations, individual corporate leaders and trial-lawyer groups actively contributed large sums directly to candidates. In the GOP primary, some trial lawyers supported Judge Moore for the chief justiceship, less because of any agreement with him than because of deep disagreement with his main opponent, Justice Harold See. That disagreement may have led the trial lawyers to support not only Moore but also another candidate in that primary, trial judge Wayne Thorn; Thorn ran advertisements attacking See, while Moore ran a positive campaign.

The uniqueness of judicial elections is brought out by the litigation over an official Judicial Inquiry Commission proceeding against Justice See about one of his TV spots that compared his record on crime with Judge Moore's.[45] The commission charged that a statement in See's ad that "Moore let convicted drug dealers off with reduced sentences or probation—at least forty times," was misleading and false, even though simultaneous with the first broadcast of See's ad, See had given the press documentation for his claim. See's supporters claimed that the commission was partisan, but a bipartisan, quasi-official Judicial Campaign Oversight Committee had declined to act on the matter. The mere pendency of the official commission's charges triggered See's disqualification from continuing on the bench, an interim sanction he was able to enjoin.[46]

Michigan and Ohio[47]

Michigan and Ohio have remarkably similar judicial elections scenes. In 2000 Michigan had three GOP state supreme court incumbents up for reelection and Ohio had two, one Republican and the court's most "anti-business" Democrat, Justice Alice Resnick.[48] All five incumbents won.

The Michigan Chamber of Commerce linked the two states' 2000 elections when it ran newspaper and radio ads in Ohio. The ads urged Ohio businesses to move to Michigan because "the judicial restraint of the Michigan Supreme Court and fair laws have helped create a healthy economic climate in Michigan."[49] The Michigan chamber viewed the Ohio court as having ruled against business by 4 to 3 majorities in workmen's compensation and other matters; and in 1999, Justice Resnick authored a 4 to 3 decision striking an important tort reform statute. The Ohio Chamber and affiliates were also active, running a TV ad that became the event of the campaign and unquestionably backfired, turning into a main cause of Resnick's victory.[50] That ad "featured a statue of Lady Justice who peeks underneath her blindfold as piles of special interest money tip her scales and state Justice Resnick ruled nearly 70 percent of the time in favor of trial lawyers who have given her more than $750,000 since 1994 . . . Concludes the announcer: 'Alice Resnick. Is justice for sale?'"[51]

In both states, "issue ads" like the one above drew regulatory efforts. In 1998 Michigan's secretary of state issued a regulation, which banned the use of corporate funds for any "communication [with the candidate's name or likeness] broadcast or distributed within 45 days before an election." This regulation was stricken immediately.[52] Ohio had similar events in 2000 when Ohio's election commission decided on a complaint against the Chamber's ads, first holding that issue ads were beyond their jurisdiction, then on the eve of the election reversing itself, being sued, and ultimately returning to its first position.[53]

In both Michigan and Ohio, campaigns opened earlier than usual. Michigan opened earlier than ever in July 2000, when Democratic Party ads showed animated trees shuddering about the Republican incumbents as a voice-over said the court "ruled against families and for corporations 82 percent of the time." A *Detroit Free Press* review found that the ad "borders on the bogus": in fourteen of the forty-three "anti-family" cases, the Democratic justices had agreed with the result. "State party officials said . . . 'defining a family or corporate entity [is not] an exact science.'"[54] On the other side, a GOP ad attacked a challenger (an intermediate appellate judge) for having upheld a light sentence for a pedophile. In this ad, "the word 'pedophile' in huge type flashes close to the judge's name." When this ad was brought into question, the GOP's reply was, 'We don't call him [a pedophile].'"[55]

Like Michigan, Ohio's campaign opened early: in November 1999, an "insurance industry-funded group aired radio attack ads" against Justice Resnick, spending an estimated $100,000.[56] The Ohio chamber also participated in funding "attack ads," which were the subject of a complaint to Ohio's Election Commission, as noted above. These ads as well as other noncandidate expenditures totaled more than $8,000,000, in addition to the $3,278,700 raised by the five candidates in Ohio (including one primary loser). Although the candidates' funds were about a million dollars lower than funds in Ohio's 1992 race, the 2000 race demonstrates an explosion in noncandidate spending.

Michigan's ten candidates' funds totaled $7,058,914, compared with a prior peak of $2,726,833 in 1998 when fourteen candidates vied for three seats. Along with the candidates' funds, at least another $6,000,000 in noncandidate funds was spent, bringing the total to around $13–15 million.[57] The local chamber spent about $2,700,000 on issue ads, and the Democratic Party and the GOP spent about $2,000,000 each on issue ads.

Two more comparisons between the two states: campaign finance regulation is only slightly different in the two states. Michigan allows PACs and individuals to make unlimited contributions to parties and individuals, while Ohio does not.[58] Also, Ohio has enjoyed a strong chief justice, Thomas J. Moyer, under whose leadership his court has, with Texas, led the nation in steps to meet problems in judicial elections.[59] In Ohio, judges and judicial candidates are required to attend an educational program about campaigning early in the year they are running. They are also subject to an expeditious process of oversight and discipline for their campaign conduct, which has been impressively effective. In sharp contrast, although Michigan had a monitoring effort conducted by its mandatory-membership bar association in 1998, it was not repeated in 2000.

The extremely expensive campaigns point out the difficulty of dealing with the problematic aspects of judicial elections. Ohio has been active in judicial election reforms, but its reforms address the problems of candidate-controlled campaigns. However, in the 2000 elections in Ohio and Michigan campaigns were largely shaped, even dominated, by noncandidate groups. This development acutely challenges the long-standing view, reflected in numerous laws, that judicial campaigns should, and can, be regulated to a unique degree.

Mississippi

Noncandidate groups also shaped judicial elections in Mississippi. The U.S. Chamber of Commerce was active in Mississippi, spending about $958,000 for TV "issue" ads on behalf of the chief justice, two other incumbents, and one challenger.[60] Two trial-lawyer PACs, Mississippians for an Independent Judiciary, and Mississippians for Fair Justice, spent $312,000 opposing the Chamber's attack ads.[61] The chief justice and the challenger even asked the chamber to halt the ads, without success.[62] But after the secretary of state and attorney general met with the chamber's lawyers and questioned the legality of the chamber's refusal to meet disclosure requirements, the chamber went to federal district court claiming these were issue ads and not subject to those requirements—the chamber's lawsuit lost six days before the election. One state judge ordered a halt to broadcasts of the ad; that order was joined shortly thereafter by a similar order from a second state judge. Justice Antonin Scalia's stay of the restraint was followed by one of those judges' reentering his order, the afternoon before the election. But the chamber never disclosed; appeals are pending in the Fifth Circuit and Mississippi supreme court.[63]

The "outsider" intervention was at least a major cause of the upset defeat of the chief justice. She had served eighteen years and never been opposed but lost 48 percent to 52 percent to a challenger who had raised only $9,000 as of mid-October.[64]

Wisconsin

Of the twenty-three states with public funding for campaigns, only Wisconsin includes funding for judicial races, and only for their supreme court races. Unfortunately this funding program, which began in 1979, was effective only in its early years. Starting in 1995, public funding has accounted for only about 3 percent of the candidates' expenditures in these judicial races.[65] One reason for the program's failure is that public funding depends on taxpayer checkoff, which has declined sharply in Wisconsin as elsewhere. And candidates' participation has been hurt because the grants are conditioned on a candidate's agreeing to a spending limit of $215,000—which has not been adjusted for inflation since 1979. Reform groups in Wisconsin are actively working to revive the state's public funding program.

Florida and Arkansas

Florida voters faced a ballot proposition to decide whether their trial judges should continue to face nonpartisan, contestable elections or should instead be selected by the same system as Florida's appellate judges, who receive "merit" appointments by the governor after screening through judicial nominating commissions with subsequent retention elections. The change was defeated in every circuit, with the affirmative vote averaging 32 percent and the highest affirmative vote in any county at 39 percent.

The change to a "merit" system was supported by the Florida Bar, which like the American Bar Association and most state associations had supported the system for decades. The change received broad editorial support as well. However, the four major minority and women's bar associations were forcefully opposed to the change. The minority and women's associations felt that they had just begun winning significant numbers of judgeships and would be severely hindered by one feature of the proposed change: all current sitting judges would not, at the end of their terms, face the new nomination process but instead only retention elections—and no Florida judge has ever lost a retention election. The proponents emphasized the number of initially elected judges who have been disciplined and the influence of campaign contributions on the judiciary. The opponents emphasized the sanctity of the vote and their fears about a "closed-door, elite" selection process.[66] The ballot proposition garnered substantial media coverage, despite competing events such as competition from the presidential race.

The Florida Bar spent $80,000, mostly for brochures, one video, and twelve large newspaper ads in major dailies just before the election. "Citizens for Judicial Integrity," a statewide group (mainly of lawyers), sided with the bar; they hoped to raise $400,000–$500,000 but only managed $37,000.[67] Most of that money was spent on direct mail to 33,000 households in Miami-Dade and some for litigation over the ballot language. The opposition "Citizens for an Open Judiciary," organized by members of the four bar associations in opposition, spent about $75,000 on Spanish-language TV and radio ads and English-language direct mail and newspaper ads, all in Miami-Dade.

In contrast to the proposition's defeat in Florida, Arkansas voters unexpectedly adopted, with a 57 percent majority, a constitutional amendment that included changing from partisan to nonpartisan judicial elections.[68] (The December 2000 "Chief Justices' Summit" recommended that "All judicial elections should be conducted in a nonpartisan manner.")[69] The *Arkansas Democrat-Gazette* reported that "not a single judicial candidate we've interviewed has the slightest objection" to the ballot proposition (Arkansas has 129 judges).[70] The campaign also received overwhelming support from interest groups. The Arkansas State Bar contributed $155,102 for the campaign; another $10,000 came from the Arkansas

Judicial Council, $15,000 from the Arkansas GOP and $26,105 from law firms and individual lawyers.[71]

The Arkansas GOP had been for this change since 1990 because few judicial candidates could win with a Republican label. Although the Democratic Party did not become engaged in the campaign, their state chairman spoke out in opposition. One reason for Democratic opposition was that the candidates' filing fees went to the parties: for the Democrats, about 10 percent of their annual budget, $110,000, came from judicial candidates, but only $20,250 for the GOP.[72]

The Arkansas-Florida contrast constitutes a blunt lesson for judicial reformers: to overcome inertia and the inevitably substantial interests that have a stake in the status quo, a well-funded campaign is a *sine qua non* for reform. However, it does not follow that spending for reform will win. The last major effort before Florida's was Ohio's 1987 ballot proposition to replace contestable elections with "merit" appointment and retention. Ohio's State Bar and League of Women Voters spent about $400,000 on signature gathering to qualify the ballot proposition, then raised $411,513 for the campaign, but lost 2 to 1 and in eighty of Ohio's eighty-eight counties. The opposition, funded exclusively with more than $300,000 from the Ohio AFL/CIO, included the Democratic and Republican parties; they ran TV ads—"Don't let them take away your vote."[73]

Lessons from 2000 and Prospects for the Future

The concluding chapter of *Financing the 1996 Election* was about "The Reinvigorated Reform Debate." Robert E. Mutch said that congressional debates, despite a presidential fund-raising scandal, just as in the "the previous two decades . . . divided those who want to limit the role of money in elections from those who do not. . . . There was no strong public demand for reform legislation," and without public demand legislators will not "change the rules under which [they] run for office."[74]

A similar question may be asked of judicial reforms: where will judicial elections go from here?

Issue advocacy was a major source of the negative campaigns in 2000. But is there a way to regulate noncandidates? In Ohio, notable support has been expressed for increased disclosure of noncandidate expenditures; moving to an appointive system (which, ironically, Ohio firmly rejected in 1987); broadening the definition of "express advocacy"; and lengthening terms.[75] Putting aside such crucial details as what specific dollar amounts should trigger disclosure, will it make much difference to learn that the chamber or other contributors spent X amount of dollars on issue ads? The disclosure data might make media coverage more effective, but any regulation beyond disclosure encounters First Amendment complexities.

The natural first reaction to judicial election problems is simple: stop electing judges. No democracy could abolish elections for legislators or executive officials;[76] but no democracy except the United States elects judges,[77] and no state that has changed from contestable elections to an appointive system (with or without retention elections) has changed back. The fact that after a century of strongly supported work to eliminate elections or at least contestable elections, 87 percent of state judges still face elections—53 percent of all appellate judges and 77 percent of trial judges face contestable elections—does not dent the drive for the simplistic solution. The problem is that, right or wrong, stopping contestable elections has been strikingly hard to sell, at least for the last twenty years. Will Florida's overwhelming rejection of change recur, or will the spread and rising severity of judicial election problems make the simple solution more attractive?[78]

There is new strength to the drive for incremental reforms within judicial elections. First, in August 1999 the ABA House of Delegates amended the Model Code of Judicial Conduct (which is adopted or adapted by court rule in almost all elective states) to call for fuller funding disclosure, contribution limits set in light of each jurisdiction's circumstances, and mandatory recusal (upon motion) if a party or lawyer exceeds the contribution limit, and so on. A few states are already considering the amendments, but adoption is never speedy.

Reform was also the topic of the December 2000 "Chief Justices' Summit," convened by seventeen chief justices (from the most populous states with judicial elections) to consider what steps may be taken to address the problematic aspects of judicial elections. The summit's "Call To Action" has twenty recommendations.[79] Among the recommendations are that all judicial elections "should be conducted in a nonpartisan manner" and that all judicial candidates should be required to attend programs on state election laws. The recommendations also urge that "non-governmental monitoring groups should be established to encourage fair and ethical judicial campaigns"; "state and local governments should prepare and disseminate judicial candidate voter guides"; Congress should provide a free mailing frank for such guides; that there be "public funding for at least some judicial elections"; and that other steps on campaign finance should be considered. The summit also recommended a symposium on the First Amendment and judicial campaigns, to consider what limits on judicial candidates' campaign speech are appropriate and what steps may be taken regarding noncandidates' participation. The symposium was held in November 2001 to address the tension between campaign limitations and First Amendment rights. An important point about the summit's recommendations is that almost all of the "Call To Action" can be implemented by state supreme court rules.

However, one recommendation calls for a constitutional change that would lengthen judges' terms.[80] Longer terms would directly reduce the need for campaign funds and the frequency of the kinds of campaigns that jeopardize public confidence in judges. For example, if Ohio's terms of six years were changed to ten years, aggregate campaign costs would be cut substantially even if not *pro tanto*. Reducing the need for repeated forays into fund-raising and the need for warlike campaigns, would make service on the bench more attractive, thus more likely to draw able people. Ensuring the caliber of our judiciary and thus promoting a "juster justice" is, surely, our whole purpose.

Some people dismiss these kinds of advances as "Band-Aids." But, in my view, incrementalism is the only feasible, or (at least) the most likely way to protect the balance between judicial independence and judicial accountability. The key question is whether, and in what ways, the spread of intense campaigning in judicial elections may affect the conduct of justice. Are we experiencing or heading into an "axial change" for state courts?[81] If so, would such change stem mainly from the change in judicial elections or from various causes? There is no question that last year's elections were qualitatively different from the ones before them, and there seems little reason to believe that we will not see nastier and costlier campaigns like the ones in 2000. However, the cost in dollars is not the cost that matters.

Notes

1. William C. Bayne, "Lynchard's Candidacy, Ads Putting Spice into [Mississippi] Judicial Race," *Commercial Appeal*, October 29, 2000, p. DS1.
2. Peter D. Webster, "Selection and Retention of Judges: Is There One Best Method?" *Florida State University Law Review*, vol. 23 (Summer 1995), p. 19.

3. The Los Angeles events are described in the American Bar Association Task Force on Lawyers' Political Contributions, *Report Part II* (Chicago, 1998), pp. 13–14 (hereafter ABA Task Force Report). For the cooling of Texas's contests as GOP dominance has discouraged opposition, see Anthony Champagne and Kyle Cheek, "Money in Texas Supreme Court Elections: 1980–1998," *Judicature*, vol. 84 (July-August 2000), p. 20.

4. Richard Woodbury, "Is Texas Justice for Sale," *Time*, January 11, 1988, p. 74.

5. In 2000: Ala., $133,035,426; Ark., $399,845; Idaho, $300,391; Ill., $8,144,965; Ga., $13,509; Ky., $509,222; La., $127,895; Mich., $7,058,914; Minn., $499,516; Miss., $3,383,000; Mont., $836,366; N. Dak., $13,925; Nev., $1,234,282; N.C., $1,792,762; Ohio, $3,278,700; Ore., $692,325; Tex., $1,213,000; Wash., $953,273; W. Va., $1,576,960; Wisc., $431,144. The average per seat sum in 2000, $995,999 (46 seats), is nearly double the average for 1990–99, $540,067 (189 seats). The prior peak was 1997's $1,072,274 but for only two states and a total of two seats. The prior peak national total for candidates' funds was 1998, $27,842,016 (19 states), with an average of $618,711 (45 seats). All these figures include primaries as well as general elections. Data, unless otherwise indicated, are as of May 30, 2001, and from a national treasure, the National Institute on Money in State Politics. I am indebted to Samantha Sanchez. For 2000 data on Illinois, data are from the hugely knowledgeable and helpful Kent Redfield. Kent Redfield, *Money Counts: How Dollars Dominate Illinois Politics and What We Can Do about It* (University of Illinois at Springfield, Institute for Public Affairs, 2001), pp. 111–12. Data for Mississippi and Texas are from their Administrative Office of the Courts. Data on either spending or receipts are used (as noted) unless any substantial difference is known; they rarely differ materially. An increasing number of states do not allow candidates to keep surpluses. As for deficits, the National Institute on Money in State Politics data include loans as contributions, and since the data include postelection reporting, postelection fund-raising is included.

The ten states in which records were broken (either for total sums or per seat sums): the four highlighted below as well as Illinois (four times the prior peak total, seven times the prior peak per seat), Idaho (50 percent over prior peak total), Kentucky (11 percent over prior peak per seat), Montana (total nearly doubled), North Carolina (total doubled), and Oregon (total nearly doubled per seat).

6. See Champagne and Cheek, "Money in Texas Supreme Court Elections," p. 21. We cannot ignore that in federal judicial selection as well, controversy has become more frequent and intense.

7. ABA Task Force Report, app. 2; for updated numbers of judges, see Court Statistics Project, *State Court Caseload Statistics, 1999–2000* (Williamsburg, Va.: National Center for State Courts, 2001), figure G.

8. See table 9-1. Besides the seven states with no elections, four have only minor elections, for example, for probate judges: Connecticut, Maine, South Carolina, and Vermont.

9. American Judicature Society "survey of thirteen elective states" (July 2000). From the study, Minnesota has 90 percent of its judges initially appointed, Geor-

gia 71 percent, Alabama 49 percent, Michigan 44 percent, Nevada only 33 percent, North Dakota 30 percent, Texas over 40 percent, and Washington about 75 percent.

Appointees must face election soon after going on the bench. While eleven states have nominating commissions for vacancy appointments, twenty-eight do not, and apparently no elective state requires advice and consent for these appointments.

10. Roy A. Schotland, "Comment: Judicial Independence and Accountability," *Law & Contemporary Problems*, vol. 61 (Summer 1998), pp. 154–55.

11. In Florida since 1986, 80 percent of incumbents were not challenged. Susan Barbosa, "Judge Selection Goes to Voter," *Lakeland Ledger*, October 29, 2000, p. A1. In Minnesota last year, sixty-two of sixty-seven district court judges faced no opposition, and in 1998, seventy-nine or eighty-nine trial judges. *Republican Party v. Kelly*, 247 F.3d 854, 896 (8th Cir. 2001) (Beam, J. dissenting), certiorari granted, *U.S. Law Week*, vol. 70, December 4, 2001, p. 3369.

12. Melinda Gann Hall, "Competition in Judicial Elections, 1980–1995," Michigan State University, paper presented at the annual meeting of the American Political Science Association, September 1998.

13. C. J. Thomas R. Phillips, "State of the Judiciary Address," February 23, 1993, p. 5. Emphasis in original.

14. A century ago, no states had retention elections; today eighteen states have them for some or all judges; and twenty-five states had partisan judicial elections, none had nonpartisan ones. Robert Darcy, "Conflict and Reform: Oklahoma Judicial Elections 1907–1998" (2000). Today, twelve states have nonpartisan elections for all judges, and another eight have them for some judges. For current arguments about nonpartisan elections, see note 69.

15. That tension has driven a major effort by the organized bar and good-government groups, since at least 1906, to eliminate judicial elections (or at least contestable elections). In 1906 Roscoe Pound delivered a major ABA address that catalyzed action, "The Causes of Popular Dissatisfaction with the Administration of Justice," *ABA Reporter*, vol. 29 (August 1906), p. 395. "We get what Michael Shapiro calls the 'clumsy institution' that tries to straddle the contradiction of independence and democratic control." Quoted in Hans Linde, "The Judge as Political Candidate," *Cleveland State Law Review*, vol. 40 (1992), p. 4.

16. Milo M. Quaife ed., *The Convention of 1846*, Wisconsin Historical Society Collections, vol. 27, Constitutional Series, vol. 1 (Madison,1919), p. 596. I am indebted to Chief Justice Shirley Abrahamson for this reference.

The United States is all but alone in having judges stand for election. Judges are elected also in some Swiss cantons and a few French municipalities and were "elected" in the Soviet Union; justices of the peace are elected in Peru and Venezuela. See "Note, For Whom the Bell Tolls . . . Judicial Selection by Election in Latin American," *Southwest Journal of Law and Trade*, vol. 4 (Fall 1997), p. 261.

17. Roy A. Schotland, "Vacancy Appointments; and, Timing of Judicial Elections Generally," Chief Justices' Summit (December 2000, unpublished)

18. In Alabama, where last year's candidates for five supreme court seats spent the most in the nation, 90 percent of the voters could not name a single candidate

except for the Chief Justice's position. Editorial, "This Is No Way to Choose Who's on Appeals Courts," *Mobile Register*, November 8, 2000, p. 12A. See also Roy A. Schotland, "Elective Judges' Campaign Financing: Are State Judges' Robes the Emperor's Clothes of American Democracy?" *Journal of Law and Politics*, vol. 2 (Spring 1985), pp. 86–88.

19. Texas Chief Justice Phillips has assembled charts showing the striking differences in support won in media markets where the candidate advertised, and where the candidate had not. For example, in the 2000 GOP primary, Justice Gonzales (now White House counsel) got 59 percent of the vote in eleven media markets where he advertised and 44 percent in eight where he did not. Similarly, winner's figures in the 1998 primary were 61 percent and 49 percent; in 1994, 65 percent and 48 percent; and in 1992, 61 percent and 43 percent. Data compiled by Philips and Karl Rove, consultant to the winning candidates (available from Chief Justice Phillips or from author). We need more such analyses, including consideration of the localities' voting tendencies.

20. Cook County's newly designed ballot had 456 positions; the old one had 320, so the punch holes were closer together. And for the first time in decades there was no "straight party punch," so voters had to "poke and hope;" as a result, Cook County's erroneous ballots in the presidential race went from 1996's 2.7 percent to 6.3 percent. John B. Judis, "Punch Drunk," *American Prospect*, March 12–16, 2001, p. 10.

21. Mark Matassa and Julie Emery, "Could Any Charles Johnson Have Won? Upset Vote Raises Qualms about How We Choose Judges," *Seattle Times*, September 20, 1990, p. A4.

22. See ABA Task Force Report, pp. 11–13.

23. ABA Task Force Report, pp. 89–95, table 2. And a recent study found that lawyers accounted for only 28 percent of the total $53,128,350 contributed in 1989–99 supreme court elections in Alabama, Idaho, Illinois, Louisiana, Montana, Oregon, Texas, and Wisconsin. National Institute, "Money in Judicial Politics," Chief Justices' Summit, 2000 (unpublished).

24. *Stretton v. Disciplinary Board of Supreme Court of Pennsylvania.*, 944 F.2d 137, 145 (3d Cir. 1991).

25. Report of the Citizens' Committee on Judicial Elections (appointed by Chief Justice Moyer), 1995, p. 1. For Pennsylvania and Arizona, see ABA Task Force Report, pp. 25–26; for recent other surveys in seven more states and a 1999 national survey, see David Rottman, "Voters in Judicial Elections: Motivation, Capability, and Trust," Chief Justices' Summit, 2000 (unpublished).

26. The pre-election window is one year in five states and shorter in eleven states, and the postelection window is six months shorter in nineteen states. ABA Task Force Report, note 82.

The thirty-nine states with elections are listed in table 9-1; as noted there, another four have minor judicial elections, for example, for probate judges.

27. Randall Shepard (Indiana Chief Justice), "Campaign Speech: Restraint and Liberty in Judicial Ethics," *Georgetown Journal of Legal Ethics*, vol. 9 (Summer 1996), p. 1059.

28. One woman commented, "You can't go to them." Another said, "You can't see them, not unless you are brought up before them." These comments were made in professionally conducted focus groups about the judiciary, for Philadelphia's Committee of Seventy, published in a report by the Committee of the Seventy, "Who Chooses? The Need for Judicial Reform in Pennsylvania," p. 5 (Committee of Seventy, 2001, info@seventy.org.) "The participants . . . felt that judges are more distant from the electorate than other elected officials."

29. For example, a Berkeley ex-law professor "played his trump card in the last week of the campaign. Shifting away from lofty remarks about the independence of the judiciary, he flooded the county with 100,000 fliers proclaiming, 'The Issue is Rape' and [declaring] that as a judge, [he] had been 30 percent tougher on average in sentencing rapists than other state judges, a statistic [his] staff came up with by extrapolating from the five rape or attempted-rape cases he had handled." Schotland, "Elective Judges' Campaign Financing," pp. 79–80.

30. The increasing involvement of interest groups brings more "signaling." "Interest groups . . . provide important cues to voters about the attitudes and values of judicial candidates. [For example, in one California trial court race] one candidate obtained the endorsements of the Sacramento County Deputy Sheriff's Association and the Sacramento Police Officers Association." Anthony Champagne, "Interest Groups and Judicial Elections," *Loyola (Los Angeles) Law Review*, vol. 34 (June 2001), p. 1391.

31. See Opinion 93–52, 1993 WL 838832 (*New York Advisory Committee on Judicial Ethics*, October 28, 1993).

32. In Kansas in 2000, a black female juvenile judge lost her seat because of a well-funded campaign led by the parents of a defendant unhappy with the judge's action. Jack Focht, Wichita attorney and unofficial archivist on judicial elections, telephone interview with author, March 26, 2001.

33. Leading campaign consultant Joe Cerrell of Los Angeles said, "Our senators have a political operation for use in retaliation. Judges are standing naked in the political process not knowing what, when, or how to do anything." Quoted in Schotland, "Electives Judges' Campaign Financing," pp. 71–72.

34. Ulf Nilsson, "Ohio's Judicial Election in 2000: Will It Prompt Change?" *For the Record—Newsletter of the Ohio Judicial Conference* (Second Quarter 2001), pp. 2–3, quoting media commentary.

35. On the increasing role of interest groups, its causes and the "unhealthy dependence between judicial candidates and interest groups," see Anthony Champagne, "Interest Groups and Judicial Elections," *Loyola (Los Angeles) Law Review*, vol. 34 (June 2001), p. 1391. "The greater role for interest group money . . . in judicial campaigns stirs concerns about the kinds of relationships that are being created." Kent D. Redfield, *Money Counts* (Springfield, Ill.: Institute for Public Affairs 2001), pp.111–12.

Although data on candidates' funds are reliable, information on participation by parties and other groups is incomplete; as a result, on much of that activity we have only unsubstantiated media estimates. The only effort better than such estimates is a major, detailed effort by Craig Holman of the New York University School of Law, Brennan Center for Justice (publication forthcoming), who found a total of $10,677,000 spent on TV ads (for time bought). In the nation's seventy-five leading TV markets, interest groups spent at least $3,105,000 in advertising on judicial campaigns, candidates spent $6,448,000 and parties $1,124,000. However, those sums seem far too low: in just Michigan and Ohio, the Chamber of Commerce alone is estimated to have spent about $5,000,000.

36. See note 5. The record single-year judicial election spending is still California's 1986 battle over whether to retain Chief Justice Rose Bird. She and two colleagues had massive financial support but lost to an even more massive outpouring of small, grassroots contributions: the two sides spent $11,400,000—when adjusted in 2000 dollars the total is $17,900,000. See Roy A. Schotland, "Personal Views," *Loyola (Los Angeles) Law Review,* vol. 34 (June 2001), p. 1361.

37. Texas Office of Court Administration, Texas Appellate Judicial Candidates: Campaign and Election Report (March 1995) data on Justice Raul Gonzalez and challenger Rene Haas (unpublished).

38. See table 9-2. All data in this chapter, unless otherwise indicated, are from the National Institute on Money in State Politics and are correct as of May 30, 2001. For extraordinary aid with their data, I am indebted to Samantha Sanchez.

Data on *either* spending or receipts are used (as noted) unless any substantial difference is known; of course they may differ but rarely materially. An increasing number of states do not allow candidates to keep surpluses; and as for deficits, the National Institute data include loans as contributions, and since the data include postelection reporting, postelection fund-raising is included.

The National Institute brings a remarkable improvement in candidates' data on judicial elections. This scene lacked "comprehensive or systematic" data, as it still does for all but the candidates' funds. For noncandidates, we still rely on a handful of studies and an array of news articles; such sources are helpful but often "frustratingly incomplete" and sometimes "biased, for example, by presenting data [about] only trial lawyers." ABA Task Force Report, p. 79.

39. To this amount must be added grassroots efforts by, for example, the Citizens for a Sound Economy in Ohio, Michigan, and Alabama. Their efforts included mailings on state supreme court candidates to 435,000 households in Ohio, 330,000 in Michigan, and 400,000 in Alabama. "Press Release: Citizens for a Strong Economy," November 18, 2000 ([June 25, 2001]).

40. The National Institute collects only supreme court data. We do have a few studies of trial-court campaign finance in Los Angeles County between 1970 and 1994; median spending for superior court (trial) judicial races rose from $3,170 to $70,000. California Commission on Campaign Financing, *The Price of Justice* (Los Angeles, Center for Governmental Studies, 1995), pp. 67–71.

41. See "Campaign Financing, Division of Elections, Florida Department of State" (June 28, 2001).

42. Leo M. Romero, University of New Mexico Law School (2001) (forthcoming publication); see also Leo M. Romero, "Judicial Selection in New Mexico: A Hybrid of Commission Nomination and Partisan Election," *New Mexico Law Review,* vol. 30 (Spring 2000), p. 177.

43. Surely a classic among campaign finance filings is the Lyn Stuart campaign's report on contributions received on the Wednesday before the 2000 election: Forest

PAC: $20,500; Guard PAC: $7,000; HOSPAC: $6,000; AG PAC: $6,750; VEND PAC: $4,500; Home Care PAC: $4,500; BAC PAC: $4,000; Lawsuit Reform PAC: $15,000; Home PAC: $4,000; Concerned Associates Employees PAC: $1,000; Retailers of Alabama PAC: $4,000; Chem PAC: $2,160. Form 2 filing by Committee to Elect Judge Lyn Stuart, with the Secretary of State. This information can be found at http://arc_sos.state.al.us/PEL/SOSELPDF.001/E0006457.PDF.

44. In 1996 two candidates for one seat averaged $2,244,252.

45. William Glaberson, "States Rein in Truth-Bending in Court Races," *New York Times,* August 23, 2000, p. A1; and George Lardner Jr., "Speech Rights and Ethics Disputed in Judicial Races," *Washington Post,* October 8, 2000, p. A13.

46. *Butler v. Alabama Judicial Inquiry Commission,* 111 F.Supp.2d (M.D. Ala. 2000). On appeal, 245 F.3d 1257 (11th Cir. 2001), the court certified questions to the Alabama Supreme Court. Separately, in May 2001 the Alabama supreme court declared the rule on which See's suspension had been based unconstitutional. Stan Bailey, "Court Says Rules Used in See Case Unconstitutional," *Birmingham News,* May 16, 2001. p. 4C.

47. Nilson, "Ohio's Judicial Election in 2000: Will It Prompt Change?" p. 3; and Hugh McDiarmid, "Little Justice Shown in Ads for High Court," *Detroit Free Press,* November 2, 2000, p. B1. See also William Glaberson, "Spirited Campaign for Ohio Court Puts Judges on New Terrain," *New York Times,* July 7, 2000, p. A11; William Glaberson, "Fierce Campaigns Signal a New Era for State Courts," *New York Times,* June 5, 2000, p. A1; and Warren Richey, "Justice for Sale? Cash Pours into Campaigns: Money, Negative Ads May Determine Bench in Ohio and Michigan, among Other States," *Christian Science Monitor,* October 25, 2000, p. 2.

48. Ratings were done by the Ohio Chamber of Commerce, which found the court voted pro-business only 31 percent of the time, and Resnick 18 percent of the time. Constance Sommers, "Ohio Supreme Court Race Gets Political: A Very Bad Campaign," *Corporate Legal Times,* May 2000, p. 72; for valuable fuller treatment, see John D. Echeverria, "Changing the Rules by Changing the Players: The Environmental Issue in State Judicial Elections," *N.Y.U. Environmental Law Journal,* vol. 9 (2001), pp. 217, 287–97.

49. Charlie Cain, "High Court Races Will Be Nasty, Pricey," *Detroit News,* June 23, 2000, p. 1A. Some Republicans joined Democrats on these 4–3s, but all dissenters were Republicans.

50. See Mike Wagner, "Despite Negative Ads, Resnick Retains Seat," *Dayton Daily News,* November 8, 2000, p. 1A.

51. Spencer Hunt, "Campaign 2000: TV Ads Help Mold Supreme Court Race," *Cincinnati Enquirer,* October 22, 2000, B1. "The anti-Resnick campaign has become infamous in the American legal community, both for its unsavoriness and for its portentous effect on future judicial campaigns." Joe Hallet, "Should Ohio Stop Electing Judges?" *Columbus Dispatch,* April 8, 2001, p. G1.

52. See *Planned Parenthood Affiliates v. Miller,* 21 F.Supp.2d 740 (E.D. Mich. 1998), and *Right to Life of Michigan v. Miller,* 23 F.Supp.2d 766 (W.D. Mich. 1998).

53. Alan Johnson and James Bradshaw, "Panel Upholds Anti-Resnick Ad," *Columbus Dispatch*, October 20, 2000, p. A1; James Bradshaw, "Panel Rules on Resnick Attacks," *Columbus Dispatch*, November 7, 2000, p. A1; and Joe Hallet, "Free Speech Protects Attack Ads, Ruling Says," *Columbus Dispatch*, April 5, 2001, p. A1.

54. See Dawson Bell, "Party Politics Enters High Court Race: TV Ads Slam Republican Judges," *Detroit Free Press,* August 3, 2000, p. B1.

55. Editorial, "Debate: Corrupting Influences Grow in Contests for Judgeships," *USA Today*, November 2, 2000, p. 16A.

56. Joe Hallet, "High-Court Race Conjures Low Blows," *Columbus Dispatch*, April 2, 2000, p. 3B; the estimate is from another informed source.

57. Robert Labrant, president of the Michigan Chamber estimated that "about $15 to $16 million" were spent. David Shephardson, "Stakes Rise in Court Race," *Detroit News,* October 31, 2000, p.1.

58. Ohio's rules also set spending limits, which a) secured compliance from the candidates but seem to have encouraged spending by the GOP on one side and union PACs on the other; and b) were stricken as unconstitutional, *Suster* v. *Marshall*, 149 F.3d 523 (6th Cir. 1998), *cert. deni.* 525 U.S. 1114 (1999), 121 F.Supp.2d 1141 (N.D.Oh. 2000).

59. Texas alone has a comprehensive statute regulating campaign finance in judicial campaigns; C. J. Thomas R. Phillips secured its enactment in 1995. Very important is Texas's setting not only a limit on contributions from individuals but also an aggregate limit on contributions from any one law firm, its partners, employees, affiliates, and so on. See Tex. Stat. Ann. § 253.157 (Supp. 2001).

60. Eric Clark, "Supreme Court Campaigns Need Disclosure," *Amory Advertiser,* February 21, 2001, p. 4A. The figure comes from an unofficial survey by the secretary's office of all TV stations.

61. Filings at office of Mississippi Secretary of State.

62. Associated Press, "Chief Justice Asks U.S. Chamber of Commerce to Stop Running TV Ads," *Commercial Appeal*, October 22, 2000, p. DS4.

63. Respectively, *Chamber of Commerce* v. *Moore*, No. 00-60779, and *Chamber of Commerce* v. *Landrum,* No. 2000-CA-2048. A petition for certiorari in *Chamber of Commerce* v. *Vollor, No. 00-1255,* was denied May 29, 2001, 121 S.Ct. 2207.

64. The challenger attacked the Chief Justice's support by the Chamber and her "liberal" participation in reversal of criminal convictions. Associated Press, "Races for Supreme Court Generating Big Bucks; Outside Money Creating Cry of 'Better Justice or Bought Justice?'" *Commercial Appeal*, October 22, 2000, p. DS4.

65. In 1979 the figure was 46 percent. But it was 3 percent in 1995, 1996, and 1997, 2 percent in 1999's very heated election, and 6 percent in 2000. Samantha Sanchez, "Campaign Contributions and the Wisconsin Supreme Court," Report of The National Institute on Money in State Politics, Helena, Montana, May 15, 2001, p. 3 (www.followthemoney.org/issues/WI_Sup_Court_study/WI_Sup_Court_study.html); data on 2000 from J.R. Ross, "Reform for State Races, Some Say More Public Money Is Needed," *Wisconsin State Journal*, April 2, 2001, p.

B3; the earliest data are from Wisconsin Election Campaign Fund, Summary (unpublished).

66. The nominating commissions include six members (lawyers and nonlawyers) with three appointed by the governor and three by the bar. Then those six members appoint another three members who must be nonlawyers. In 2001 this was amended to enlarge the governor's role.

67. For perspective on the reformers' spending under $120,000: first, in the same election, $8,638,000 was spent in trial-court races, only seventeen of which were contested. See "Campaign Financing, Division of Elections, Florida Department of State" ([June 28, 2001]); second, the Arkansas reform effort noted spent almost double the Florida sum, despite obviously lower media costs; last, in just two judicial districts in Kansas, reform committees spent $97,841 to defeat ballot propositions aimed at returning to partisan elections. Report of Citizens to Keep Politics Out of Our Courts (January 21, 2001)(unpublished).

68. This was only one part of an overhaul of their constitutional provision on the judiciary. The overhaul enjoyed bipartisan support—the state's Republican lieutenant governor and its incoming Democratic president of the Senate participated in events supporting the amendment.

69. See National Center for State Courts, "Call To Action," *Loyola (Los Angeles) Law Review,* vol. 34 (June 2001), p. 1353.

Two concerns explain the drive to end partisan elections: (1) Any suggestion that judges can offer "Democratic" or "Republican" judging is misleading and jeopardizes public confidence in judicial integrity. (2) In states that allow party-line voting, a strong year for one party will unseat many fine judges in the other party.

In 2000 nonpartisan elections were under attack in three states—Idaho, Kansas, and Minnesota. The major question is whether or not it is constitutionally legal to bar party endorsements. Two decisions in California have already held this barring unconstitutional. However, in Minnesota, a Republican candidate who wanted party endorsement challenged Minnesota's limitations, but his arguments were rejected by the Eighth Circuit in a lengthy 2–1 decision. *Republican Party* v. *Kelly,* 247 F.3d 854, certiorari granted, *U.S. Law Week*, vol. 70, December 4, 2001, p. 3369.

70. However, there were substantial complaints about the inadequacy of the proposition's mere twelve-word explanation on the ballot.

71. Don Hollingsworth, executive director, Arkansas Bar Association, letter to author, March 13, 2001.

72. Long ago, the parties had paid for primaries; that had changed, but the provision routing the filing fees to the parties had not.

73. John D. Felice and John C. Kilwein, "Strike One, Strike Two: The History of and Prospect for Judicial Reform in Ohio," *Judicature*, vol. 75 (December–January 1992), p. 193.

74. Robert E. Mutch, "The Reinvigorated Reform Debate," in John C. Green, ed., *Financing the 1996 Election* (M.E. Sharpe, 1999), pp. 216, 237.

75. See Nilsson, "Ohio's Judicial Election in 2000: Will It Prompt Change?" pp. 3–6.

76. Parliamentary systems of course do not elect those officials separately.

77. See note 16.

78. A major test is coming in Pennsylvania, where Governor Ridge, preparing to end his term as governor, was promoting as his "legacy" an all-out drive to end elections for their appellate judges, see "Press Release: Governor Ridge Begins Historic Effort to Create Appointive System for Selecting Appellate Judges" ([June 25, 2001]). The change would require passage of a constitutional amendment in two consecutive legislative sessions and the voters' adopting a referendum.

79. National Center for State Courts, "Call To Action."

80. See note 10.

81. "Axial change" is philosopher Karl Jaspers's phrase for a "radical metamorphosis," "a deep cut dividing line" as distinct from mere "synchronistic curiosities." *The Origin and Goal of History* (Yale University Press, 1953), pp. 1, 11, 139.

TEN   *Lessons for*
Reformers

THOMAS E. MANN

T HE FLOW OF MONEY in the 2000 elections docu-
mented thoroughly in this volume could easily reinforce the aura of futil-
ity that envelops most discussions of campaign finance reform. The
explosive growth of funding in targeted contests, the diminishing role of
public financing in presidential elections, the increasing importance of unregulated spending by parties and groups, and the loss of transparency as
disclosure requirements are circumvented by candidate-specific issue advocacy and by a dizzying pattern of financial transfers among party organizations together confirm how far campaign finance practice has departed
from the intentions of the law's framers. If the 1996 elections revealed the
first widespread avoidance of federal election law strictures, the 2000 elections witnessed the near collapse of the Federal Election Campaign Act
(FECA) regulatory regime.

Many analysts will not be surprised or dismayed by this revelation.
They believe that money in elections is like gambling in casinos, and efforts to restrict campaign contributions and expenditures are doomed to
fail. First Amendment guarantees properly limit the reach of regulators.
Political money is fungible, and legal constraints on its flow will merely
divert it to less accountable passageways. Politicians and interest groups
will exploit the weaknesses of the regulatory fabric to advance their interests. These overriding realities, they argue, are encompassed in the infamous Law of Unintended Consequences: the intended purposes of
campaign finance regulation will inevitably be overwhelmed by effects
not desired or anticipated.

This characterization of campaign finance contains elements of truth, and reformers would be wise to acknowledge the complexity of money and politics and the inherent difficulty of formulating policies that are workable and sustainable. But a healthy dose of skepticism is a far cry from certitude that any attempt to regulate campaign financing will be counterproductive.

The record of the 1974 amendments to the FECA, the first comprehensive scheme for regulating federal election financing, is actually more mixed than critics would have us believe. Important elements of the legislative plan—mandatory spending caps in congressional elections, limits on self-financing by candidates and on independent spending by individuals and groups, and regulation of electioneering communications broadly defined—were struck down by the Court in *Buckley* v. *Valeo*, leaving a regulatory residue designed by no one on the statute books. And yet parts of that system worked as intended, and in a positive way, for a substantial period. Public financing slowed the money chase in presidential elections and contributed to a rough parity between the parties in campaign spending and competitive opportunities for challengers. Disclosure of contributions and expenditures improved dramatically. Very large contributions from individuals and organizations to candidates and parties ceased. Well before the explosion of soft money, political parties took advantage of the opportunities afforded them in the law and became significant players in federal election campaigns.

Other consequences of the FECA may not have been intended by policymakers, but they surely could have been anticipated. For example, setting contribution limits to candidates from political committees at five times the level of that for contributions from individuals, with no aggregate limit on what those committees can contribute, helped fuel the growth of political action committees. The streak of pragmatism and concern about access so evident (and predictable) in corporate and trade association PACs in turn contributed to the advantages enjoyed by incumbents. Failure to index contribution limits for inflation spawned an important new role for money brokers and intensified the money chase. And it was no surprise that the Court's banishment of limits on congressional campaign spending, independent expenditures, and self-financing by wealthy candidates quickened that same money chase.

Indeed, the critical factors largely responsible for the difficulties of the FECA regime originated not in the legislation passed by Congress but in administrative and judicial decisions. Party soft money, ostensibly used for purposes other than federal election campaigning, was created and then expanded in a series of rulings by the Federal Election Commission (FEC). Candidate-specific issue advocacy, the current campaign weapon of choice for parties and groups, had its roots in the famous *Buckley* footnote listing "magic words" of express advocacy. It took ambitious politicians and their consultants many years to exploit soft money and issue advocacy and push the boundaries of the law. Any system of regulation is bound to develop problems as new conditions arise and regulated actors wear down its constraints on their behavior. Congress has had ample opportunity to repair the breach in the FECA, within the constitutional constraints defined by the Court, but for a variety of reasons has been unable to agree to do so.

The present campaign finance system combines an elaborate legal and administrative edifice governing the flow of political money with a widespread recognition that the constraints imposed by that system are easily circumvented. This is a recipe for cynicism and loss of legitimacy for the rule of law. The question is not whether change in the present arrangements for financing elections is needed—defenders of the status quo are nowhere in sight—but rather the direction of that change. The fundamental choice is between deregulation and attempts at more effective regulation.

Deregulation has the virtue of simplicity and clarity. Its adherents, ranging from Stanford Law School Dean Kathleen Sullivan and the American Civil Liberties Union (ACLU) on the left to FEC Commissioner Bradley Smith and the National Right to Life Committee on the right, embrace one central argument: the *Buckley* distinction between contributions (which can be regulated) and expenditures (which cannot) is deeply flawed.[1] In their minds, all contribution restrictions, including source prohibitions (for example, from corporate and union treasuries) and limits on amounts, are unconstitutional, unworkable, and unwise. Such restrictions should be eliminated by judicial ruling or legislative enactment.

Most advocates of deregulation offer mandatory disclosure of contributions and expenditures as a tool for preventing abusive finance practices, but it is not at all clear how far they would go toward requiring disclosure of the fastest growing component of campaign finance—electioneering activities that do not meet the Supreme Court's current test of express advocacy. Some advocates prefer anonymity to transparency. They argue a regime of mandated anonymity would be much more effective than disclosure at reducing influence peddling and deterring politicians from extorting donations.[2]

Champions of deregulation also disagree on the virtue of public subsidies of election campaigns. The major "deregulate and disclose" bill in the Congress, introduced by Representative John T. Doolittle (R-Calif.), would repeal the presidential public financing component of existing law.[3] Sullivan and the ACLU instead would extend public subsidies to congressional elections but avoid any link to voluntary spending limits or other mechanisms designed to restrict private donations.

As a practical matter, deregulation alone will not likely be embraced in the near term by the Supreme Court or Congress. In the Court's two most recent decisions on campaign finance, *Nixon* v. *Shrink Missouri Government PAC* (2000) and *FEC* v. *Colorado Republican Federal Campaign Committee* (2001), six justices (including Chief Justice William Rehnquist) stoutly defended the *Buckley* framework insofar as it permitted the regulation of campaign contributions.[4] That majority sentiment is unlikely to change during President George W. Bush's first term. And the Doolittle bill shows little sign of life in Congress. At the peak of its popularity, the bill garnered only 71 House cosponsors and 131 votes on the floor.[5] Given the history of past efforts to limit the direct involvement of corporations and unions in federal election financing and the widespread populist view in the country that political money buys special interest influence, relatively few politicians feel comfortable publicly defending a repeal of all limits on political donations.

If an immediate return to a "state of nature" in political financing seems politically infeasible, so too does the strategy of eliminating all private funding through full public financing of elections. Although four states (Maine, Vermont, Arizona, and Massachusetts) have enacted some form of voluntary full public financing of elections, enough complications and obstacles have arisen there and elsewhere to suggest this approach is hardly the wave of the future.[6] As Anthony Corrado and John Green and Nathan Bigelow detail in their chapters, the public financing of presidential elections is rapidly being undermined both in the nomination process and the general election. Support in Congress for extending public funding to congressional elections has also declined in recent years, and it is no longer actively on the policy agenda.

For better or worse, then, reformers understandably will devote most of their energies to repairing the present regulatory structure rather than repealing it or replacing it wholesale. Efforts to pass the McCain-Feingold/Shays-Meehan bill in the 107th Congress are the most visible manifestation of that strategy.[7]

The Costs of Election Campaigns

Every contributor to this volume has been struck by the high and rapidly increasing costs of elections. George W. Bush raised $94 million from private donors in his quest for his party's presidential nomination, shattering the previous record. Senate and House candidate spending topped $1 billion, exceeding the previous high by $240 million. New Jersey Democrat Jon Corzine spent $63 million in his successful bid for a Senate seat, $60 million of it from his own pocket. Party soft money almost doubled between the 1996 and 2000 elections. PACs increased their federal election activity in 2000 by 20 percent over the previous cycle. Election-oriented issue advocacy spending by outside groups also increased dramatically. State and local elections showed similar increases, and expenditures in judicial elections exploded.

What is one to make of this evidence of and concern about the rising costs of elections? In several respects the concern is exaggerated. The total amount expended on elections in the United States, a populous, sprawling, federal polity whose citizens are generally inattentive to communications about politics and public affairs, is not self-evidently unreasonable. As reform critics have often observed, political advertising budgets are dwarfed by commercial advertising. Moreover, conditions were ripe for a major increase in political spending in the 2000 election cycle. As David Magleby makes clear in chapter 1, with the parties at parity, an open-seat contest for the presidency, razor-thin majorities in the House and Senate, the ideological division of the Supreme Court, the specter of redistricting, and a set of policy issues before legislatures and courts of immense importance to affected groups, the political stakes were exceptionally high in 2000. No one should be surprised that political money flowed freely in this last election.

Nonetheless, a host of troublesome issues surrounds electioneering costs. As political scientist Frank Sorauf observed, rapid increases over a series of elections suggest a dynamic less like a hydraulic system than an international arms race. Such a dynamic can easily lead "to a destabilization of the system, the result of which is a lack of confidence in all limits, a declining sense of how much is enough, an escalating insecurity, and a consequent scrambling for more weapons." What follows, Sorauf continues, "is overkill, the raising and spending of money out of all proportion to a reality-based assessment of need."[8]

Focusing on total costs almost certainly understates the existence of this arms race in political financing. As the national competition between the parties intensifies, more and more money is being spent on fewer and fewer contests. The acceleration of spending in these targeted constituencies is much more rapid than the aggregate figures suggest. If outlays by candidates, parties, and outside groups are taken into account, for example, average spending for a successful House challenge has jumped from a half million to several million dollars in less than a decade.[9] While concentrating resources in marginal seats is rational, particularly when party control of Congress and many state legislatures hangs on the outcome of a handful of races, most other contests are starved for resources, and most voters receive much too little information about competing candidates. Ironically, funding patterns associated with more intense competition between the parties for majority control have contributed to a decline in the number of competitive seats.

Apart from the instability and concentration of political funding, increasing costs bring a host of problems associated with new demands on fund-raising. What kind of candidate skills and endowments are favored? Are capable and promising individuals discouraged from seeking office? How do elected officials allocate their time and legislative energies? Do serious conflicts of interest arise when huge political contributions are extracted from individuals and organizations with substantial stakes in the policy process? Does party-based fund-raising insulate or facilitate linkages between contributors and policymakers? And do voters have any reasonable ways of knowing what interests have financed the political communications sponsored by outside groups?

These questions may not have conclusive answers or obvious cures, but they certify that concern about the costs of American elections is not misplaced.

Presidential Campaign Finance

Public financing of presidential elections has been a centerpiece of federal election law since 1974. This includes a public matching system tied to voluntary spending limits for the nominations process and a full public grant contingent on an agreement to not raise or spend private dollars in the general election. As chapters 3 and 4 make crystal clear, both elements of this system are under extreme stress.

Nominations

George W. Bush was the first successful candidate to decline matching public funds in the presidential nominating process. Other decisions to opt out of public financing (John Connally in 1980, Steve Forbes in 1996 and 2000) were inconsequential; Bush's decision may well be a harbinger of future nomination contests. Since many factors were involved in Bush's choice, it is not obvious whether or how the financing rules can be altered to diminish those prospects. Increasing the voluntary spending limit—which has been indexed for inflation but has not kept up with more rapidly rising campaign costs—would be a start. Raising the size of private donations that is matched with public funds, which has remained at $250 since the 1974 law, would also help. Eliminating state-by-state spending limits, which have no relationship to the political importance of individual primaries, and consolidating the three separate fund-raising limitations (for spending, fund-raising, and compliance) would remove minor irritants to candidates accepting matching public funds. Taking immediate steps to avoid a likely 2004 shortfall in public funds presently earmarked through the tax checkoff is essential.[10] These might include increasing the amount that can be designated for public financing on individual tax returns, authorizing and financing a public education campaign about the checkoff, or substituting a direct appropriation for the checkoff. None of these options will be easy to achieve.

Ironically, other reforms could increase the incentives for presidential candidates to decline matching funds. Raising individual contribution limits, while important for recovering some of the value of contributions lost to inflation, might persuade candidates that relying exclusively on private donations and freeing themselves from spending limits, as George W. Bush did, is feasible. Banning party soft money and reining in party issue ads makes more perilous the fate of publicly financed candidates who have wrapped up their party's nomination but run out of spending room months before the national convention. Under these new rules, front-running candidates might think twice before agreeing to the spending limits associated with the public match.

General Election

While no major party candidate has declined full public financing of their general election campaign, the last election cycle witnessed the virtual collapse of the spending limits provided for in the law. As Corrado details in chapter 4, as much spending occurred outside the public funding grants in the 2000 presidential general election campaign as within them. Banning party soft money, requiring candidate-specific issue ads broadcast near the election to be treated as electioneering communication subject to regulation, and tightening current regulations governing allowable coordination between candidates and outside groups would rein in much of current spending activity not anticipated by the 1974 law.

If these measures were truly effective, which is by no means certain, additional resources would be required for the general election campaign. These resources might be provided through an increase in the amount of the public grant to presidential candidates, an increase in the hard money parties may spend in coordination with their candidates, or the provision of free broadcast time for the candidates and parties. If the major party presidential nominees believe the public grant is too small to wage a strong campaign, and alternative channels are blocked, they could well opt out of public financing in the general election as well as the nomination campaign.

Congressional Elections

The intense competition for control of the House and Senate in 2000 accelerated long-standing trends. None is more significant than the strategic role of the political parties. The congressional party campaign committees are playing an increasingly prominent role in financing congressional elections. Candidate-specific issue ads funded largely with soft money have become the major weapon in the arsenal of party committees, making coordinated party spending and independent expenditures financed with hard money much less important. Current and aspiring congressional party and committee leaders take a very active role in fund-raising (hard and soft) for their party campaign committees and contributing from their leadership PACs or personal campaign funds to candidates in marginal seats. Party leaders now routinely assess members in safe seats to provide the party with substantial sums from their individual campaign war chests for redistribution to targeted races. This party involvement has led to a further concentration of resources on a very small number of congressional races, a concentration reinforced by the campaign activities of outside groups working with the same list of targeted seats.

The intensified strategic involvement of party leaders in congressional elections is an inevitable consequence of the close party balance in Congress. But that party engagement could have proceeded apace without the reliance on soft money and candidate-specific issue ads. If reform forces the congressional party campaign committees to operate in a world confined to hard money, express advocacy (coordinated or independent), and generic party activity, they are very likely to adapt successfully. And by returning to a regime of limits on source and size of contributions in congressional campaign finance, parties will be less vulnerable to exploitation as conduits and facilitators of linkages between large donors and policymakers.

Even with a return to an exclusively hard money world in congressional elections, it would be foolish to forecast any measurable diminution in the money chase. Without limits on expenditures (and voluntary limits tied to public financing, while in place in a number of states and major cities, are nowhere in political sight in Washington), the pressure to steer more and more funds to swing districts and states will continue at least as long as the two parties compete seriously for majority control of Congress. And now that the practice of party assessments of safe incumbents has been established, the scramble for money will routinely extend well beyond competitive districts and states

Some steps could be taken to lighten the burdens of fund-raising by easing supply. They have the additional virtue of providing help to challengers and possibly increasing the number of competitive contests. Adjusting contribution limits for the effects of inflation over the past twenty-five years; providing tax credits for small donors, free broadcast time for candidates, and subsidized mailings and voter brochures; and increasing the amounts of hard money that parties can spend in coordination with their candidates are prime examples of these supply-side measures. Clearly, they would work most effectively if soft money and electioneering masquerading as issue ads were no longer the norm in competitive congressional elections.

The success of three self-financed Senate candidates in 2000—Jon Corzine, Maria Cantwell, and Mark Dayton—raises the legitimate issue of whether personal wealth is becoming the best ticket to public office. The record of self-financed candidates is decidedly mixed. Millions have been squandered by wealthy individuals who learned the painful lesson that personal wealth does not convert easily to electoral success.[11] Yet there can be no doubt that recruiters from party campaign committees are attracted to candidates who can raise money easily, and nothing is easier than writing a check from one's own account. It is likely that the number of candidates able and willing to finance their own campaigns will increase.

The *Buckley* Court's ruling that limits on self-financing are unconstitutional severely restricts the ability of reformers to alter that trend. Curbs must be voluntary, tied to the acceptance of public funds. And a potentially workable public financing system in congressional elections now garners relatively little support. Alternatively, parties can be unleashed to counter the funding of wealthy candidates. Some party soft money is used for that purpose now. Examples in the 2000 campaign included West Virginia Republican Shelley Moore Capito, who won an open House seat against a wealthy opponent with the help of party-financed issue ads, and New Jersey Republican Bob Franks, who had the unenviable task of running against free-spending Senate candidate Jon Corzine.[12] If soft money is eliminated, the supply-side measures to ease the burdens of fund-raising discussed above would help raise the funding floors on which candidates opposing self-financed candidates wage their candidacies.

One new idea on this subject did emerge in the form of a successful amendment during the Senate debate on the McCain-Feingold legislation. Introduced by Senator Pete Domenici (R-N.M.) and dubbed the "Millionaires' Amendment," it would raise the individual contribution limits and party coordinated spending limits for candidates facing self-financed opponents.[13] Whether such a measure would pass constitutional muster is doubtful, but its popularity in the Senate dramatically illustrates the fear, irrational as it may be, incumbents have of wealthy challengers.

Parties and Soft Money

Every chapter in this volume discusses the ways in which soft money has transformed the conduct and financing of elections and undermined the objectives of federal election law. Although campaign finance statutes prohibit contributions from corporate and union treasuries to federal election campaigns and strictly limit the amount that can be contributed by individuals and political committees, the national parties have utilized nonfederal accounts and transfers to state parties to render those restrictions largely ineffective. All of the concerns raised by a reliance on very large contributions—conflicts of interest, distortion of policy agendas, abuse of public authority in soliciting these funds, the appearance of impropriety—have returned to the center of American politics.

Consequently, it is no surprise that soft money is at the top of the reform agenda. A ban on soft money is the centerpiece of the McCain-
Feingold/Shays-Meehan legislation considered during the 107th Congress.
Critics of this proposal have raised a host of objections. National parties
and federal officeholders have legitimate interests in nonfederal election
activities, such as promoting issue positions, strengthening party organizations, supporting candidates in state and local elections, registering voters, getting out the party vote, and advertising generic party messages.
They should not be limited, it is argued, to financing these activities under
legal restrictions written for federal election campaigns. Financing a share
of these activities with funds raised under operative state law is entirely
reasonable. Some critics go so far as to argue that a ban on soft money is
unconstitutional.[14] Others simply assert it is unjustified and unwise.[15]

The constitutional argument is less compelling than the substantive one,
especially after the Court's recent decisions affirming the *Buckley* framework for limiting contributions and coordinated party spending limits. If
corruption or the appearance of corruption is a legitimate basis for Congress setting $1,000 contribution limits, it ought to be sufficient to ratio-
nalize a ban on $1 million contributions. The practical questions about
soft money naturally turn on the underlying empirical reality. To what
extent do parties rely on a small number of very large donors? Is soft
money used for nonfederal election activities? Have parties been strengthened by soft money? Would they be weakened by its abolition? If national parties are prohibited from raising soft money, would the same
resources be redirected through less accountable passageways?

The evidence is decidedly on the side of the reformers. In the 2000
election cycle about $300 million of the $487 million in party soft money
came from only eight hundred donors.[16] Fifty corporations, unions, and
individuals each contributed more than $1 million in soft money.[17] The
dominant use of party soft money is for funding candidate-specific television and radio ads and direct mail in a small number of highly competitive House and Senate races.[18] Less than 10 percent of party soft money
goes toward party building and grassroots political activity. Substantial
sums go to administrative, staff, and fund-raising costs at the national
and state party level.

If party strength is measured by the amount of money crossing party
ledgers and the presence of party-financed issue ads in highly competitive
races, then soft money has indeed strengthened parties. But there is little
sign of strength from soft money expenditures beyond these indicators.

Parties began their revival in the late 1970s and 1980s, well before the explosion of soft money. They adapted well to the new electoral environment, becoming repositories of professional campaign expertise and building strong national organizations to boost their candidates.[19] In the new world of soft money and issue advocacy, however, parties have become instruments of incumbent officeholders to launder large contributions that would otherwise be illegal and channel these resources to a handful of races. There is no pretense of party building or party activity of any sort in the vast majority of districts and states that are deemed noncompetitive. The only game in town for the parties is raising and steering resources to the few targeted races to hold or gain majority control. And that requires pressuring and courting those with the resources to give a lot.

The evidence suggests that parties would adapt well to a post-soft money world, especially if limits on contributions to parties are increased and separate aggregate limits are set for individual contributions to parties and candidates. (Both of these provisions were included in the new Shays-Meehan legislation in the summer of 2001.) The parties raised $717 million in hard money during the 2000 cycle, a sum that would certainly increase as parties redirect their fund-raising strategies to raise only hard money. The pool of potential contributors, from individuals and PACs that currently make substantial soft money donations, is large. It would not be difficult for parties to fund current voter registration and mobilization activities exclusively from hard dollars. And without the incentive to spend huge sums on candidate-specific issue ads in a few hotly contested races, parties would likely spread their resources a bit more widely and invest more heavily in grassroots political activities. These latter activities would also be facilitated by a provision of the reform bill added by Senator Carl Levin (D-Mich.) that would permit state and local party committees to raise nonfederal contributions of up to $10,000 for voter registration and generic party mobilization.[20]

Even if parties convert some portion of existing soft money into hard money contributions, significant soft money sums might flow to other electoral actors in support of the same campaign activities now financed with soft money. The extent of this diversion would depend partly on what other reforms accompany a soft money ban. A prohibition on corporate and union funding of candidate-specific television and radio issue ads near the election would close off one obvious outlet. Extending that prohibition to nonprofit groups, though of dubious constitutionality, would tighten that spigot even further. Nonetheless, outside groups would retain ample scope for engaging in "ground war" campaign activities that do not meet the Court's current standard of express advocacy.[21] And unions, corporations, and membership groups would be completely free to direct additional resources into "internal communications" not limited by the FECA.

Nonetheless, the inevitable porousness of a soft money ban would be limited in one important respect. A larger part of the soft money now raised by the parties materializes because of the extraordinary efforts of federal officeholders and party officials. Some attribute their success to persuasion, others to extortion. Breaking the link between soft money donors and public officials would remove a major incentive for many of these large contributions. Some evidence exists that a number of corporations would be delighted if they were freed from the importuning of soft money fund-raisers.[22] In any case, with a soft money ban, parties would lose one critical incentive to facilitate links between large contributors and elected officials.

Issue Advocacy

As several authors in this book have pointed out, the market for party soft money was transformed in 1995 when (thanks to Bill Clinton and Dick Morris) the parties discovered they could use the cover of issue advocacy to finance broadcast ads for their candidates outside the reach of federal regulation. By avoiding the terms of express advocacy illustrated in the *Buckley* footnote, they could fund aggressive campaign advertising with a large dollop of soft money. And by transferring funds to state parties, which then place the candidate-specific issue ads, they could reduce the percentage of hard dollars required to match the soft dollars. Outside groups, in turn, realized they too could finance electioneering communications in the guise of issue advocacy, avoiding the need to expend precious dollars raised under the limits of federal law.[23]

The constitutional case for keeping issue advocacy free from federal regulation is compelling. But the *Buckley* test for distinguishing between express and issue advocacy is utterly bankrupt. A substantial body of research on the 1998 and 2000 elections has produced powerful evidence that the Court's magic words test fails to differentiate electioneering and issue discussion.[24] Fewer than one-in-ten candidate ads, which because of their sponsorship are by definition express advocacy, invoke the magic words.[25] While most key votes in Congress during election years occurred before Labor Day, almost all so-called issue ads appeared after. Party-sponsored issue ads almost never mentioned the name of the party, but almost always (95 to 99 percent) named a particular candidate running in the district or state in which the ad is targeted. Candidate-specific issue ads are more likely to attack rather than advocate or compare than candidate ads are.

Most important, from a reform perspective, this research makes clear that the bright-line test in the McCain-Feingold/Shays-Meehan legislation for regulating sham issue advocacy would not be constitutionally over-broad.[26] That is, by defining electioneering communication as targeted broadcast ads that refer to a clearly identified candidate within sixty days of a general election or thirty days of a primary, the proposal would regulate transparent campaign ads without touching genuine issue ads. What appears to be a serious constitutional problem in theory evaporates in practice.

More difficult is the question of how these electioneering communications are regulated. The most ambitious proposal is to treat them as a form of express advocacy and, therefore, subject to the legal requirements attached to independent expenditures. That entails financing with funds raised under the FECA, which prohibits coordination with the candidates, and public disclosure. Alternatively, as proposed by Senators Olympia Snowe and Jim Jeffords (and incorporated into McCain-Feingold), direct and indirect financing of such ads by corporations and unions could be prohibited. The tricky constitutional and practical issue is how to treat nonprofit organizations, which do not receive corporate or union funding. At the very least they might be required to disclose their sponsorship of electioneering communications and the donors who financed their broadcast.

A final issue involving issue advocacy concerns the ground war tactics of direct mail, phone banks, and personal contact. In recent election cycles, parties and outside groups have financed extensive ground campaigns in hotly contested races off the FECA books by avoiding express advocacy.[27] Abolishing party soft money and more strictly defining federal election activity, as proposed in McCain-Feingold, would force parties to finance these activities with hard money. But outside groups would not be so constrained. Some critics of reform argue this would be the next loophole in campaign finance practice, one certain to be exploited aggressively by political consultants and their clients. But at least it would more closely serve the purpose originally intended for soft money.

Disclosure and Enforcement

Election law in the United States provides for more extensive and timely disclosure of political contributions and expenditures than any other democracy in the world. The FEC receives, processes, and publicly releases an extraordinary array of data. Journalists, citizen groups, political actors, and scholars make extensive use of these data, in many cases refining them for broader public consumption. The FEC has encouraged electronic submission of financial reports by political committees, which are required for all filers except Senate candidates in the 2002 election cycle. Most reform proposals provide for mandatory electronic filing and immediate posting of the reports on the Internet.

The problem is that a large and growing share of campaign activity is exempted from disclosure requirements. Issue advocacy by outside groups is not subject to federal law. National party committees must disclose their soft money donors and expenditures, but the precise uses of funds transferred to state parties are often difficult to track. Reports on expenditures by unions and corporations for internal communications with their restricted classes (members, managers, shareholders) are not readily available. Nonprofit groups organized under section 527 of the Internal Revenue code have largely escaped disclosure of their political activities, even after a recent change in the law designed to correct the problem.[28]

Some changes in campaign finance law discussed above—such as banning soft money and regulating electioneering communications—would reduce the disclosure deficit. But the lesson of 2000 is that the greatest disclosure challenge is not accelerating the submission and release of currently reported information but instead finding ways of bringing more campaign activity under the disclosure regime.

Another lesson of the 2000 election cycle is that a weak enforcement agency will hasten the unraveling of campaign finance law. In chapter 4, Corrado reports how the FEC facilitated transforming what in 1996 was a brazen test of the boundaries of election law into settled practice on the eve of the 2000 campaign. This is only the latest in a series of actions and inactions that underscore that the FEC is a weak and ineffectual agency, precisely what Congress had in mind when creating it in 1974.[29] Nothing short of a major restructuring will overcome the constraints built into its charter.[30] And without a stronger enforcement agency, new campaign finance law is likely to founder on the shoals of implementation.

Lessons from State and Judicial Elections

Any thought that the strains on the campaign finance system are largely limited to federal elections is belied by the analysis of funding patterns in state and judicial elections in chapters 8 and 9. What Corrado argues about presidential elections holds across levels of elective office: financing practices are shaped by the strategic context of the election and the regulations governing them. As the perceived stakes of an election increase—because of its competitiveness, the power accruing to the victor, and the perceived impact of the election on group interests—money will flow more freely. The velocity, shape, and direction of that money flow will depend on how campaign finance law is written, interpreted by the courts, and implemented by administrative agencies. The strategic context and legal environment of state and judicial elections have produced escalating costs, a mobilization of parties and interest groups, uneven disclosure, an increase in unregulated campaign activity, concerns about access and influence associated with large contributions, an intensified money chase, waves of reform, and sober reflections the morning after.

The states serve usefully as laboratories of democracy, but no clear pattern of success in the states has yet emerged to guide federal reformers. States clearly play a crucial role in the federal campaign finance system, because state law governs how national parties can raise and spend nonfederal funds and state parties serve as indispensable agents for implementing the funding strategies of their national counterparts. If every state were to adopt contribution limits as restrictive as federal law, soft money could not exist.

However, campaign finance reformers in the states operate under constraints similar to those faced at the national level. Parties often disagree sharply over what constitutes constructive reform. Incumbents are reluctant to change the financing rules that brought and returned them to office. Powerful interests oppose new limits on their election activity. The courts limit the tools available to policymakers. Taxpayers decline to make voluntary (and usually costless) checkoffs to support public financing. Citizens seldom make campaign finance reform a top priority. And yet in spite of these constraints, the states have been a hotbed of activity during the past decade to regulate the role of money in elections. Partial public financing tied to spending limits has been tried in a number of state and local elections. Together with the more ambitious Clean Money Option of voluntary full public financing, these reform initiatives in the states provide fertile ground for exploring what might work in federal elections.

As Roy A. Schotland relates in chapter 9, the financing of judicial elections presents a special and uniquely disturbing case. One sympathizes with those who advocate a simple solution: stop electing judges. But after reading Schotland, one also understands why a strategy of making incremental reforms within judicial elections is likely to bear more fruit. More broadly, as Schotland documents, issue advocacy attacks on judges up for election and expressions of concern about possible conflicts of interest in fund-raising by judges have elevated the importance of campaign finance in the judicial branch and may influence how judges see the issue in other contexts too.

Conclusion

Financing practices in the 2000 elections bear little resemblance to the letter or intended purposes of the laws under which they occurred. This disjuncture between theory and practice weakens the legitimacy of the electoral system. The critical question is what can be done to reconcile these differences. Some solutions—such as the deregulation of political finance—would cleanly achieve that objective but do violence to other values that citizens hold dear. A less glamorous but more practical approach is to acknowledge the inherent problems surrounding money and politics and to strive to contain and manage them as best as possible.

Reformers need to recognize the limits and the possibilities of regulation, and to acknowledge the extent to which the strategic environment shapes the behavior of rational political actors. As reviewed in this chapter and throughout the volume, the 2000 elections provide many lessons for reformers. The most important lesson is that campaign finance reform is an ongoing process of maintenance and repair, unlikely to provide any lasting solutions but nonetheless capable of enhancing the quality of and respect for our democratic system.

Notes

1. Kathleen M. Sullivan, "Against Campaign Finance Reform," *Utah Law Review* 311 (1998); Ira Glasser, *Testimony of Ira Glasser, Executive Director of the American Civil Liberties Union, before the United States Senate Committee on Rules and Administration*, March 22, 2000, Committee on Rules and Administration of the U.S. Senate (rules.senate.gov/hearings/2000/ /032200glas.htm [July

19, 2001]); Bradley A. Smith, *Unfree Speech: The Folly of Campaign Finance Reform* (Princeton University Press, 2001); and James Bopp Jr., *Testimony of James Bopp, Jr. before the Senate Committee on Rules and Administration Regarding Federal Election Commission Authorization and Campaign Finance Reforms*, January 30, 1997, National Right to Life Committee website (www.nrlc.org/bopptest.html [July 18, 2001]).

2. Ian Ayres, "Should Campaign Donors Be Identified?" *Regulation*, vol. 24 (Summer 2001), pp. 12–17.

3. Congress, House, 106 Congress, 1 sess. *H.R. 1922, Citizen Legislature and Political Freedom Act (Doolittle Bill)*, August 5, 1999, GPO Access (frwebgate.access.gpo.gov/ /cgi-bin/getdoc.cgi?dbname=106_cong_bills&docid=f:h1922rh.txt.pdf [July 19, 2001]).

4. Brookings Institution Campaign Finance website, *Key Court Cases* (www.brook.edu/gs/cf/courts.htm [July 19, 2001]).

5. *Congressional Quarterly Almanac*, vol. LIV, 1998, s.v. "House Vote 403. HR2183. Overhaul Campaign Finance Laws/Doolittle Substitute (Washington: Congressional Quarterly, 1999); and U.S. Congress, House, *H.R. 1922, Bill Summary & Status for the 106th Congress*, Thomas website (thomas.loc.gov/cgi-bin/bdquery/z?d106:HR01922:@@@L&summ2=m& [July 5, 2001]).

6. Abby Scher, "Cleaning Up Politics, Clearing Out Big Money: Citizen Groups Win State Reforms," *Dollars and Sense*, no. 230 (July-August 2000), pp. 24–27; and Carey Goldberg, "Publicly Paid Elections Put to the Test in Three States," *New York Times East Coast Late Edition*, November 19, 2000, p. 1.44.

7. Brookings Institution Campaign Finance website, *A Guide to the Current Congressional Campaign Finance Debate* (www.brook.edu/GS/CF/debate/ / debate_hp.htm [July 19, 2001]).

8. Frank J. Sorauf, "What Buckley Wrought," in E. Joshua Rosenkranz, *If Buckley Fell* (New York: Century Foundation Press, 1999), pp. 11 62.

9. David B. Magleby, ed., *Outside Money: Soft Money and Issue Advocacy in the 1998 Congressional Elections* (Rowman and Littlefield, 2000).

10. Federal Election Commission, *Annual Report 2000* (Washington: Federal Election Commission, 2000), p. 15. This report is also available online (www.fec.gov/pdf/ar00.pdf.)

11. Jennifer Steen, "Maybe You Can Buy an Election, but Not with Your Own Money," *Washington Post*, June 25, 2000, p. B01; and Jennifer A. Steen, *Money Isn't Everything: Self-Financing Candidates in U.S. House Elections, 1992–98*, Ph.D. dissertation, University of California, Berkeley.

12. Philip D. Duncan and Brian Nutting, eds., *CQ's Politics in America 2002: The 107th Congress* (Washington: Congressional Quarterly, 2001).

13. Congress, Senate, *Bill Summary and Status for the 107th Congress*, 2001, Thomas website (thomas.loc.gov/cgi-bin/bdquery/z?d107:SP00115: [July 19, 2001]).

14. Bradley A. Smith, *Unfree Speech: The Folly of Campaign Finance Reform* (Princeton University Press, 2001).

15. Raymond La Raja and Elizabeth Jarvis-Shean, *Assessing the Impact of a Ban on Soft Money: Party Soft Money Spending in the 2000 Elections*, Institute

of Governmental Studies and Citizens' Research Foundation Policy Brief, Berkeley, Calif., July 6, 2001 (www.cfinst.org/parties/papers/laraja_softmoney.pdf [July 20, 2001]); and John C. Green and others, *CFI Cyber-Forum: Parties under McCain-Feingold: Topic III: Soft Money and the Appearance of Corruption* (www.cfinst.org/parties/ /mf_responses.html#T3Intro [July 19, 2001]).

16. David Rogers, "'Soft Money' Study Shows Concentration of Donations by Wealthy Contributors," *Wall Street Journal Eastern Edition,* March 16, 2001, p. A16.

17. Sheila Krumholz, Center for Responsive Politics, telephone interview by David Magleby, July 16, 2001.

18. New York University School of Law, Brennan Center for Justice, *The Purposes and Beneficiaries of Party "Soft Money"* (2001).

19. Paul S. Herrnson, *Party Campaigning in the 1980s* (Harvard University Press, 1988).

20. Congress, House, 107 Cong. 1 sess., *H.R. 2356, Bipartisan Campaign Reform Act of 2001 (Shays-Meehan Bill),* June 28, 2001, GPO Access (frwebgate.access.gpo.gov/ /cgi-bin/getdoc.cgi?dbname=107_cong_bills&docid=f:h2356rh.txt.pdf [July 19, 2001]); Brookings Institution Campaign Finance website, *Shays-Meehan Analysis by the Campaign Finance Institute* (www.brook.edu/gs/cf/debate/new_amendment.pdf [July 19, 2001]).

21. Magleby, *Outside Money*; and David B. Magleby, ed., *Election Advocacy: Soft Money and Issue Advocacy in the 2000 Congressional Elections* (Brigham Young University, Center for the Study of Elections and Democracy, 2001).

22. Research and Policy Committee of the Committee for Economic Development, *Investing in the People's Business: A Business Proposal for Campaign Finance Reform* (New York: Committee for Economic Development, 1999).

23. The origins and legal basis for electioneering issue advocacy are summarized in Trevor Potter, "Issue Advocacy and Express Advocacy," in Anthony Corrado and others, eds., *Campaign Finance Reform: A Soucebook* (Brookings, 1997).

24. Jonathan S. Krasno and Daniel E. Seltz, *Buying Time: Television Advertising in the 1998 Congressional Elections* (New York University School of Law, Brennan Center for Justice, 2000); Jonathan Krasno and Kenneth Goldstein, *The Facts about Television Advertising and the McCain-Feingold Bill,* Brookings Institution Campaign Finance website (www.brook.edu/ /campaignfinance/debate/ senate%5Fhp.htm [July 20, 2001]); Magleby, ed., *Outside Money*; Magleby, ed., *Election Advocacy*; David B. Magleby, *Dictum without Data: The Myth of Issue Advocacy and Party Building* (Brigham Young University, Center for the Study of Elections and Democracy, 2000).

25. Jonathan Krasno and Kenneth Goldstein, *The Facts about Television,* Brookings Institution Campaign Finance website (www.brook.edu/ campaignfinance/debate/senate%5fhp.htm [July 20, 2001]).

26. Richard L. Hasen, "Measuring Overbreadth: Using Empirical Evidence to Determine the Constitutionality of Campaign Finance Laws Targeting Sham Issue Advocacy," *Minnesota Law Review,* vol. 85 (June 2001), pp. 1773–1807.

27. Magleby, *Outside Money*; and Magleby, *Election Advocacy*.

28. Brookings Institution Campaign Finance website, *Recent Developments in Campaign Finance Regulation: Section 527 Organizations* (www.brook.edu/gs/cf/headlines/527_intro.htm [July 20, 2001]).

29. Thomas E. Mann, "The FEC: Implementing and Enforcing Federal Campaign Finance Law," in Corrado and others, eds., *Campaign Finance Reform* (Brookings, 1997).

30. Project FEC, *Statement of Principles for Achieving Effective Enforcement of Federal Campaign Finance Laws*, Brookings Institution Campaign Finance website (www.brook.edu/gs/cf/headlines/projfec_sop.pdf [July 20, 2001]).

Contributors

Anthony Corrado is a professor of government at Colby College and a nonresident senior fellow at the Brookings Institution.

Nathan S. Bigelow is a Ph.D. student at the University of Maryland, College Park.

Allan J. Cigler is the Chancellors Club Teaching Professor of Political Science at the University of Kansas.

Diana Dwyre is associate professor of political science and director of graduate studies at California State University, Chico, and coauthor of *Legislative Labyrinth: Congress and Campaign Finance Reform.*

Anthony Gierzynski is professor of political science at the University of Vermont and author of *Money Rules: Financing Elections in America.*

John C. Green is professor of political science and director of the Ray C. Bliss Institute of Applied Politics at the University of Akron.

Paul S. Herrnson is director of the Center for American Politics and Citizenship and professor in the Department of Government and Politics, University of Maryland.

Robin Kolodny is associate professor of political science at Temple University and the author of *Pursuing Majorities: Congressional Campaign Committees in American Politics.*

David B. Magleby is dean of the College of Family, Home and Social Sciences, distinguished professor of political science, and director of the Center for the Study of Elections and Democracy at Brigham Young University.

Thomas E. Mann is the W. Averell Harriman Chair and senior fellow in the Governmental Studies program at the Brookings Institution.

Candice J. Nelson is associate professor of government and director of the Campaign Management Institute at American University.

Kelly D. Patterson is associate professor and department chair of political science at Brigham Young University.

Roy A. Schotland is a professor at Georgetown University Law Center.

Index

ABC News polls, 40
Abraham, Spencer, 3, 42, 175
Access-oriented PACs, 116–17, 129
ACLU (American Civil Liberties Union), 240, 241
Adams, Stephen, 96
Advertising: attack ads, 157–58, 222, 254; DCCC ad not allowed in Kentucky congressional race, 114; presidential general campaign, 2, 95–99; Spanish-language ads, 151. See also Broadcast advertising; Issue advocacy
AFL-CIO. See American Federation of Labor and Congress of Industrial Organizations
AFT (American Federation of Teachers), 178
Agency agreements for spending national party's and state party's coordinated expenditure on candidate, 153
Alabama judicial elections, 4, 218–19, 220–21
Alaska: gubernatorial elections, 194; soft money regulation, 189
Albuquerque, New Mexico's spending limits, 190–91

Alexander, Lamar, 28, 56, 63
Allen, George, 175, 179
American Civil Liberties Union (ACLU), 240, 241
American Federation of Labor and Congress of Industrial Organizations (AFL-CIO), 32, 74; advertising for Gore, 99; campaign activities, 7, 164, 166–67, 177–78; political activities investigated by FEC, 83; soft money from, 143
American Federation of Teachers (AFT), 178
Americans for Equality, 182
Americans for Job Security, 98
Americans for Tax Reform (ATR), 39, 167
Annenberg Public Policy Center of the University of Pennsylvania, 23, 25, 33, 176
Arizona: Clean Elections public financing programs, 189, 190; public funding of state candidates, 189, 241
Arkansas: judicial elections, 224–26; tax credits for contributions, 190
Ashcroft, John, 3, 112

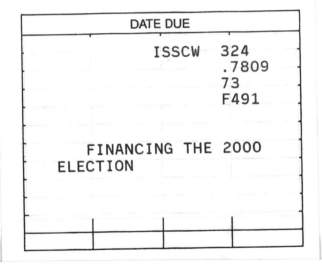